The foreman

International Library of Sociology

Founded by Karl Mannheim
Editor: John Rex, University of Warwick

Arbor Scientiae
Arbor Vitae

A catalogue of the books available in the **International Library of Sociology** and other series of Social Science books published by Routledge & Kegan Paul will be found at the end of this volume.

The foreman

Aspects of task and structure

David Dunkerley
Department of Sociology
University of Leeds

Routledge & Kegan Paul
London and Boston

First published in 1975
by Routledge & Kegan Paul Ltd
Broadway House, 68–74 Carter Lane,
London EC4V 5EL and
9 Park Street,
Boston, Mass. 02108, USA
Set in Monotype Times
and printed in Great Britain by
Western Printing Services Ltd, Bristol
© David Dunkerley 1975

ISBN 0 7100 8158 8

Contents

Preface

Professor Ray Thomas and Dr George Bain critically analysed an earlier draft of this study and their help in identifying defects is much appreciated. The particular part played by Professor George Thomason needs to be separately acknowledged as his encouragement and criticism have enabled the work to be completed. Despite this scholarly assistance the defects remaining are solely attributable to me.

DAVID DUNKERLEY

1 Introduction

This is a study of a position within complex organisations and the performance of people in that position. From this statement of intent can be seen two key words and concepts for the study—organisation and position. The translation of these two words into behavioural concepts provides the cornerstone for this analysis of the industrial foreman. Organisations which are studied are primarily industrial in nature and the role concentrated upon is that of the foremen in such organisations.

Taking the notion of organisation first, social scientists have frequently noted that there has been a significant shift towards larger organisations in modern society—whether they be industrial organisations or not. In modern society, individuals are surrounded by organisations from 'the cradle to the grave'; they are instrumental in shaping the whole essence of social life. This in itself provides sufficient justification for why the social scientist should be interested in complex organisations.

It is really the specific nature of the functions of modern organisations that has led to the dependency of society upon them. In orientation, organisations are basically purposive—they are orientated towards the achievement of goals. These goals can take the form of material products or of providing services. The extent to which the goals of an organisation are actually achieved is usually seen as one measure of how effective the organisation is. The nature of the configuration of the characteristics of organisations in relation to goal achievement has led many social observers to the conclusion that complex organisations are among the most important social inventions of the twentieth century. Such a claim is obviously disputable and, without exploring its validity, it is clear that organisations have provided the opportunity for the realisation, by rational means, of many of the desired ends of society.

1

It is a feature of complex organisations that they are basically rational structures. They are uniquely capable of combining various functions in a rational way in order to achieve their goals. Beyond the rational combination of functions, however, organisations can only achieve their goals by the utilisation of human skills. Therefore, there must also be a rational combination of human functions, again orientated towards the achievement of goals. In order to do this, organisations can be viewed as large and complex role systems. That is, roles are assigned to different organisation positions which in turn are structured to enhance the realisation of organisation goals.

The use of role systems for the rational pursuit of organisational objectives implies, *inter alia*, that it is necessary for the organisation to ensure a certain dependability in the performance of these roles. There is, therefore, the requirement that superimposed upon the role system there should be a control system. There must be predictable patterns of role performance and a need for conformity within the organisation. In larger organisations where there is greater interdependence of individual roles arising from a more complex division of labour, the notion of a control system becomes even more of a prerequisite.

It has always been one of the defining characteristics of complex organisations that there should be formal structures of control. There are several ramifications of such an observation. One of the most important, at least from the point of view of this study, is that there are some positions within organisations that must be defined in such a way that they are able to influence other positions. It is to such a position of influence that the present study addresses itself—the position of foreman.

An understanding of both the position and role of the foreman in industry is important for social scientist and practising manager alike. As the study demonstrates, the foreman occupies a position in the industrial hierarchy that enables many unusual social relationships to be explored. The power and status relationships can be explored by taking such a crucial role and position; organisational change in terms of the changing role of the foreman can also be analysed. The pressures on role performance of this position present another area to the social scientist. In brief, such a study could make a contribution to our knowledge of organisation functioning. In both of these senses, therefore, the use of both role theory and organisation theory in the study are crucial.

Equally important is the part that the study can play in furthering the knowledge of supervisory roles for the practising manager. The kinds of problems that the industrial foreman experiences in the performance of his role are of interest to industrial management, particularly when looked at 'from a distance' and, hopefully, with a greater degree of objectivity than the working manager could hope to achieve. Again, an understanding of the role is of interest to the manager since most industrial organisations have gone through, or are at present going through, a period when they have to take a fresh look at their foremen. New job definitions and job schedules often need to be written for foremen because of the changing industrial circumstances. Thus, for example, the changes that are discussed at some length later in the study relate to the traditional functions of the foreman and the way in which many of these functions have been given to staff specialists of all kinds such as personnel officers, quality control specialists, and so on. These changes have led to new power structures and new structures dictating social relationships, so that the working manager needs to be aware both of the actual changes that have occurred and the nature of possible future changes.

The case being made for a study of this nature, therefore, is that both social scientists and managers need to know more about supervisory positions in so far as individuals in these positions represent a very important function in the modern industrial organisation. Foremen play a crucial part in determining whether organisational goals are realised or not. Central to the thesis being put forward here is the point that the effectiveness of foremen is the responsibility of management. The way in which the job of foreman is designed, the functions allocated to the foreman and the responsibilities allowed the foreman are all determined by management. In this sense, therefore, management can determine the extent to which the organisation is performing effectively. But likewise, it is argued, management can only produce an effective supervisory body within its organisation when it has sufficient knowledge of that body. It is here that the social scientist can aid the manager. Should a rationalisation be necessary for such a study, it could be stated in terms of sequential influence. The social scientist is able to derive information relating to the foreman and to foreman performance. This information can be transmitted to the manager who in turn is able to have an influence upon the foreman role. Such influence is designed to produce greater organisational effectiveness. A study such as this, therefore, has a two-fold purpose. First, to increase our knowledge relating to industrial organisations and organisational roles; and, second, to aid the manager in making his organisation more effective by providing badly needed information about a key organisational role.

The major task set for this study—examining the theory and practice of the foreman role—must inevitably have various residual consequences. Such consequences can be seen in both the research strategy or methodology and in the theoretical perspectives employed. Taking the first point of methodology, any brief survey of the literature on industrial behaviour and practice shows that there has already been a great deal of work carried out to investigate the nature of the role of the industrial foreman. One of the guiding propositions, and to some extent the impetus as well, for this analysis is that little of this work is of much relevance to the theorist or practitioner. Such a broad generalisation can be defended, as in fact it is later in the study, on the grounds that very little attempt has been made to relate the work of one researcher to another. As far as the present writer knows, there is nowhere to be found a comprehensive survey of research findings which integrate the results into a comprehensive analysis of the foreman role.

Past research differs from the present in the emphasis placed upon the descriptive features of the foreman role. In effect, the emphasis used by many previous writers has been a mainly demographic one, rather than a more analytical one, say within the discipline of sociology. Taking these two approaches of demography and sociology, they are similar in that both examine the effect of one factor upon another factor. The factors or variables chosen are really only relevant for the purpose of prediction. But this represents the particular method of demography rather than the method and purpose of sociology. Thus, both demographers and sociologists make use of 'social indicators' such as the social and economic status of the foreman, the organisational climate in which the role operates and the organisational context. For a descriptive level of understanding the method of social indicators is adequate, but the method becomes inadequate when the social process needs analysis. Such a process might be the effect of the foreman's class position upon the functioning of his role. As sociological analysis frequently uses social indicators and often such a method can add to our knowledge, the method should not be rejected out of hand. But the relative usage of such a method is the important factor. Thus, sociological research uses social indicators as a kind of shorthand—a method for increasing our understanding of a particular social process of interest. Social indicators are then used as a secondary method and are not of primary concern.

Another aim of sociological research is explanation. Thus, sociology is concerned with how X can affect Y in a particular way and under certain conditions. The 'particular way' and the 'certain conditions' can be specified—the result is a quantification of the actual process of interaction amongst variables. Demographic research is concerned with a similar relationship but does not quantify this process. Instead, its primary aim is the provision of an outline of knowledge aiding prediction. Whereas sociology is concerned with the 'how' of the relationship, demography is concerned with other ends. The amount of directly relevant knowledge is thus reduced.

4

Social research can take many forms, depending on the nature of the problem and the kind of information desired from the research. Thus, it is possible to distinguish descriptive, formulative, exploratory and explanatory research. One of the aims of this study is to provide both an exploratory and explanatory study of the foreman role, making every effort to avoid the specifically demographic analysis as discussed above.

Compared with the natural and physical sciences, the social sciences are at a disadvantage because of their relative youth. In any one branch of the social sciences there is not enough evidence on any particular subject, or at most there is enough evidence but this is so scattered that it is difficult to comprehend the nature of the social reality being examined. The lack of evidence, or lack of collated evidence, means that there is rarely a well-developed theory for future research problems or for hypotheses to be deduced from the theory. Where theory does exist in the social sciences, it is often either too general or too specific to be of great assistance in restructuring further hypotheses for future research.

Given this situation, it is possible to discuss the nature of exploratory research since this particular analysis takes that form more than any other. In essence, exploratory research enables the researcher to gain experience which will be of value in further research for the formulation of hypotheses and the posing of specific problems associated with the research. Exploratory research fulfils several functions in addition to this. First, by examining the area in which further research points, it is possible to discuss the way in which practical problems may arise in further research. Second, such research can provide, as Selltiz points out, 'a census of problems regarded as urgent by social practitioners' (1959, p. 33).

Some writers have suggested that exploratory research has little significance for the development of knowledge in the social sciences, since it rarely, in isolation, provides much of a contribution to knowledge. This charge, however, is unfounded. At the very least, research of this nature provides information which is of value to future research and can aid in problems that have a high priority for 'social practitioners'. Also, there is implicit in the charge made an assumption that only experimental and explanatory research is of any scientific value. Again, this assumption is an erroneous one. Explanatory and experimental research, for them to have any social significance, must be more or less relevant to wider issues than the specific area of the research itself. For this relevance, there must be an exploration of all the parameters of the problem in question.

The analysis of an area such as the foreman role requires a strict theoretical base. The role is taken at a universal level and, as mentioned, an attempt is made at integrating the important variables affecting supervisory behaviour. Clearly, these variables need to be integrated in some way if any sense is to be made of the role in question. The problem of inter-relating and integrating the variables is really a problem of a strong theoretical framework.

Many theoretical frameworks are available to the social scientist working in the broad area of organisational roles, but the choice of one over the others is not one of random selection. Rather, it is a problem of choice based on the objectives or goals of the study. With the goal of integration in mind, an adaptive open systems model is used in this study. Such a theoretical approach, as advocated in Chapter 2, is advanced because, being open in character, the systems view can incorporate the many variables that are analysed in this study.

The systems viewpoint has the added advantage that it does enable other theoretical approaches to be incorporated in the analysis. Two of the most 'popular' frameworks available to the social scientist in the contemporary literature are considered as viable alternatives in Chapter 2, but the systems approach is decided upon because this does enable the inclusion of many of the important points from both 'grounded theory' and 'social action theory'. Grounded theory, as advanced by Glaser and Strauss (1967), emphasises that social research should be used to generate theories—theory should be discovered from data. Thus, if the proposition made earlier regarding the non-integration of data on foremen into a coherent theoretical framework is accepted, this study, by re-analysing the data, is capable of generating grounded theory. With the other theoretical approach of social action theory the emphasis is upon the meaning of social action for the individual. Thus, the ends of action, the means available to attain these ends and the consequences of action are examined. The systems approach used in this study, by concentrating upon the performance of an organisational role, is able to incorporate many aspects of social action theory.

Although, as Chapter 2 shows, the model used is that of a complex adaptive system, the actual operationalisation is remarkably simple. A system is taken as a construction of inputs, conversions and outputs, or, in terms of the variables analysed, one of independent, intervening and dependent variables respectively. The foreman role, for analytical purposes only, is taken to be the total system and this can be seen as being divided into three broad sub-systems, each with varying types of variables.

Before the three sub-systems can be examined in detail, it is necessary to examine the role of the foreman in general terms. Chapter 3 makes some attempt at clearing the confusion that surrounds the meaning of the term 'foreman'. It is shown that the actual identification of foremen in the industrial setting is difficult and that any attempt at a definition becomes even more difficult because of the heterogeneity of supervisory tasks in modern industry. Aspects of the foreman role that are often discussed in the literature are also examined in this chapter and include features such as role ambiguity and marginality, the nature of role conflict and the application of the historical perspective in the analysis of the foreman role.

Once this confusion concerning the foreman role has been cleared, the analysis of the role in terms of the theoretical perspective developed in Chapter 2 is attempted. Chapters 4, 5 and 6 examine the three sub-systems of the role at the organisation, group and individual levels respectively. As mentioned, at each of these sub-system levels the variables influencing the role are analysed and discussed in terms of the nature of their dependency. At each sub-system level a portion of the total model is built up, but integration of these 'portions' cannot take place until the final chapter.

It might be argued that by taking each variable separately and compartmentalising it, perhaps at times rather arbitrarily, into the three sub-systems delineated could lead to methodological problems, particularly the problem of reductionism. Initially, there might be a valid argument, but when all the variables are integrated into the total system model of the foreman role, the usefulness and validity of the approach is demonstrated. Again, it might be argued that some variables are wrongly placed in terms of their general dependency and here there might be a more reasoned basis for disputing the approach used. To counter such an argument would be difficult, except to say that the 'positioning' of variables in the total system model is done on the basis of the available evidence which appears most relevant to the study. Although arbitrariness might appear to be present, for this study the positioning developed throughout seems to be most appropriate. This is not to say, however, that another study of another organisational role would necessarily follow such a schema. Given different task and situational variables a great deal of 're-shuffling' of the variables might take place.

As discussed above, the final chapter attempts to integrate the findings relating to foremen into a coherent framework. It is hoped that the initial objective of providing coherence to a scattered area of analysis is achieved by this method. But in addition to this, the study is capable of looking at some of the practical issues involved in supervisory behaviour. In the final chapter some of these issues are examined in the hope that the practising foreman and manager may derive some useful information from the study. In particular, the two aspects of supervisory training and motivation are concentrated upon because of the great deal of confusion that appears to be present in the current literature on these matters and because these appear to be two aspects of the foreman role that managers seem most concerned with at the present time.

It is hoped, then, that the study has relevance for both the social scientist interested in analytical techniques and for the manager and foreman looking for ways of improving supervisory effectiveness. Obviously the satisfaction of the needs of such a wide 'audience' is difficult, but, if nothing more, the claim by some writers that the foreman is 'the forgotten man of industry' now has fewer foundations.

2   The theoretical model

In his book *Sociology and Modern Systems Theory*, Buckley (1967) presents a cogent argument against what he sees as being the two predominant themes for the analysis of society in modern sociology. Basically, he terms these two themes the mechanical and organic models of society. In essence, these two models are better thought of as the mechanical equilibrium and the organismic homeostatic models of society. Whatever name is given to them, they are expressing the same ideas, and for Buckley at least, in terms of social theory, they have little usefulness for the analysis of modern society and modern societal processes. Before examining these two models, it needs to be pointed out that Buckley proposes a new model for the analysis of society—what he calls the complex adaptive system. This model, as shown below, is consistent with societal reality and with modern systems thinking by the use of concepts such as cybernetics, information and communication theory, and other related fields of study.

The mechanical equilibrium model of society is well illustrated by Sorokin (1928) as deriving its influence from the writings associated with 'social physics' in the eighteenth and early nineteenth centuries. Concepts such as social entropy and the transformation were typical of such writings of the mechanical model theorists. Perhaps the best known of these early mechanical model theorists was Pareto who, whilst using a system concept for the analysis of society, held that the parts of the system should be in a state of equilibrium, no matter what the state of change within society.

The ideas put forward by the early 'mechanical' theorists have been used by later influential writers in sociological theory, particularly Homans and Parsons. Again, there is the notion of a system having inter-related parts with their special boundaries, but maintaining a state of equilibrium.

To some extent it cannot be doubted that the mechanical model theorist of society is correct, particularly in stressing that if we take a society and view it as a social system, there is always within that system a set or a complex of sets of norms, expectations and values which maintain the equilibrium of the system under discussion. But in concentrating upon the 'functional' parts of the system—the parts that inevitably lead to this state of equilibrium—the elements of the system leading to dysfunctioning and to disequilibrium are missed. For example, the deviant values and expectations to be found in any social system may be just as stable as the 'functional' ones and yet they will inevitably lead to parts of the system experiencing a state of disequilibrium. By presenting only a part of the total picture in this sense, it suggests that the mechanical model theorists need to be either rejected completely or, at the very least, they need to be fundamentally revised to account for factors such as the deviant values and all the aspects of the system that contribute to a state of disequilibrium.

Thus, in theoretical terms, the equilibrial systems presented by the writers of the mechanical school of thought are relatively closed systems and to a certain extent they are entropic. This state arises from the continual striving for equilibrium. In doing so, the systems lose energy and they have, in Buckley's terms, only a minimum of free energy. Change in such systems is the result of external disturbances; nowhere is it possible, in equilibrium terms, to see change arising from within the system itself; endogenous sources of change are not catered for in these terms. Taking the idea of the system itself as being composed of interdependent parts in a state of equilibrium, these parts are viewed in relatively simple terms and, since they are interdependent, they are linked to one another directly. But, furthermore, the linking operation is carried out by means of energy exchange and not by, say, information exchange. Finally, if the point regarding their relatively closed state is taken, it follows that there can be no mechanism that allows for feedback, self-regulating mechanisms or adaptive contingencies at all.

The other major theme that can be seen in the history of sociological thought is the organic model of society, or, as expressed above, the organismic homeostatic model. The major influence upon the rise of this approach was the transformation of biological concepts to sociological theory, as seen particularly in the work of Spencer (cf. Andreski, 1969). As with the mechanical model, the social system is seen as being composed of interdependent parts, but they are discussed in the sense that the interdependent parts of an organism might be.

Again, like the mechanical model, the organic model of society sees that the parts of the system are related functionally and that the parts are in a state of co-operation rather than one of conflict. The work of Spencer and the early social organicists led to 'social Darwinism', but later writings using the same organic theme have given rise to 'structural functionalism', as best portrayed in the writings of Talcott Parsons. The functionalists stress the notion of order within society—order in the sense of consensus and co-operation. The organic model is used to reach a similar conclusion to that of the mechanical equilibrium theorists, that the parts of the social system are in close co-operation and that there is little opportunity for deviation from the norms, values and expectations of the society. The way in which the organic model is used in contemporary sociological theory is such that it stresses the nature of social homeostasis, that is a process within the social system that ensures that the parts maintain equilibrium.

Criticisms of functionalism abound in the writings of many contemporary social theorists and this is not the place to either review these criticisms or to add to the already growing list of them. It is sufficient to say that increasingly there is discontent concerning structural functionalism and that in system terms this discontent may be expressed in the following way.

In pure terms, the homeostatic system deriving from the organic model of society is an open one and, in Buckley's terms, it is also negentropic. A fairly high level of energy is maintained within strictly controlled limits. As seen above, however, the social system's chief characteristic is in terms of its ability to maintain the given structure within limits set down previously. Unlike the mechanical model, there are feedback loops with the environment and interchanges are based both upon energy (as with the mechanical model) and information. But, the interchanges that occur are designed to produce self-regulation for the system and not, in fact, to give rise to adaptation. In functional terms, the interchange that occurs is designed principally for structure and boundary maintenance and not for change of system structure.

If both of the main streams of thought in the contemporary sociological literature are unsatisfactory, as the above analysis suggests, there is clearly a need for a new approach. Even if a new approach were merely a synthesis of the equilibrium and homeostasis models, it would present a much more realistic model of societal functioning. Such a model has been suggested by Buckley—the complex adaptive system.

Complex adaptive systems are open in nature and, like the organic model, such systems are negentropic. They differ from the two previous types of system to the extent that they are open, not only externally but also internally. Using an adaptive model is to recognise that the component parts of the system may interchange and

11

that such interchanges can result in significant changes in the nature of the component parts. Because of the inter-relatedness of the parts, a change in one part may give rise to changes in other parts and ultimately in the total system. Interchanges may be of an energy kind and these are subject to wide fluctuations, unlike those in the two previous models. There are also information interchanges at the internal and external levels. Feedback control loops exist, making possible self-regulation as in the organic model. But, in addition to this, the feedback loops enable self-direction and adaptation to a changing environment. Thus, the complex adaptive system may, in fact, change its structure as a response to a changing environment, particularly if this is seen as a prerequisite for survival or viability.

For an adequate analysis of society and its component parts, it is suggested that such an adaptive complex system model is required in so far as it is not restricted solely to the social system but also incorporates the whole socio-cultural system. Such a model is discussed in more detail below, drawing upon the basic essential characteristics briefly discussed above. Buckley sees the usefulness of such an approach because for him it develops (Buckley, 1967, p. 39):

1 A common vocabulary unifying the several 'behavioural' disciplines;

2 A technique for treating large scale complex organisations;

3 A synthetic approach where piecemeal analysis is not possible due to the intricate interrelationships of parts that cannot be treated out of context of the whole;

4 A viewpoint that gets at the heart of sociology because it sees the socio-cultural system in terms of information and communication nets;

5 The study of relations rather than 'entities', with an emphasis on process and transition probabilities as the basis of a flexible structure with many degrees of freedom;

6 An operationally definable, objective, non-anthropomorphic study of purposiveness, goal-seeking system behaviour, symbolic cognitive processes, consciousness and self-awareness and socio-cultural emergence and dynamics in general.

The three approaches discussed above can be represented diagrammatically in order to show the main distinctions between them. Figure 2.1 shows that the equilibrium model (I) moves to a point of equilibrium and stays there, allowing for little variation. The homeostatic model (II) is seen as applying to those systems with a given high level of organisation, where there are constant pressures to alter the structure of the system. And, lastly, the adaptive system (III) shows that variation is a key component and that the system is capable of accommodating to such changes as may occur.

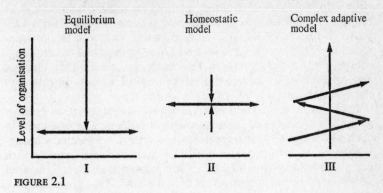

FIGURE 2.1

A paradigm for the analysis of complex adaptive systems

A theme running throughout Buckley's work is that modern systems research is attempting, among other things, to produce a general paradigm relating to the mechanisms which lead to the discussion of complex adaptive systems. In fact, Buckley himself attempts to do this, at least implicitly. At this stage of the analysis a more explicit attempt is made to produce such a paradigm and one which, consistent with common contemporarily expressed ideas in modern systems thinking, attempts to use the language of information theory and cybernetics. The concepts of such an approach need to be delineated in the first place.

The term *environment* is commonly used in systems analysis. Basically, what is meant by this concept in this context is that there is a set of distinguishable elements, states or events. These properties are distinguishable by various differences, as seen below, and for this reason it is possible to talk of a *variety* referring to these distinguishable differences. The variety of distinguishable aspects of the properties composing the environment is usually seen as being fairly stable and to this extent it is possible to delineate the next concept—that of *constraint*. Typically, the environment displays a high level of constraint since this enables both the development and the elaboration of adaptive systems. Of course, it is possible that the elements in the environment are only loosely related and in a situation such as this it is possible to think in terms of lack of constraint, an extreme form of which might be seen as chaos.

Turning to the internal organisation of an adaptive system, when it has developed to such a stage that it is possible to think in terms of it being in a state of interaction with the environment, it is usual to refer to the term *mapping*, that is that the system has mapped parts of the environment variety and constraints into the organisation as either structure or information, or even in some circumstances as both. The way in which such mapping processes work is for a sub-set to be formed containing the constrained variety in the environment. In some way this is coded and then transmitted to result in a change in the receiving system. This receiving system and its changes are isomorphic to some degree to the original variety. In this way, the system becomes adjusted to its environment.

Using these and other widely accepted concepts, it is possible to build a paradigm of complex adaptive systems. The first point in such a paradigm is that there is, for any system, a potentially changing environment that has as one of its characteristics a variety with constraints. Also, it can be taken for granted that there is a given adaptive system or organisation of some kind. This given adaptive system persists and elaborates to higher levels of system by a successful mapping procedure of some of the environmental variety and constraints into its own organisation on at least a semi-permanent basis.

Taking these basic system characteristics, the adaptive system must manifest certain typical characteristics that can now be distinguished. For the present purposes, this notion of an adaptive system is taken at the socio-cultural level, but equally the paradigm is applicable to biological and psychological systems as well. The characteristics can be thought of as follows:

1 There must be a degree of 'friction' between the system and its environment. This is necessary so that there is an ongoing interaction between the two. Also, of course, this leads to on-going reaction between them.
2 There must be a mechanism for variety as distinguished earlier. This mechanism could be regarded as a pool of variability designed to meet the need and problem of mapping new variety and for mapping new constraints in a changing environment.
3 There must be a set of selective criteria or mechanisms against which the 'variety pool' may be sifted into those variations in the organisation or system that more closely map the environment and those that do not.
4 There must be an arrangement for preserving or propagating these successful mappings.

As Buckley points out, a paradigm such as this is relational in its perspective. It is also consistent with the ideas presented in contemporary information theory—that is as a process of selection of a sub-set that only acquires meaning when it is matched with another sub-set from a similar environment. Also, it is by communication that the constrained variety is transmitted through the environment; coding and decoding takes place throughout the whole process so that the original variety and its constraints are 'relatively invariant' at the end of the process.

This process can be seen in terms of a socio-cultural system. In such a system there are variously patterned and predictable actions of individuals and groups. These are an important feature of the environment. Over any period of time a process of selective elaboration occurs, but, simultaneously, some parts of the social process are preserved and these are transformed or become part of the culture, the personality structure and the social organisation of the society or socio-cultural system.

Having looked at the paradigmatic characteristics of systems in general, it is possible to turn to the specific socio-cultural system. As shown, the characteristics of, say, biological and psychological systems are similar to those of the socio-cultural systems, but more specific refinements can be made.

There is still the notion of friction between the system and its environment. This is usually manifested in the form of tension and is a universal feature of complex adaptive systems. In discussing this feature, Buckley refers to Thelen (1956) who maintains that life for the average individual can be seen as a set of reactions to stress where energy is mobilised. Since tension and stress are both disturbing for the individual there are continual attempts made to reduce both. In the language of the psychologist, impulses are created to take direct action for tension management. This is clear at the individual level of analysis, but can also be seen at higher levels. Tension is ubiquitous in any social system for a variety of reasons, the important thing is that attempts are always made to reduce or to manage this tension.

Following sequentially from the first feature of socio-cultural systems, it is true to say that taking a system as a whole, it is impossible to talk about a state of equilibrium pertaining. Only if the system were completely closed would it be possible to talk of a state of equilibrium. Having said this, however, it does not follow that the homeostatic model of system functioning is any more realistic. Buckley suggests that the term 'morphogenesis' is appropriate for the analysis of socio-cultural systems. This is because it covers the structure-maintaining feature of the equilibrium model and the structure-elaborating and -changing feature of the homeostatic model.

Taking into account the above description of some of the features of a socio-cultural system, such a system can be defined as 'a complex of elements or components directly or indirectly related in a causal network, such that at least some of the components are related to some others in a more or less stable way at any one time'. Clearly, from this definition, it follows that the inter-relationships of the components that become established can be seen as constituting the structure of the particular system. For this reason, it is important to recognise that the complex adaptive system is something different and can be distinguished from the structure that the system displays at any point in time.

Recognising that the system can be distinguished from the structure enables a further feature to be noted—that the continuity of the system may require a change in structure over time if, in fact, the system is to persist. The amount or degree of change that is necessary can be analysed by examining the internal state of the system, the state of the system environment and the nature of the interaction between the system and the environment.

A perspective such as this is useful since it goes beyond the structural functionalist analysis of social systems. In the latter, a major system problem is seen as pattern maintenance, together with that of tension management. In the present analysis, for the system to continue and persist (though not necessarily in its present form) there must be the maintenance of certain essential variables. These variables may be seen in terms of functional prerequisites. The maintenance of the system's essential variables may depend on pattern reorganisation or change, although there will be a necessity for some maintenance of these essential variables through patterning. Again, the statement by other system theorists that order and integration are achieved in the system through a process of institutionalisation is not completely adequate since deviance, social disorder and even disintegration of the system can also arise through the same process of institutionalisation.

In dealing with the complex adaptive system, therefore, it is necessary to recognise the continually changing state of the system. This can be seen as a process of structuring, de-structuring and re-structuring.

Deviance and deviation are crucial in any complex adaptive system and in the model presented here they are emphasised by concepts such as self-regulation and cybernetic control. Deviance, of course, may be either functional or dysfunctional for the system. From the dysfunctional viewpoint, deviance can be seen as arising from a negative feedback somewhere in the system. Functionally, cybernetic control shows the necessity for deviation in the system in so far as deviation provides a 'pool' of potential transformations of structure that the adaptive system may have reason to call upon at some time. Deviance, then, may act as a pool of alternative ideas and

16

behaviour in juxtaposition to the traditional institutionalised ideologies and role behaviours of the system.

If the above argument is accepted concerning the necessity for deviance in the adaptive system, it then follows that within the system there must be processes or mechanisms that function to select and to preserve part of the deviance in the system. In a socio-cultural system, the selectors and preservers are common; they are manifested in conflict, competition, collective behaviour, social movements of all kinds, and so on. It should be noted that such mechanisms and processes are often not of a rational kind.

A socio-cultural system is capable of adjusting to deviance in this way because of its very adaptive structure. Almost instantly, such a system is capable of temporary shifts in structure that will meet the exigencies of deviance in the system. Of course, these structural shifts may only be temporary because in any system there is need for a minimum level of integration, but there are usually structural alternatives internal to the system.

Deriving from this paradigm elaborated, other comments need to be made before turning to the organisation as an adaptive complex system. Most sociological studies have analysed society in terms of structural concepts such as institutions, culture, norms, roles, groups, and so on. Often, as Silverman (1968) has argued, these structural concepts have been reified in the course of analysis and lead to a static, deterministic view of the operation of society. The unit of analysis needs to be the systemic matrix of interacting, goal-seeking, deciding individuals and sub-groups. This matrix may be part of a total organisation or part of a loose collectivity. Society in these terms can be seen as a continuous morphogenic process.

The organisation model

Two basic assumptions are made about organisations when they are being discussed by social scientists or by the layman. They are that, first, organisations exist in some identifiable form or another and that, second, these identifiable forms are purposive in that they are orientated towards the attainment of relatively specific goals. In terms of the general system model developed above, these two assumptions tell us little about the nature of organisations either as social systems or as part of a larger complex adaptive system.

These are important problems, as can be seen when the overall complex adaptive system is examined. It is difficult to determine whether an organisation is, in fact, being dealt with in so far as the boundaries of the organisation are difficult to determine. Organisational behaviour relating to the individual is often indistinguishable from extra-organisational behaviour. Problems such as these support

17

the proposition that it is difficult to determine what an organisation actually is, let alone the difficulties of attempting to identify the organisation.

In terms of the second assumption relating to purposiveness, this is perhaps an even greater problem. A cursory examination of any organisation, once it has been identified, shows clearly enough that the objectives of the organisation cannot always be equated with the directives and goals of the chief executive, even though there needs to be recognition that there is purposive behaviour within any organisation. It has been recognised for a long time that the goals of the organisation members (particularly lower level participants) are often divergent to the manifestly stated goals of the organisation as a unit. The 'logic of activity' and the 'logic of sentiment' that Homans (1951) refers to in his re-analysis of the Hawthorne Studies exemplifies this argument, as does Merton's (1957) account of the latent functions of bureaucratic structures and the subsequent dysfunctioning of the organisation.

The proposition is made here that in developing an organisation model for present purposes it is better to take the organisation as a complex adaptive system first of all and only later to attempt to build into this system the notion of objectives, goals, purposes, and so on. Consistent with the general systems model already developed, it is necessary to examine the organisation as an energy input–output system and as an information input–output system. At its most simple level, the organisation can be seen in terms of input, output and functioning.

When the organisation is viewed as an information and energic input–output system there must be provision for feedback so that any information or energic return from the output re-activates the system as a whole. In this way, and by allowing for input from the environment as described earlier, the system is manifestly an open one.

The level of stability talked of earlier (whilst allowing for the functionality of a degree of deviation) enables the term 'organisation' to be used. Stability is evident in both the social and non-social spheres of activity, over time. The factor of endurance and stability enables the system to be understood in terms of an input into the system (energic and informational), a transformation within the system itself and a resultant output in terms again of energy and information, but usually seen as a product or service. To avoid the problems of reification referred to earlier, such a process can best be illustrated by reference to an industrial organisation. The input is the combination of raw materials and human labour; the transformation is seen in the actual stages of production; and the output is the finished product. A cycle of events is thus completed and a new cycle can be activated. The product at the output end of the cycle is often transformed into cash which supplies new energy for the system. This, of course, refers to the 'physical' system based on energy exchange and, as shown below, other 'systems' operate simultaneously producing informational and affective outputs.

Other types of organisation follow this same basic pattern—hospitals, social work agencies (for example the Probation Service) and educational organisations. But if the process is analogued in this way, it becomes clear that the source of energy feedback differs. Thus, the majority of organisations use both intrinsic and extrinsic sources and are very much dependent upon the output in social terms for the feedback of energy in whatever form.

Taking the organisation as a social system, therefore, has two important dimensions. First, there is the process of translating the input into an output by examining the activities of individuals within the system. Second, there is the process of feeding back the output energy into the system as a further input.

A model of organisation in these terms is not new (cf. Von Bertalanffy, 1956; Thomason, 1970), but the emphasis upon the two dimensions delineated above does add a new perspective to systems thinking, particularly as seen later when an organisational role is analysed in these kinds of terms. Before any attempt is made at such an exercise, it is necessary to comprehend fully the notion of system as it is being used in this context and, more particularly, how the general model of a complex adaptive system as distinguished earlier can be utilised at the organisational level in terms of the open system concept.

It has already been shown that the primary emphasis in general systems theory, whether an open or closed system is being advocated, is upon the question of the interdependence of the parts of the system, the actual relationships between the parts and an examination of the structure of the system.

Open systems have various characteristics in common with one another and each of the characteristics goes some way in defining the concept of a system when applied to complex organisations (cf. Katz and Kahn, 1966).

1 The input of energy: energy is an input into the system from the wider external environment of the system.
2 The conversion: energy at the input stage is transformed within the system into an identifiable output.
3 The output: transformed energy from the input is exported into the environment.
4 A cycle of events: the exported energy may act as a further input to the system, thus producing a cycle of events.

5 Negentropy: this is a mechanism to ensure the survival of the system. One method is by using the cycle of events described above.

6 Feedback, coding processes and information: these are similar to the functions as described in the general model above. Feedback, of course, may be seen in terms of information, producing a homeostatic state within the system; usually this is seen as a kind of negative feedback. The coding processes that occur ensure that input into the system is done on a selective basis. The nature of the coding mechanism, of course, depends upon the task that the system is oriented towards.

7 Homeostasis: in general open systems display a fairly steady state through homeostatic procedures. The reason for homeostasis is to ensure that the basic character of the system remains the same, notwithstanding that separate parts of the system may themselves alter radically. Also, homeostasis can really only be understood by examining the system over a period of time; at any one time there may be a very 'unsteady state' existing within the system.

8 Differentiation: this arises through the homeostatic processes of the system. Over time there is movement towards more elaboration of the parts of the system which may occur through a variety of processes such as mechanisation.

9 Equifinality: this was originally suggested by Von Bertalanffy. Basically what equifinality states is that although different conditions may obtain at the beginning, and though the system may reach the final outcome by different routes, the output may be the same.

Discussion

From the above analysis, it is clear that the concept of a system and the use of a system perspective have useful implications for any social analysis. The same is true, of course, in any scientific activity. Increasingly, the systems approach is being used in order to further the interests and activities of the scientific discipline. This idea of a systems approach being used in all types of scientific ventures, however, does present drawbacks. Perhaps the greatest of these is that there is a strong tendency to believe that what is permissible and what works in, say, the biological sphere will operate equally in the social and psychological spheres. There are obvious differences between these two, as the earlier analysis relating to the general systems model has shown. Therefore, the system concept as used in differing situations ought to be clearly specified.

The fact that social systems are man-made means that there are differences between them and biological systems. Again, in so far as they are man-made, they are subject to a high level of variation in their functioning, particularly when compared to the level of variation in biological systems. This reduces the degree of prediction that is possible in such systems. Nevertheless, within social systems, there are always pressures to reduce the amount of potential variation by a number of mechanisms such as roles having fairly specific expectations associated with them, the existence of a fairly stable normative system as a part of the social system, and so on. The prevailing value structure of a social system is further evidence of the striving to reduce variation.

System parts

It has been shown above that the concept of a system can be applied to various levels of social phenomena, particularly the societal level and the organisational level. In addition to this, it is possible to conceive of there being distinct systems at a lower level of analysis. They can, in fact, be regarded as systems so long as the general notions of openness and adaptability are used. For the purposes of the present analysis, however, it is proposed to take some component parts of a system as sub-systems rather than as total systems, whilst other phenomena are regarded as total open systems. Thus, as seen below, the *role* of the foreman is regarded as a total system, though interacting with other systems, whilst the *technical component* of the organisation system is viewed as a sub-system of the organisation.

It is a common observation that organisations are itemised according to the major organisational objectives. Thus, those organisations concerned chiefly with educational objectives are usually classified as educational organisations. So it is with production or business organisations. They are called such because this label is consistent with the major system objective—production or business. The production element in an organisation, however, comprises only a part of the organisation and so for the present purposes is known as a sub-system couched within a total organisation. The main task of this sub-system is to get the work done, and in that sense it can be seen in the input–conversion–output schema as a definite conversion factor. In fact, it is the major conversion factor within an organisation of this nature. Nevertheless, it has to be recognised that there are, in addition, distinct inputs and outputs within a production organisation.

A further sub-system within an organisation is the supportive sub-system. It is given this name because its main function is to interact with the wider environment, usually ensuring that there is an accommodation of the output of the total system. There is then a close link between this sub-system and the production sub-system.

In production organisations, the supportive sub-system might well go under the heading of 'marketing' or 'sales'.

One other sub-system that can be distinguished is the maintenance sub-system. As the name implies, the main function of this sub-system is not actually to produce whatever the system is directed towards achieving, but to ensure that the means for such production are available. Thus, using the word in its widest possible sense, it is possible to talk of the maintenance sub-systems as being concerned with the equipment of the organisation. In production organisations the maintenance departments such as engineering come to mind readily, but equally important are the maintenance functions of personnel and industrial relations.

Role systems

The concept of role is a widely used one in the social science literature. When used as such, roles are taken to mean specific forms of behaviour which have certain expectations associated with them. In complex organisations, roles invariably derive from the requirements as laid down by the tasks of the organisation. When organisational roles are referred to, it is usual to perceive them as characterising and characterised by standardised patterns of behaviour, at least more so than in the non-organisational sphere of society. For these reasons, it is difficult to envisage the concept of role without the related concepts of norms (expectations) and values. The norms associated with a particular role are in effect the expectations laid down for the individuals occupying the particular role. Values are similar, but do tend to represent rather more generalised belief systems or social ideologies, again associated in many instances with particular roles, although usually more than one, as with the notion of norm.

Some writers have suggested that organisations can only be understood as systems of role structures. There is evidence to support such suggestions in so far as organisational roles are interdependent and reciprocal. The role system of an organisation is therefore integrative.

Complex organisations give the clearest examples of roles in operation. Such roles have strong normative pressures attached to them; the strength is often indicated by the fact that there are sanctions available in the case of any deviation from the role. More directly, this refers to deviation from the norm associated with the role. Organisations have formalised role systems in which there is a system of rules prescribing the patterns of behaviour for each organisational role. In this sense, it is possible to talk of there being standardised role systems.

The managerial role system

It has been shown how organisations can be construed as systems and as sets of systems. Re-capping, a system has been taken to mean a set of interdependent parts which receives inputs, converts these inputs by a set of planned activities and, as a result, produces specific outputs. It has also been shown that part of the output may 'feed back' to constitute part of the input in the next cycle of events. There is common agreement that part of the managerial role system's function is to act as a feedback system through control and authority. This can be demonstrated with the example of industrial management. Part of the managerial function is to report on outputs such as production costs, quality risks, manhours, morale measurements, and so on. These are supplied by management for action. If there is any deviation between the output and the planned output or standard, then corrective action is taken, often through adjustment of the input. Feedback processes within organisations such as these may be regarded as regulatory mechanisms. They are often very highly developed with respect to the control that they exert over input decisions. A very simple way in which the managerial feedback process operates can be demonstrated diagrammatically, as shown in Figure 2.2.

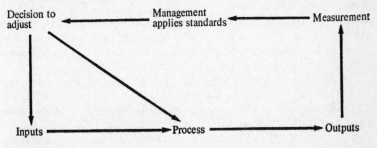

FIGURE 2.2

Another major function of the managerial role system is that of decision-making and again this can be seen in terms of the general systems model already distinguished. March and Simon (1958) see the organisation as a total system—as a composite of all the sub-systems which serve to produce the desired outputs. The basic assumption is that the elements of organisation structure and function emanate from the characteristics of human problem-solving processes and rational human choice. Therefore, the organisation is people making choices and behaving on the basis of their reactions to their needs and environment. The emphasis for practical employment of the theory is placed upon identification of the

23

decision centres and the communication media through which information is passed within the organisation system.

Acceptance of the March and Simon theory of decision-making has many consequences, but in the present context the main consequence can be seen to be the acceptance of the system model. This, in turn, has many sub-consequences for organisation and management theory. First, there is the fact that as we move to the top of the hierarchy, decisions lose rationality due to the increase in the number of systems and the manager's incapacity to deal in the aggregate form. Also, the division of labour within the organisation causes organisation members to build biases towards their sub-goals which insulate them from the other systems that make up the organisation. Third, there is the point that participation and the delegation of authority may be a necessity because of lack of adequate information or communication media. This results in poor co-ordination. Fourth, influence within an organisation is determined largely by the organisation's communication system. It is possible that influence may be gained as a result of expert knowledge in relation to an organisation problem. Influence centres, therefore, may be separated from the decision-making centres within an organisation.

Consequences such as these are discussed in more detail later. They are important since, for one thing, the logical conclusion to draw, even on the basis of the cursory examination so far, is that perhaps the notion of a hierarchical structure in an organisation is no longer a useful one to employ and that perhaps organisations should be looking for alternative forms of structure.

Summarising, then, at the most elementary level the system can be seen in terms of inputs, conversions and outputs, and feedbacks. For the managerial role system, the main emphasis is really upon organisational problems of one sort or another (but usually concerned with control and decision-making). The managerial system, therefore, can also be represented very simply, as shown in Figure 2.3.

FIGURE 2.3

This is still an input–conversion–output model in so far as the inputs are organisational problems, the conversions can be viewed as the problem-solving and decision-making processes and mechanisms, and the outputs are organisational solutions.

24

The foreman role system

By now it is clear that a pattern is emerging in this analysis of the general system model. A system can be broken down into other total systems or into sub-systems until the basic components are arrived at. Three levels of systems have now been discussed—the general model applicable to the societal level, the organisational level and the managerial level. And this 'breaking-down' process can go on almost *ad infinitum*. There is a danger, however, in that it is pointless discussing many sub-systems unless there is an awareness that those sub-systems are integrated into a total whole—that is that there is system synthesis of some kind or another.

The whole of this study is an exercise in examining the foreman role in system terms as discussed earlier. Before any attempt can be made to distinguish the system parts of the role, there must be recognition and acceptance that the role is not isolated, that it is an integral part of a larger system and that without this larger system

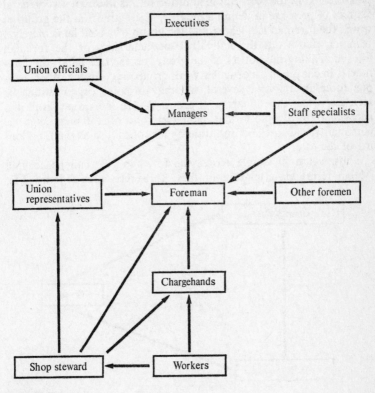

FIGURE 2.4

the role becomes meaningless. Therefore, the foreman role can be represented as being couched within an organisation, as Figure 2.4 demonstrates.

From the diagram, complex though it is, it can be seen that there is not representation of the total system. It has to be recalled that the view is taken here that a system should be seen in terms of complete openness and in terms of adaptability. The model represented in the diagram has shortcomings in that the interaction of the organisation with the external environment is not shown. Nevertheless, the figure is useful in that it shows that the role of foreman (or any other organisational role for that matter) cannot be discussed in isolation from other organisational roles. It does demonstrate the important point made above that the role of foreman is an organisational role and that unless the total organisation is recognised the role is meaningless.

From another point of view, there are inadequacies in such a representation. The figure demonstrates some of the organisational pressures upon the role. But in addition to this there are two general sources of pressure in defining the role. These are from the group of which the foreman is a leader and the group of which he is merely a member, and from the individual characteristics of the foreman himself. Taking the notion of the group, on the one hand, the foreman is in charge of a particular work group, and, on the other, he is one foreman amongst several and may in some organisations be seen as part of the management group. At the individual level, it is necessary to recognise that characteristics of foremen such as personality, background and training all contribute to the functioning of the role.

Thus, again in simple terms, the foreman role can be seen in system terms as a mixture of these three pressures (Figure 2.5).

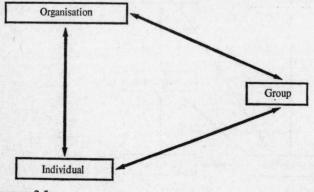

FIGURE 2.5

These three pressures are in interaction with one another in the organisational context and determine how the role is performed.

Although the model is displayed in the most simple of terms here, it is proposed that such a model should guide this study of foremen. Each of the three levels is analysed in detail and is regarded as a sub-system of the total system constituting the foreman role. To be consistent with the general system model developed here, if each of the three types of pressure upon the role are taken to be sub-systems of the total role, then they need to be considered in terms of the input–conversion–output process. As the analysis below shows, this can be done for the organisation and individual sub-system, but for the group sub-system there is a complication. It is proposed to take the inputs of the group sub-system as the outputs of the other two sub-systems so that only conversions and outputs are examined and discussed. The methodological reasons for this decision are explained later.

Conclusions

The model used here for the analysis of the foreman role is a basic system model utilising the notions of inputs, conversions and outputs. These are analysed at three levels of analysis—organisation, group and individual—taking each level as a sub-system of the total role. Recognition is made and stressed that the foreman role is an organisational role and that it can only be understood in organisation terms.

Before any attempt can be made at using the model of the foreman role developed here, it is necessary to discuss the role in general terms in an attempt to provide clarity at defining and identifying it. It is to these problems that the next chapter turns.

3 Identifying and defining the foreman

Introduction

The role of the foreman is a well-known one; the foreman is widely recognised as occupying a position within industrial organisations. However, few people would know how to describe the role in any detail. Most people would recognise that this particular role involves being in a position of formal and given authority over 'men'. For most people this is the important criterion in distinguishing the role of foreman. Many terms are used synonymously with the term 'foreman'—overlooker, supervisor, section hand, overseer, and so on. In all of these terms there is the fundamental idea that the distinguishing criterion is that of an individual being in charge of other individuals.

The view that the foreman himself has may well differ from this in several important respects. He probably accepts that he is in charge of men, but simultaneously he sees himself as being severely restricted in his authority over them. This may arise either because management does not give him enough authority or because the men deny him the right to use it in the form it is given. As a result, the foreman is likely to see himself as a 'dogsbody', at everyone's beck and call, and as the runner-about for everybody else. The outsider may attach a degree of prestige to the role of foreman, but regardless of this the foreman himself is unlikely to express too much satisfaction with the way it is shaped for him.

The sociologist's view of the foreman role has usually been expressed in terms of 'marginality' and 'ambiguity'. The commonest observation in the literature is that the role is defined—by management or workers or by the organisation in some abstract sense—in very ambiguous terms. The expectations of the role are seen to be at least ambiguous and more probably as conflicting. As they impinge upon the position-incumbent, they make him a 'marginal man' (cf. Berger, 1964, pp. 86–7):

As the lowest man on the managerial ladder, with meagre authority and reward, his identification with management tends to be weak; at the same time, he is not likely to develop a strong identification with the rank-and-file subordinates who tend to define his role as a representative of management.

The foreman is thus seen as being on the margin of two different cultures or two groups, whose expectations conflict to the detriment of his forming adequate perspectives of the role. In identifying and defining the foreman role, these aspects of marginality, role conflict and ambiguity can be examined.

Strain in the foreman role

Probably no other organisational role has attracted to itself so many ambiguity-implying epithets as that of the foreman in industry. He has been described as the 'man in the middle' (Gardner and Whyte, 1945), 'a master and victim' (Roethlisberger, 1951) and as a 'marginal man' (Wray, 1949). These epithets arise partly because of the foreman's position in a hierarchy of command; he stands between the management proper and the workforce proper, and by this token at least he is clearly in the middle or on the margin of both. But it is not this simple factor of spatial location which accounts for the very real concern about the foreman's role. The problem arises from ambiguity of both role and position.

Schneider (1957), for example, has suggested that the strains in the foreman role may be attributed to two complex sources: first, the strain which arises simply from the 'man in the middle' position, caught between groups whose power has been increasing (the management, the functional specialists and the unionised workers); second, the general decline in the total structure of rewards and satisfactions attached to the foreman role itself, both absolutely and relative to those attaching to other roles, both managerial and workers. Detailed descriptions of the conditions under which each occurs have been provided by a number of writers; Argyris (1954), Dalton (1959) and Walker, Guest and Turner (1956) have provided fairly detailed case studies of developments in America, and Lupton (1963) has provided a similar but more tangential study in Britain.

Schneider sums up the position as a generally weakened claim to managerial status and a reduction in importance as a role (Schneider, 1957, p. 143):

there is less authority, less prestige, less superiority in remuneration [and] less and less does it represent a way up, a means of escape from the bottom. The foreman is caught between the conflicting forces of an expanding bureaucracy; he is suspended between management and 'managed', between the hierarchy and an increasingly powerful laity.

Using the language developed in another context by the Tavistock researchers, it might also be summarised as a change from a fairly central and important *composite* managerial role to a more peripheral and less important *specialist and dependent* role outside the mainstream of management decision, which has in turn reflected itself in decreased relative rewards (cf. Trist *et al.*, 1963).

This general approach is, however, one which implies a temporal change in the role and status of the foreman as the cause of current problems. This is to suggest that the problems arise because the foreman employs a historical reference group (Shibutani, 1962) in expressing relative deprivation. If the foreman is allowed to speak for himself, as in Walker, Guest and Turner's study (1956), this may well emerge, but it should not be assumed to exist independently of detailed examination. In fact, one interpretation of the pattern of response obtained by Walker is that the foreman is so concerned with immediate situational problems, whether technical or interpersonal, that he has little time to compare himself favourably or unfavourably with the traditional conception of the foreman role. An alternative view, therefore, would be that the foreman's role strain is the product of his current position in a network of control and status, which may be the product of a historical development (but then what position is not?) but which also contains its own inherent strains which may not be tackled by reversion to a past age but could be by analysis and rectification of the current situation and structure.

Nor is Schneider alone in presenting this inference. Most representations see the 'reason' for the problem in the changes which have been occurring in industry. 'The role of the foreman today is one of transition', says Schneider (1957, p. 137) and it has been the victim 'of certain underlying forces which have tended to reduce the importance and uniqueness of his role'. He assigned these to categories: changes in size, mechanisation, specialisation, rationalisation and unionisation 'have all combined to alter drastically the content of the foreman's role, the relation of the role to managerial roles, the skills needed for the job, and the way in which the foreman must operate in the social structure of the plant' (ibid.). The conditions of aggressive de-formation and re-formation of occupations (Hughes, 1959) have apparently hit the traditional foreman role with particular severity, after a period of slow change since the beginning of the industrial revolution (NIIP, 1951, p. 15).

Although he is not the only member of the staff whose role has been changed by these factors (for example the clerical worker's role has also been affected drastically), the effect has not in his case been to assimilate it to manual workers' roles (as in the case of clerical workers); the position of the foreman remains differentiated from those, even after all the changes.

Furthermore, his role loses nothing of its complexity, even if the influences making for this role are different from those which applied before. It remains a complex role because of the increasing complexity of the production system itself, and not because of the centrality of the role in the management system. Partly because of this, attention tends to focus upon the consequences of the changes, not so much for their effect upon the role *per se* but for their effect upon the foreman's generalised status. He has lost position, power, authority and reward (in the sense that the position is no longer an indication of either 'success' or 'upward mobility').

But this aspect of the change has also led to the suggestion that the foreman's skills not only are changing but should change to make him more able to deal with all the new specialists and the more powerful workers. This tends to focus upon the skills of human relations or human management, and through a long period attention to the training of the foreman has concentrated on giving him these skills to enable him to get along better with others, or 'handle' men, as well as on developing appropriate 'attitudes' congruent with management objectives.

Writing in 1951, the NIIP researchers pointed towards the 'current trend in industry . . . towards a far more free and full-two-way communication between all levels within a factory' and the implication this carried for the job specification of the foreman. Given this scope of the 'discussion' the 'supervisor must be able to play his part as an important individual link in the communication system, as well as in conference and as a member of committees'. If this did not happen, then he would be relegated to the role of progress-chaser, concerned only 'with production details'. Because of this situation the role was seen to be changing in these ways (NIIP, 1951, p. 45):

> The changed role means that the new-pattern supervisor needs a degree of intellectual capacity and verbal ability, to comprehend and discuss abstract matters, considerably above that which was sufficient for the old-type foreman, whose main requirement was confined to knowing his immediate job and being able to get the men under him to push on with theirs. For example, it probably requires a higher level of mental ability to co-operate effectively under complicated centrally-run progress control systems than it does to be responsible for rough-and-ready progress control within a shop or department.

31

These systems save the supervisor time and effort but make greater demands on his understanding and on his powers of explanation and discussion. The new role also demands attitudes, maturity and qualities of personality, which, however desirable, were by no means essential in the old-type foreman; whilst there is an obvious tendency to require higher standards of general and technical education and training.

From this it follows that 'training in human relations and in appropriate social techniques is immensely more important than is generally realised either by supervisors or by managers' because conditions of full employment and the trend towards democratic control make it 'not only socially desirable but also economically essential that new and better methods of securing human efficiency and co-operative effort should be adopted' (ibid., p. 65). Of course, fashions are always good devices for securing the adoption of something which is undesirable, but this particular fashion may have given too much weight to one particular aspect of the supervisor's new role—that which included 'communications as a skill'. It was only later that the balance in favour of technical knowledge and skill came to be redressed, by which time the human relations approach had bestowed its charms widely.

One consequence of this was that many of the studies, particularly of the foreman role, assumed a basic human relations model of system operation before beginning. In the outcome, therefore, the findings tended to suggest that the model was supported by the facts: when the foreman spoke for himself he confirmed the view that the big problem was 'people . . . you have to get the men to see things your way' (Walker, Guest and Turner, 1956, p. 12); when an exploration was made of what the foreman actually did, using behavioural categories such as talking, writing or taking decisions, he was found to behave like a communicator; and since he needed so much training in human relations skills, he could clearly not be paid the full 'man's rate' for the new job until he had qualified.

As Thurley (1964) has suggested, the 'human relations' honeymoon may have proved a snare and a delusion as a substitute for the old style definition of the foreman's role. It tended to switch the emphasis away from the power structure within the plant and focus it upon the more personal and interpersonal elements in the situation. It is true that when the authority of the foreman in the formal sense was weakened by these various changes, he often sought to compensate by developing informal relationships with subordinates. But this could scarcely be regarded as a functional solution to the problems as posed, since it often meant the development of an 'indulgency pattern' (Gouldner, 1959) or of a network of reciprocal arrangements by which the foreman could exact production from the men in return for the connivance at various practices which might have specifically been denied by company policy. This could also be extended into relationships with specialists who sought to obtain line management acceptance of some change (Dalton, 1959). If some of these proved functional, they did so at the expense of control in the system as a whole.

Identifying the foreman role

Before any attempt can be made to define the foreman role, it is necessary to identify who the foreman is in industrial organisations. This is a major problem and is an area in which there is little uni-vocality. One part of the problem is indicated by Walker, Guest and Turner (1956). They say (p. 3) that

> the foreman is one species of a very large genus of human beings. The genus may be said to include all who directly supervise men and women, such as the power ranks of officers and non-commissioned officers in the armed forces, head nurses in hospitals, senior clerks in banks and law offices, and many others.

Their own study, as shown below, is focused upon the sub-species of foremen on the assembly line, as a part of the species of industrial foremen, which in turn is a part of the genus of supervisors—those who supervise or control the work of others.

The approach used by Walker, Guest and Turner is important in that there is the implication that the foreman can be recognised in the form of the person who stands in a particular position *vis-à-vis* a system of technology (for example, an assembly line) or of organisa-tion (for example, a factory in a particular industry). Many writers have commented, however, on the difficulties of defining the role within the socio-technical system and have sought to do so, either in terms of recognisable persons with titles or in terms of a generic control function.

Taking the first of these two approaches to resolving the difficulty, the study of foremen by the National Institute for Industrial Psycho-logy (1951) can be examined. Almost from the outset, the NIIP researchers recognised that it was 'not easy to define either the upper or lower limit of the supervisory strata in the pyramid of control' (p. 16), and so, for heuristic reasons, the supervisory strata was divided into four levels, each of which had generally recognised job or position titles. In delineating these four levels, the word 'supervisor' was taken to cover everyone in industry who had any responsibility for planning and controlling the work of others up to but excluding 'managers' as that term is generally understood (NIIP, 1951, pp. 15–17):

> *Level A* is intended to include the most senior supervisors, usually bearing some such title as Shop Superintendent, General Foreman or Senior Foreman. At this level, too, there are a certain number of people whose titles may include the word 'Manager' but who are really senior supervisors rather than junior managers. Level A usually occurs only in large concerns, and to be assigned to it, a supervisor would be in charge of a large or important shop or section and would carry considerable responsibilities and authority; he would normally have Level B supervisors under him.
>
> *Level B* includes the men and women who are probably most generally in mind when the terms 'Foreman' or 'Forewoman' are used, although here again there is a wide range of titles. The Level B supervisor would be engaged wholly in supervisory work, would normally have some responsibilities for planning and organising the work of his section, and he would usually have one or more junior supervisors under him.
>
> *Level C* covers the Assistant Foreman, Junior Foreman and those who are normally responsible to a Level B supervisor but who are themselves engaged almost entirely in supervisory rather than operative work. Except when acting as deputy for an absent Level B supervisor, the Level C supervisor would have limited responsibilities and authority. There might be several Level C supervisors, each with a section of his own, working under a Level B supervisor, or in some cases, there might be only one acting as deputy or second-in-command.
>
> *Level D* is intended to include the 'working' supervisor, the Chargehand or Leading Hand who is normally an operative but who carries some specific responsibilities for supervision for which he is separately rewarded.

Even with a schema such as this, the purely practical problem of identification still exists, even though the scheme does provide a useful and usable generalisation. The researchers in this study report that over 300 different job titles were found which had a supervisory connotation consistent with these four categorisations. They provide a list of fifteen sub-generic titles in an appendix, ranging from manager, assistant manager and department head through to superintendent, supervisor and senior (or other grade of) foreman, to leading hand, chargehand and working chargehand. But any of these might be a composite of a number of similar titles: assistant foreman, for example, is used to embrace deputy foreman, junior foreman, under-foreman, sub-foreman, junior shift foreman and foreman grade III.

Clearly, the job titles by themselves are not really going to facilitate the task of identifying the foreman role in industry or anywhere else. To define the genus of industrial foreman it is necessary to consider the function and the role within the undertaking. To describe these is not easy: it is possible to set up an abstract definition of a category, but, without careful consideration of what functionally links the titles just mentioned, this might be as sterile as any other that might be devised. Most people tend to agree that the role is 'executive' in that it involves carrying out policies, practices and procedures which have already been determined upon at a higher level of authority and that it has to do with day-to-day control. It is possible, therefore, to turn to the other way in which attempts have been made to identify and define the role—in terms of a generic control system.

Thurley (1964) uses two criteria to determine whether individual roles belong to a supervisory system or not. These are, first, the individuals concerned had to be directly in control over day-to-day variations and problems in the production system; and, second, they had to have recognised authority as immediate 'bosses' over the shop floor workers. The control systems of supervision were seen as exercised over some or all aspects of production systems, that is plant, materials, and so on. The individuals concerned might have technical rather than supervisory job titles and might be spread over a number of levels within the organisation. Thurley suggests that in spite of variations in particular plants supervisory systems will comprise four main levels (in some combination). These levels almost mirror the Glacier manifest pattern:

Level A Supervisors who directed the whole system and linked it with higher management; for example shift heads.

Level B The first-line supervisor or the man regarded by work people as their immediate boss.

Level C The semi-supervisor; e.g. the leading toolsetter, leading hand, etc., combining supervising with operative duties.

Level D The specialist operative carrying out special supervisory duties.

Thurley (1964) suggests that the most meaningful way of clarifying and classifying supervisory systems is by the main purpose of the system as shown by role behaviour. In his paper he distinguishes six main systems:

1 *Work flow systems:* here the supervisory system functions primarily

35

to get work out on time. Supervisors concentrate on easing bottle-necks, planning component flow, and so on.

2 *Work standard systems:* the premium here is on work or job specifications and methods of production. Inspection is the chief activity of supervisors and quality control the major function.

3 *Machine control systems:* these exist basically to control machine variations and breakdowns. Supervisors monitor behaviour and take correcting action if this is necessary.

4 *Labour control systems:* this is the traditional supervisory system which aims at controlling the speed of operatives and the amount of worker effort.

5 *Cost control systems:* supervisors here concentrate on the mini-misation of waste, reduction of costs and economy of effort.

6 *Work methods control systems:* here the system attempts to control and standardise types of operative method.

There are two observations that may be made in relation to these six systems. First, they may be regarded as specialised elements in a total control system, such that all must be operating at some level and be allocated at someone's responsibility. In the conception which Brown (1960) advances, they may all be seen as the ultimate responsibility of the unit manager, but any or all may be delegated to subordinates. The depth of delegation may then vary, such that, for example, the cost control system may be retained in the hands of the unit manager and the work standards system delegated to a specialist inspector without acknowledged supervisory status. In the more specific area of the relationship between the section manager and the supervisor (operating as his 'staff'), considerable possibility of functionalising the supervisor's tasks according to these systems of control may exist, so that the notion of a supervisor as a part of a *line* organisation may be thereby denied.

The *line* position may need to be a composite role of the type given by the description of the section manager. The following description of it is taken from Kelly (1966, p. 279):

The Section Manager's job is managerial in the full sense—he carries responsibilities for *engaging his operators* and supervisors, *setting standards* for them and *ensuring that standards are met*, and *rewarding* his subordinates with wages appropriate to the work they are doing. He is responsible for *training* his sub-ordinates and ensuring that they have the skills needed to get the work done; for *planning* his production to meet his current and forward load; and for *deploying* his men and machines in the most effective way. Line-shop activity is characterised by sudden changes in demand which must be coped with by equally rapid changes in plans to meet the new demands. The section manager is responsible for maintaining a high level of technical efficiency on his lines. He must continuously make decisions about production methods, interpreting manufacturing instructions where necessary. Although the development of production methods is normally the work of the production engineers, the manager has to see that the best possible standards are being used in production. He must meet standards of efficient operation set by his unit manager. His duties include the requisitioning of supplies and services needed to maintain his machines.

The section manager is responsible for establishing adequate relationships with his colleagues, with other section managers, and with staff specialists of his unit manager. He must be able to contact and use the services of inspectors, personnel specialists, work engineers, the tool room and other staff in an effective manner. He must be able to work with representatives so that problems that arise are dealt with quickly and effectively. He has to carry out all his activities in conformity with established company and factory policy. He is responsible for establishing and maintaining on his section safe standards and a high standard of cleanliness and tidiness.

The second observation that can be made with regard to the six systems of control suggested by Thurley is in fact made by Thurley. That is, that the aggregate and relative weight of these may vary from situation to situation for any one of a number of reasons, three of which he singles out for special mention:

1 The degree of planned variation in the operations supervised.
2 The degree of complexity in the operations supervised.
3 The degree of mechanisation of the process.

Whilst recognising that these factors might not exhaust the list of factors producing variation, he does suggest that these can be used to develop some notion of what supervisory system is requisite in the particular case. Nevertheless, changes in the market or technological situation of the firm could quite easily influence the pattern of supervision to be found in a particular part of the department, as shown later in the study.

Taken together these observations suggest that there may be no one single supervisor/foreman role which can be inserted, as into an appropriate status slot, regardless of the situation. It has become fashionable to follow Trist in his recognition of 'progress' in the development of management as passing from a machine theory as expounded by Taylor, through a human relations phase associated with Hawthorne, to a 'task' or 'situation' theory which lies beneath Brown's exposition (1960). All three might be challenged on the grounds that they all in their own ways seek out the long-range propositions relevant to a given category of role and are to this extent each likely to produce their own mis-matching fashion. Recognition of the possibility that there may be a number of middle-range propositions which cut in at the level of the influence of specific situationally defined ends/means might have more to commend it as a basis for prescription of management action.

Therefore, it may be in vain to search for a single role description which would prove generally valid. As a later discussion shows in more detail, Kelly (1966) seeks to validate his own foremen findings in relation to their activities with reference to four other studies of foremen or positions of a similar level, which are 'in broad agreement'. Validation is only possible if three separately identified functions are aggregated, to give a category of 'close details of work'. Then the lowest percentage is 63 per cent of time and the highest is 83 per cent, compared with Glacier's 89 per cent. The three aggregated categories are, however, programming (51 per cent for Glacier's section managers, but ranging from 20 to 40 per cent in other studies), technical (26 per cent compared with a range of 14 to 34·5 per cent) and personnel (12 per cent compared with 12 to 23 per cent). This suggests wide variation and, furthermore, the Glacier average for the three is *above* those in other studies. Kelly concludes: 'Compared with other studies . . . the section manager . . . spends more time on the close details of the work. In a phrase, he is a "task specialist" ' (1966, p. 285).

It is not absolutely clear whether Kelly attaches significance to these differences compared with other studies, but he does question whether the increased emphasis on the details of work is brought about by Brown's task approach to management, and concludes that the study does support Brown's view which 'minimises the importance of personal style and emphasises that effective organisation is a function of the work to be done and the resources and techniques available to do it' (1966, p. 286). Apart from the fact that it is difficult to conclude in this way because of the implication that the findings both support the influence of Brown himself as head of the firm and deny the significance of personal style, the full implications of Brown's own contention as to the conditions for effective organisation are perhaps unrecognised.

The views put forward by Brown are congruent both with the views advanced above and with the observations made throughout the study—that for a particular situation the particular shape and nature of the market, the particular type and level of technology and the particular pattern of organisation (particularly the pattern of division of labour) will influence the supervisory system which is adopted or promulgated at a particular level. This theme and observation allows also that the personal style will be minimised, since all these cogent influences upon the role are likely to have their contributory effects. It also admits that the marginal differences observed by Kelly between his own findings and those of other writers may have a greater significance related to these other factors than Kelly seems to acknowledge.

The requisite pattern of foreman behaviour may, in other words, remain to be worked out *in situ*, not imposed on the basis of an assumption as to what it ought to be like simply because it is like this elsewhere. The indications from these various studies may be used as a guide as to the limits of variation which are theoretically possible (or seem to be in terms of our knowledge to date), but for the particular company the determination of the requisite may require detailed internal analysis, as is indicated by Thurley.

4 Foremen and the organisational sub-system

Introduction

By now it is clear that whenever any organisational role is being discussed, the specific organisational variables need to be taken into account. The context and task corresponding to a role have already been delineated as major areas for analysis. So far in the study, the general system model has been distinguished and there it was concluded that one major area affecting the performance of the foreman role (or any other role for that matter) was that of the organisation structure.

In this chapter, the significant organisational or structural variables are analysed. Consistent with the earlier theoretical model, these variables can be viewed in terms of their being inputs, conversions and outputs. In this sense, the chapter is divided into three parts, with specific variables in each of them.

The analysis presupposes the existence of an organisation structure and it is felt to be unnecessary to discuss either the general theories of organisation that are relevant in the literature or to define the major areas comprising the characteristics of organisations. Both of these have been well documented in the past (for example, Silverman, 1970; Dunkerley, 1972). Thus, taking structure as given, major variables are analysed individually and an attempt at summation is made towards the end.

1 Organisational input variables

Technology

The variable of technology or the cluster of variables known as technology has only comparatively recently assumed any degree of importance in the analysis of industrial organisations. The consideration of technology is difficult for the social scientist if only because of the specialised knowledge needed for adequately approaching data on technology. Until recently, technology was subordinated to being of peripheral interest in organisational analysis, the ownership of the particular organisation being viewed as rather more important in the determination of structural relations and interpersonal relations (Berle and Means, 1932).

Before examining the effect that different types of technological situation have upon supervisory roles, it is necessary to look at the attempts made by social scientists to categorise types of technical production systems and relate them to the social structure of the organisation.

The concept of technology has to be taken in a broad sense, and not taken merely to be the actual machines and equipment used (Parker *et al.*, 1967, p. 113). The process of technical advance has to be seen as part of a social process, and the actual machine as the end-product is in part a social product. Technology in its generic sense, therefore, can refer to the whole body of knowledge and ideas which make production in an organisation possible.

The newness of the concept of technology viewed as a social process is reflected in the simplistic approach taken by social scientists in analysing it. Of course, this simplicity is also a reflection of the difficulties involved in ordering the data about technology. Several schemes are available for the analysis of technology, and to some extent these are both simple and arbitrary. The function of the various schemes of analysis is to distinguish various types of production system (that is the technology) and then to associate with these production systems various social characteristics. Some of the currently available schemes need to be examined before analysing the role of the foreman in relation to the technical system of production.

The most widely acclaimed schema of analysis is that of Woodward (1958; 1965). She distinguished between unit and small batch production, mass and large batch production, and process production. As discussed below, her schema appears to be the most appropriate one for the analysis of technology's impact on the supervisor's role. Woodward points out that her scheme does show a kind of chronological development of industry towards an increased standardisation of product and also towards an increased mechanisation in industry. This process is also seen by two other writers on technology—Blauner (1964) and Touraine (1955). The stage of development that an industrial organisation is at, in terms of its technology, is not an evaluation of how 'good' or successful that organisation is. It should be clear that the type of production system of an organisation is dependent upon the objectives of that organisation. Thus the development from, say, mass production to process production is not inevitable.

Blauner's classification of technology is a four-fold one and is characterised by an increased standardisation of product and an increase in the degree of mechanisation. Thus, craft industries have the least standardisation and mechanisation; next come machine-minding industries; then assembly-line industries; and, last, process industries (Blauner, 1964). Touraine's scheme has three stages of development; and these stages arise from the interaction of, first, the decreasing amount of skill required from each worker and, second, an increase in the degree of automation and mechanisation for the carrying out of skills. The three stages in Touraine's scheme then become work based upon craft skills and then a stage in which work is relatively unskilled and is mainly composed of machine-minding. The final stage is the automated factory, where the task is set and is more one of inspection and control rather than one of direction of the production process (Touraine, 1965). Other schemes for the analysis of technology on the social structure of an organisation are available, and these are referred to in passing in the course of the analysis.

As mentioned, for the present purposes Woodward's scheme of analysis will be used, though with reference to other sources as well. The three types of production process can be analysed with reference to their effect upon the supervisory role. Unit and small batch production was found to give rise to a median of three levels of authority in the management hierarchy. A median of twenty-one to thirty operators in the span of control of first-line supervisors was found. The actual process of supervision and the 'brainwork of production' were found to be integrated under this form of production. There was a particular reason for the low ratio of supervisors to operators to be found in the fact of a skilled labour force, which in turn lead to a particular 'quality of human relations', which was very high.

There are cases in unit production industries where the role of the supervisor is a very non-involved one. The construction industry has many of the characteristics of a unit production industry, and for the present purposes will be treated as such. Stinchcombe (1959) found construction workers to be 'highly professionalised' (p. 168), and this element of professionalism did away with the necessity for bureaucratic administration. The actual supervisory role involved their accepting the allocation of work and discipline that was exercised by the operators themselves and communicated to them by their union. Again, as Woodward found, there was a low ratio of supervisors to operators.

Since the Woodward classification of technology is being used in this analysis, the category of craft technology can be listed as being unit production. Blauner (1964), in his study of the printing industry, gives further evidence as to the nature of supervision in such a production system. The craftsman, as in the printing industry, has developed a high degree of personal control over the work situation, and this in itself leads to freedom from control by supervisors. Close supervision is abhorrent to the craftsman, and any attempt to impose close supervision leads to successful resistance in most cases (Blauner, 1964, p. 43). In fact, there is no need for close supervision since the craftsman has his own internalised standards of work. Discipline is unnecessary because of the intense self-discipline. Blauner found that the craftsmen he studied considered themselves to be as good as their supervisors both in terms of status and competence. In several instances, the printing industry does represent an extreme in terms of the degree of control the worker has over his work environment. Thus, in American printing firms, the supervisor has to be a member of a trade union, thereby reducing the social distance between him and the craftsman. There is some evidence that the same kind of situation pertains in the British printing industry (Cannon, 1967).

Other examples can be quoted of the nature of supervision in unit production industry (Lupton, 1963) and it is difficult to synthesise the various reports of supervisory behaviour in such an industry. In general, though, it can be said that there are usually few operators to each supervisor and this makes for more informal relations between the supervisor and his work group. The nature of the production system demands the kind of supervisor–operator ratio that is to be found. The supervisor in a unit production system may experience problems which are not found in other types of production system. For example, the work group is more able to set its own norms of conduct and output, which the supervisor has no power over. In many cases, then, the supervisor may find himself in a position of declining power, but relationships between the work group and himself may remain friendly (Roethlisberger and Dickson, 1939).

The case of the large batch and mass production industry is a familiar one. A considerable amount of work has been carried out in such plants by social scientists and there is a measure of agreement as to the nature of the supervisory roles in them. Taking Woodward's findings first, she found in her sample of firms that the median for span of control increased to as high as forty-one to fifty (Woodward, 1958). Moreover, the pressure on people at all levels of the industrial hierarchy seemed to build up as technology advanced and became heaviest in assembly-line production (p. 18). This pressure caused the employees to 'resent authority' and its incentives. It also encouraged conflict with the supervisor: 'the foremen had to work hard to prevent their operators from slipping off to wash their hands or to gather at the clock before finishing time' (p. 30).

Sociological studies of mass production industries are usually of motor car assembly plants, since such plants characterise mass production more than any other type of factory. Blauner (1964) carried out a case study in a car assembly plant and found that his dimensions of alienation—powerlessness, meaninglessness, social alienation and self-estrangement—were at their highest in such a plant. The plant was composed of 75 per cent semi-skilled labour and this was in a narrow age range. Alienation for the worker which arose as a result of the production system underlined supervisor–worker conflict. Taking the car industry from an objective viewpoint, however, we see that personal supervision is not a necessary pre-requisite for maximum production. The worker is controlled not by the supervisor but by the assembly line itself. Thus, many of the traditional functions of the foreman in other industries are taken over by the assembly line itself. Pressure to maintain output, in other words, comes from the line, not from the supervisor. The major function of the supervisor on the assembly line is making sure that the line is correctly manned and in developing good personal relationships with the men to lessen the potentiality for conflict.

Blauner found that, in many cases, good relationships did develop between the supervisor and his group. 'First line foremen can become the focus for the identity of the group in their department when they identify with their workers as well as management and view their role as that of group leader' (Blauner, 1964, p. 114).

In discussing assembly-line production, Blau and Scott (1963) point out that this form of production acts as an impersonal mechanism of social control and as such it reduces the supervisor's area of control. The supervisor, as Blauner found, loses many of his traditional functions and these are subordinated to the assembly line itself. The important functions for supervisors in assembly-line production, as Blau and Scott see them, are dealing with the problems of labour turnover and absenteeism. Training new workers also becomes an important function, as well as quality control and adequate manning. In essence, then, the foreman's task is no longer one of checking and directing but one of helping (the workers) and 'being their trouble shooter' (Blau and Scott, 1963, p. 177). This change in role was given as the explanation for the apparent good relations to be found between foremen and workers in the plant studied by Blau and Scott. The fact that the foreman becomes an advisor rather than a director would tend to substantiate this claim.

Walker, Guest and Turner (1956) discuss the position of the foreman on the assembly line in great depth, and here it is worth noting and considering the conclusions that they come to about the supervisory role under this form of production process. The previous studies discussed give the impression that supervision was made easier by the existence of assembly-line working. Walker and his colleagues found that only a minority of their foremen found line working easier (in terms of letting the line itself carry out many of the traditional functions). The majority saw their roles as being as difficult or more difficult as a result of line working. The reasons for this were the problems of manning, noted in previous studies, and the problems of morale. The assembly line was the direct cause of both of these problems. Foremen in the Walker study felt that they should treat the men under them as separate individuals, that there should be good personal relations with the men, that they should identify with the men and act as a spokesman for them and that as far as possible there should be delegation of authority to the men. If the foremen could create such an atmosphere then it was felt that this would act as a buffer to the strains and pressures which the men were subject to as a result of line working. Thus the impersonal and to some extent anonymous approach to supervision found in many industries should be shaped into a highly personal one (Walker, Guest and Turner, 1956, p. 31).

With regard to the actual production process of mass production, Walker and his colleagues found, as in previous studies, that the supervisor had little direct responsibility. The maintenance of proper manning on the line was the real relationship that the supervisor had to the production process, since if the line was not adequately manned (due mainly to voluntary absenteeism) the continuous flow process would be disrupted. Most foremen tried to introduce flexibility into the production process so that the problems associated with absenteeism could be overcome. As a result, men were taught to do more than one job, the foremen knew how to 'borrow' men from other sections in the plant, and so on.

Management regarded quality to be one of the most important factors for supervisors on the assembly line, and to help the standard of quality in the plant supervisors attempted to build up strong work groups. Given such a situation, the foreman became the group's informal leader in non-supervisory matters; he became both a member and a representative of the group. The supervisor working on the assembly line thus typifies the position that the foreman is usually seen as being in. He performs a dual role, being a member of the work group and of management simultaneously. Perhaps more than any other type of supervisor, the assembly-line foreman is the marginal man of industry (Wray, 1949).

The study described by Walker, Guest and Turner has been

categorised into the Human Relations School of writing (Silverman, 1968). There are valid reasons for doing so, since they emphasise the building up of strong personal ties with production workers and for supervisors to act as spokesmen for their work groups against management. But Walker and his colleagues not only advocated this approach to supervision in mass production industry, they also found it in the plant they studied, as the brief review of their work above shows. It may well be that enlightened management in some assembly-line plants recognise the need for a 'human relations' approach in supervision, despite the inherent conflicts this has for the supervisor himself.

A British study by Goldthorpe *et al.* (1968; 1969) was, in part, concerned with assembly-line industry as demonstrated in car assembly again. They found that their sample of workers differed from those in the American studies previously discussed. They did not find an emphasis upon human relations. 'Indeed [our findings] throw considerable doubt upon the basic assumption that industrial workers will *in general* attach high value to contact with their superiors of an informal and personalised kind' (Goldthorpe *et al.*, 1968, p. 64). The study showed that supervisors were regarded by workers as 'highly significant others' but not as members of the work team.

Despite the reluctance of workers to enter into close relations with supervisors, the Goldthorpe study showed that 86 per cent of the men had reasonably amicable relations with their foremen. There was, however, little in the way of foreman–worker contact and this gave rise to *laissez faire* supervision which was valued by the work group. Workers, in fact, saw little reason for having supervisors at all. On the one hand, Goldthorpe and his colleagues argue for a human relations approach to supervision, given assembly-line production. They argue that if a foreman takes little interest in his men and rarely interacts with them, then this will give rise to resentment and hostility. But, if the foreman takes too positive an interest, this may lead to too positive a response and hence put the foreman in a dilemma. Under these circumstances a human relations approach has a great deal of attraction. On the other hand, they argue that assembly-line workers are not concerned with having human relations-type foremen; they are simply concerned with economic considerations and do not expect any more from their employment. Thus no matter what attitude the supervisor takes, he will not engender greater enthusiasm from his men. Because of the instrumental orientation to work of the assembly-line workers, it would appear to make little difference whether the supervisor adopts a personal 'human relations' approach or an impersonal anonymous approach to supervision.

In concluding this section on Woodward's category of technology —large batch and mass—several comments are in order. It would appear that supervisor–worker conflict in such a system of production may be less important than supervisor role conflict. Sadler (1966) states that management's expectations of their foremen include keeping a high standard of discipline on the shop-floor and checking time-keeping to make sure that lost time is kept to a minimum. These production expectations, however, are at variance with the service and social expectations of the foreman by the operators. So, the 'man in the middle' in mass production may well be really the 'marginal man of industry' (Wray, 1949).

This conclusion may be an oversimplification. The 'set-up man' (Strauss, 1954), it appears, can often be in a more conflict-ridden position as a result of the foreman's greater power. In this case study, the foremen actually initiated a change in the structure that improved the relations between them and this points to the possibility of at least a small amount of room for flexibility in the supervisor's role.

The last category in Woodward's scheme is that of process production industries. It appears to offer a very varied comparison. In her study, Woodward found that the median number of levels of authority increased to six, whilst the span of control of first-line supervision dropped to a median of from eleven to twenty (Woodward, 1958). Woodward also found that the production system itself determined the quality of human relations. Thus, in process production, the existence of several factors such as the increased ratio of supervisors to operators, smaller working groups, the reduced need for labour economy, and so on, all led to a situation where there was general industrial peace. A further point is that (Woodward, 1958, p. 30):

> As technology advances the entire concept of authority in industry may have to change. In process firms the relationships between superior and subordinate was much more like that between a travel agent and his clients than that between a foreman and operators in mass production. The process foreman's job was to arrange things within limits, set by the plant, which both he and the operators accepted.

Blauner's analysis of process industry is presented in the form of a case study of a chemical plant (Blauner, 1964). In the chemical industry, he found a high degree of social integration, particularly integration of the workforce into an occupational community. One of the chief factors leading to such integration was the nature of supervision in process industry. This was found to be very different to supervision found in other types of industry. This was due to a lot of outdoor work, the existence of responsible workers who did not require much supervision and also the fact of decentralised operations. These characteristics of the chemical industry mean that operators are often out of sight of their supervisors for much of the time. The 'distance' of the supervisors is also caused by the ratio of supervisors to operators, as Woodward found.

In all instances, chemical workers found that there was a very low degree of supervision, and this they valued. It was possible to have such low supervision because many of the traditional supervisory functions are carried out by operators themselves. Even the co-ordinating and administrative functions of the operator are carried out by senior operators rather than by the supervisor himself.

Despite the distance of the supervisor from the workers in process industry, Blauner maintains that in many cases the operator has more contact with supervisors and managers than in mass production (1964, p. 147). Usually, this contact takes the form of consultation on production problems—this is to some extent a characteristic of process production, where the worker has as his main function the exercise of responsibility rather than the exercise of skill. Factors such as these led Blauner to the conclusion that the nature of the technology structures the supervisory role, and this in turn leads to a high level of social integration that is to be found in process production.

The scheme of analysis delineated by Woodward in terms of unit and small batch, mass and large batch, and process production is not exhaustive in any sense. Many industrial organisations do not fit simply into these categories, and in Woodward's original study several organisations were not studied because they could not easily be categorised. The coal industry, for example, is difficult to categorise. The 'travel agent' relationship referred to by Woodward in process production is rarely found in this industry. Various factors arising from the work situation give rise to a special kind of relationship between supervisors and the work group. Physical effort, specialised knowledge and the continuous threat of danger all combine to demand a supply function and leadership of a team from the supervisors, rather than the superior–subordinate relationship found elsewhere (Gouldner, 1955; Dennis, Henriques and Slaughter, 1956). These studies and the findings from them do not detail the technology involved. A study of technological change in the mines attributes the increases and decreases in supervisor–worker conflict to the changes in the supervisory role and the group structure necessitated by the hand-got, wall and conveyor-belt methods of extraction (Goldthorpe, 1959). These methods may be comparable to unit, mass and process production.

Another case of Woodward's scheme not being exhaustive is that of deep-sea fishermen. They have a great threat of danger and their work demands precise teamwork. And yet, their captain is supposedly highly autocratic (Tunstall, 1962). Also, there is the case of non-production industrial organisations. These have 'technologies' that bear on their supervisors. The routine nature of the majority of the operations in a bank make almost total structuring of each activity inevitable, and a passive–dependent–submissive personality configuration has been found (McMurray, 1958).

One factor that has not yet been discussed and yet which can be included under the heading of technology is that of automation. Basically, automation needs to be understood and considered as a special case of process production. A study by Emery and Marek (1962) reports the effects of the automation in two power plants. In essence, the effects were that it brought an increased complexity of the total process, a decreased tolerance for disturbance and an increased separation of operators from the process. These changes had an effect upon most operative roles and also upon the supervisory role.

With automation, supervisory roles changed in the following ways. The operator's role became far more unified to the extent that each role was now more integrated into the production process and so each operator was able to have authority in the case of any disturbances which arose in the production process. As a result of this, the supervisor was able to get away from the routine checking of operators which is a characteristic of the supervisory role under unit and mass production. The supervisor then becomes a kind of 'trouble shooter'—his role is one of maintaining a state of equilibrium for the operator, to minimise the number of disturbances that are likely to arise.

A second consequence of automation for the supervisor's role is that the time-span of the job is lengthened considerably. With the change in the operator's role, the supervisor is no longer concerned with minute checking on performance—the automated process itself can deal with this. There is also the point that the 'key functions of the operators are performed only in crises and cannot be subject to routine supervision' (Emery and Marek, 1962, p. 23).

A third change in the supervisory role due to automation observed by Emery and Marek is that the supervisor only interacts with operators when asked to by the operator himself and that the technical knowledge possessed by the supervisor is at the kind of level of the professional engineer. All of these factors lead to there being a far narrower supervisory role under automation. It would appear that both operative and supervisory roles display a greater homogeneity of content with greater supervision over the more numerous and complex tasks and much less of a gap between respective responsibilities.

The findings of Emery and Marek support the findings listed above for process production. They are supported by a comparative report that states that whilst direct supervision may increase the technical content of the supervisory role increases (Mann, 1962). The same report, however, states that office tasks 'become more like work on the assembly line' and supervisors exert more pressures on clerks.

One further point about automation is that it affects the quantity and content of the supervisor's communications with the organisational hierarchy. In effect, computerisation enables management to obtain production data without consulting the supervisor (Ward and Mumford, 1965). The bulk of communication is downwards and the supervisor may well feel isolated and depressed, since the sole purpose of contact will be in crises.

This analysis of the impact of technology on supervisors and upon their roles has shown that this impact is both great and very varied. There are as yet no standard measures for technology in organisations and no accurate means whereby this organisational input can be related to the position. Despite this, its importance is evident.

Organisation size

There is general agreement amongst writers on complex organisations that the size of an organisation either directly or indirectly affects the internal characteristics of that organisation. However, the level of this agreement is extremely low. Size, as an organisational variable, has been neglected in favour of other variables, despite the fact that it has been recognised for a long time to be an important variable.

The actual influence that size of organisation has upon other structural characteristics has produced considerable disagreement amongst social scientists. Only a general proposition to the effect that size does have some influence on other characteristics can be made. Blau and Scott (1963, p. 7) question the degree or intensity of this influence. They maintain that size can only realistically be understood in conjunction with the concept of complexity, which is discussed later. They reject the terms 'large scale' or 'complex' organisations in favour of the term 'formal' organisations, because of the confusion which the term 'size' can create. Zelditch and Hopkins (1961) would agree with Blau and Scott; to them 'large size . . . is not in itself a critical characteristic of organisations. Rather, what appears to be important here is complexity, which is often indicated by size but is quite distinct from it' (p. 470).

Presenting the other side of the argument over organisational size are Caplow (1957) and Grusky (1961) who view size as a crucial determinant of influence over other structural characteristics. The assumption is that large organisations (in terms of size) are necessarily more complex and more formalised than smaller organisations.

If it is possible to weigh one side of this argument against the other and to produce a synthetic appraisal, the result would be that organisational size, in some way, affects other structural characteristics. In line with the general proposition made above, the degree of influence one variable has upon another or upon others is in dispute.

In the same way in which the theorists have disagreed upon the importance of organisational size, empirical research into this matter provides no definitive answer. Many writers have found empirical evidence to support the proposition that bureaucratisation increases in direct proportion to an increase in organisational size (see, for example, Chapin, 1951; Tsouderos, 1955; Parkinson, 1957). On the other hand, Hall (1963) refuted these empirically derived propositions in his empirical study showing that size did not lead to greater bureaucratisation.

Other aspects of organisational size are in dispute. Many studies have been carried out into the size of the administrative component of organisations. Terrien and Mills (1955) put forward and proved the hypothesis for school districts that 'the relationship between the size of an administrative component and the total size of its containing organisation is such that the larger the size of the containing organisation the greater will be the proportion given over to its administrative component' (p. 11). That is, the administrative section increases disproportionately in size as organisational size increases. In fact, this is little more than a re-formulation of Parkinson's Law (Parkinson, 1957).

Contrary to the Terrien and Mills finding is the result of a study by Anderson and Warkov (1961). Their study of administration in hospitals showed that the administrative section was proportionately smaller in large organisations compared with that in smaller organisations. Their findings can be summarised by three propositions (p. 27):

1 As the number of individuals performing identical tasks in the same place increases, the relative size of the administrative component decreases.
2 As the number of places at which work is performed increases, so the relative size of the administrative component increases.
3 As the number of tasks performed at the same place increases, so the relative size of the administrative component increases.

There is, in fact, a third side to the argument concerning size and the administrative section of an organisation. Hawley, Boland and

Boland (1965) hypothesise that the relationship between the two is a curvilinear one. Thus, at first the administration increases disproportionately to the increase in organisation size and then it decreases as the organisation grows further still.

Before turning to the effects that organisational size has upon supervisory roles, one or two conclusions can be drawn concerning the general issue. First, consistent with the initial proposition, it would appear that size has some influence upon other structural characteristics. Later studies such as those of Hall, Haas and Johnson (1967) and Pugh, Hickson and Hinings (1968) are mainly in agreement about this. A level of agreement may have been reached since these were comparative studies of a fairly large number of organisations (seventy-five and fifty-two organisations respectively), whereas previous research tended to be exclusive to one organisation. Second, the variable of organisational size has an influence upon other structural variables when it is possible to compare different types of organisation. Again, the tendency in the past was for conclusions to be drawn from the analysis of only one 'type' of organisation, such as the hospital or the school. By comparative analysis the influence of the factor of size has been more conclusively studied.

Much research into the variable of size has centred around the interactions of size and technology. By examining this relationship, it is possible to make predictions about the nature of supervisory roles and size. Traditionally, size has been regarded as an intervening variable between technology and structure. The work of Woodward (1958; 1965) and of later researchers has shown that to view size as an intervening variable in this way does not stand up to empirical testing. Briefly, Woodward's study of firms in south-east Essex showed that there was no relationship between size and structure. However, in terms of technological groupings as distinguished above—unit, mass and process production—various internal organisational characteristics varied with size. For one thing, the span of supervisory control could be predicted by examining the interaction of size and technology. This finding can be more rigorously examined.

In each of the three production groups delineated on the basis of technology, there were varying sizes of organisation. Thus, no relationship was found to exist between the size of the organisation and the production process. However, when the organisations were analysed on the basis of technology, patterns did begin to emerge which were found to be statistically significant. As organisations became more technologically advanced, so the number of levels of authority within the organisations increased. Thus, the longest lines of command were to be found in process industry (the actual median numbers were three levels in small batch; four levels in mass; and six levels in process production).

Parallel to the growth in the number of levels of authority was an increase in the ratio of supervisory staff to non-supervisory staff. Thus, in unit production there was one manager or supervisor to twenty-three employees; one to sixteen employees in mass production and one to eight non-supervisory employees in process production. From this Woodward concludes that technical change (in terms of technical advance) indicates an additional demand for managerial and supervisory skill (Woodward, 1965, p. 55). Also, she concludes that taking the size of the managerial and supervisory group within an organisation provides a better guide to organisational size than merely taking the total number of individuals employed by an organisation.

On a further point there was not a direct increase in the span of control of supervisors as there was technical advance. Rather, there was what Woodward called 'similarity at the extremes' (Woodward, 1965, p. 60). By this she meant that the average number of workers controlled by supervisors (first-line supervisors) was highest in mass production organisations. This again shows the usefulness of breaking organisations down into production types. The small spans of control on the 'extremes'—small batch and process industries—reflect that the small working group predominated in such organisations. Given such a work situation there is a need for more supervisors and Woodward makes the suggestion that this contributes to greater informality between supervisors and workers, which ultimately leads to a better climate of industrial relations (Woodward, 1965, p. 60).

It is interesting to note that the relationship which Woodward found between size, technology and span of control of supervisors can be compared with growth models of biological organisms (Haire, 1959). Haire studied the growth of four firms and pointed out that the span of control of the first-line supervisor is a variable that is not defined by the work area. He reaches this conclusion since the number was the same for firms of the same age and size, but not for the same technology. In this sense, Haire challenges the conclusions that Woodward arrived at.

So far in this analysis, the emphasis has been upon the structural consequences of organisational size (which is itself a structural factor). If the variable of the size of an organisation is to achieve any fundamental significance for the analysis of the supervisory role, it is necessary to develop some kind of relationship between this variable and the behavioural consequences and attitudes of organisation members. Thus, the proposition can be made that the size of an organisation has certain behavioural and attitudinal consequences for the organisation member. In discussing this proposition, the work of Indick (1963) can first of all be examined. Of relevance for the

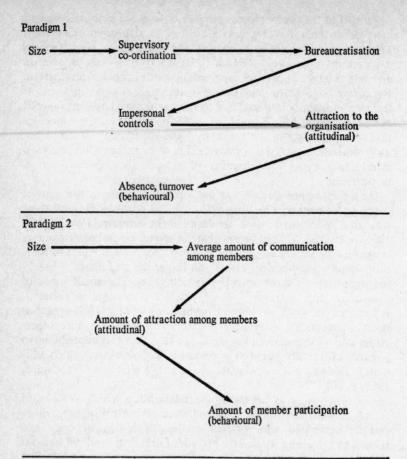

Paradigm 1

Size ⟶ Supervisory co-ordination ⟶ Bureaucratisation

Impersonal controls ⟶ **Attraction to the organisation (attitudinal)**

Absence, turnover (behavioural)

Paradigm 2

Size ⟶ Average amount of communication among members

Amount of attraction among members (attitudinal)

Amount of member participation (behavioural)

Paradigm 3

Size ⟶ Role specification

Job complexity ⟶ Intrinsic job satisfaction

Attraction to the organisation ⟶ Member participation (behavioural)

FIGURE 4.1

consideration of supervisory roles, Indick indicates that there are three possible paradigms to explain the effects of organisational size on attitudes and behaviour of members towards the organisation (see Figure 4.1).

The first paradigm shows that size and the problems of organisational control (which can be more or less formal in character) and a decrease in attraction to the organisation will be indicated by an increase in absence and turnover and, commensurate with this, an increase in the number of problems presented for the supervisor to solve. Consistent with one of Woodward's findings up to a certain point, this paradigm also shows that as the size of the organisation increases there is greater need for a supervisory function within the organisation. In part, this supervisory function is one of co-ordination, and to bring this about may require an increase in the amount of bureaucratisation in the organisation (Merton *et al.*, 1952; Gouldner, 1954). All of this in turn produces the behavioural and attitudinal consequences as shown by the paradigm.

This then is a structural–functional type of paradigm. The organisational structure can be seen to affect the functioning of the organisation; the functioning also affects the structure; and both of these— structure and function—affect the behaviour and attitudes of individuals within the organisation.

The second paradigm has an important indirect relevance for an understanding of the supervisory role. As an organisation increases in size, the potential for communication among individuals within that organisation decreases, although theoretically, as Caplow (1957) shows, the potential increases enormously. As the relative amount of communication decreases in an organisation, so that organisation becomes less attractive to organisation members and this can have attitudinal and/or behavioural consequences for them.

The consequences this has for the supervisor are obvious enough. He has to adopt a far more positive role to attempt to increase the amount of attractiveness for the rank-and-file organisation member. As Homans (1951) points out, a paradigm of this nature is of importance for the supervisor and his role as a leader of a work group. The nature of the supervisor's role in this respect is examined below, but it is sufficient to point out here that the supervisor has a centrally important role to play in an organisation as it increases in size by increasing the amount of member participation as measured by rates of absenteeism and turnover, as in the first paradigm.

The third paradigm can be spelled out in the following way. As the size of an organisation increases, so the tasks performed by individuals in that organisation become more specialised. This is consistent with the basic assumptions of the division of labour and with the fact that increasing role specialisation is a prerequisite to the development of a bureaucratic organisation (Weber, 1947). As each task or work role becomes more specialised, it is in the very nature of this specialisation that there is a decrease in the complexity of that task. Empirical studies indicate that as role complexity decreases, there is a greater propensity for job satisfaction and motivation to decrease accordingly (Vroom, 1964). Thus, here again, because of a change in organisational size, there are both attitudinal and behavioural consequences.

As far as the role of the supervisor is concerned, size can be related to structure in the form of bureaucratisation. It can also be related to social groupings in terms of the average amount of member communication and to skill in terms of role specialisation. If there is less formalisation within an organisation, the factors of social groupings, job skill and job satisfaction are likely to be more intense. The greater the size of the organisation the more formalised the supervisor's role is likely to be. And the more formalised the supervisor's role the less the likelihood of social groupings, job skill and job satisfaction for rank-and-file members of the organisation.

Many issues arise from the variable of organisational size which can affect the role of the supervisor. In general, these have not been systematically investigated and proved, but they are, nevertheless, worthy of consideration in this context. Again, most of these issues relate to the behavioural and attitudinal consequences of organisational size. If it can be established that such consequences arise, then there are clear repercussions for the role of the foreman.

As was demonstrated in the paradigmatic approach to the issue, absenteeism and turnover rates within an organisation can be related to the size of those organisations (Revans, 1958). Again, Revans has shown that the size of an organisation is curvilinearly related to job performance measures. Morale, also, has been found to be negatively related to organisational size (Hewitt and Parfit, 1953) and Thomas (1959) has shown that there is more organisational effectiveness and a better quality of work in smaller organisations. The three paradigms Indick proposed explain these general findings related to organisational size. Most of these and related studies are concerned with wider issues, but in all of them it is possible to re-trace the problem to that of a problem of organisational size and the supervisory (and management) structure of an organisation.

Revans's paper on *Size and Morale in the Mining Industry* (1959) is a good example to take in order to demonstrate the above contention. He is not specifically concerned with the role of the supervisor, but from his study it becomes clear that the supervisor is intimately affected by any change in his environment—here, that aspect of environment, organisational size.

In a modern pit there are two managerial tasks. First, to control work operations at the coal face. This involves interaction between the work group and the deputy (the equivalent of a first-line foreman). Second, the provision of services for the seam. This involves not only the deputy but also various technical experts who are responsible for methods of working. Revans found that, if the pits he studied were ranked in order of size, the average number of men under each deputy increased and, also, that the number of deputies to be co-ordinated by each under-manager also increased. He also found that if the deputy has a large number of men to supervise, the morale of the work group tends to be low. Revans himself is cautious about the conclusions to be drawn from his study, but the results are consistent with other studies.

General conclusions can be drawn concerning the relationship between organisation size and the role of the supervisor. First, as an organisation increases in size, the ratio of supervisory to non-supervisory personnel will increase. This is consistent with the essential ideas of Parkinson's Law and also with the mathematical findings of Kephart (1950). Kephart showed that there is a necessity in organisations, and certainly a great deal of pressure, to increase the ratio of supervisors at a faster rate than that by which the organisation itself grows. This conclusion concerning a direct relationship between the increase in supervisory staff and increase in organisation size requires some qualification, particularly in the light of what appear to be contradictory research findings (for example Terrien and Mills arriving at different conclusions to Anderson and Warkov).

In some circumstances it is possible that the ratio of supervisory to non-supervisory personnel in an organisation will decrease with an increase in organisation size. This is likely to be the case when the tasks to be performed by rank-and-file members of the organisation do not change with a change in organisation size. If work roles do change—and this will usually be the case since organisation change is usually brought about by technological change—then the ratio of supervisory personnel is likely to increase.

In fact, what may occur in practice may be similar to the relationship found by Hawley, Boland and Boland (1965) in terms of a curvilinear relationship between size and the administrative component. The same probably holds true for the supervisory component. A logarithmic relationship can be postulated since as the organisation becomes larger other forms of control emerge from the organisation and it becomes easier for one supervisor to control more individuals after this point. Control might take the form of increased bureaucratisation, the writing of job descriptions or other aspects of formalisation.

The second major conclusion to be drawn is that with increasing size of organisation there will be behavioural and attitudinal consequences for the rank-and-file member. These consequences may be dysfunctional for the organisation in the sense that they are likely to take the form of absenteeism and high labour turnover. As such, the supervisor's task becomes more important for the organisation in attempting to make the task (and the organisation) more attractive for the ordinary member.

Thus, finally, if the supervisor makes his role as little formalised as possible, despite the possibility of increasing formalisation around him (since this is usually associated with an increase in size), the organisational objectives, in terms of the fulfilment of individual roles, are more likely to be achieved.

Ownership

In taking the industrial situation as it is to be found in the United Kingdom at the present time, there are basically three alternatives for forms of ownership of industry. These are private, public company and state-owned. There are, of course, other types of ownership, but they represent such a small percentage of the total ownership that for the purposes of the present analysis they will be ignored.

The interest in examining the factor of industrial ownership is to discover whether the type of ownership does have any significant effects upon the style of supervision, the pressures by the organisation on the supervisor, and so on. From an ideological point of view, there ought to be differences between different types of industry—for example, differences between private and state-owned industries. This analysis will attempt to examine the relationship in terms of empirical research and then add some theoretical points which appear to be of some relevance.

The major problem in examining the influence of ownership is that most published studies of organisations deal with capitalistic organisations. Those studies which do exist of state-owned industries do not take the variable of ownership into account, but merely treat the organisation in question as any other type of organisation. There may, of course, be good reasons for this. The ideological differences may exist, but these have little influence on what takes place in practice.

Governmental legislation in the past few decades has introduced a new form of ownership and control in industry. State ownership is a relatively new dimension to the input of ownership. Chester and Forsyth (1961), in discussing the nationalisation programme in Great Britain, have pointed out that this phenomenon has accentuated the concentration of industry. They go on to point out that rank-and-file members of nationalised industries have exerted considerable pressures on the management of the industries in terms of increased wages and better conditions of employment. This is by no means a new development in any system of industrial relations, but what is new about it is that pressure is exerted without the aid of trade unions. Clearly this is a generalisation, but Chester and Forsyth do see this as being a new phenomenon.

Parallel to the development of non-union activity in nationalised industries, the role of the supervisor has also changed to that found in private industry. It is said that supervisors have had to examine their own roles themselves and to make necessary adjustments in their behaviour. This has come about for several reasons. One of these is the suggested new form of worker-negotiation (notwithstanding the fact that this is a generalisation and empirically unsubstantiated). Also, some nationalised industries, according to Chester and Forsyth, have suffered or are suffering from 'top-heavy administration'. This, of course, means that there are increased pressures on the supervisor, and in many cases these pressures take the form of more qualitative checks on individual and group performance.

Two other features have developed in nationalised industries which are not so readily apparent in privately owned industry. One is an increased conflict between line and staff. Such conflict appears universal in all types of industry (Dalton, 1951), but in nationalised industries Chester and Forsyth suggest that it has become accentuated because of an increase in the number of staff specialists. Again, it is necessary for the supervisor to be able to accommodate such conflicts and the mechanisms which he adopts to do so may hinder his primary objective. The other main feature is that nationalised industries have in some cases developed inflexible promotion procedures, which in turn lead to an increase in the degree of dissatisfaction with the job by supervisors.

One result of these generalised differences in nationalised industries in this country for the supervisor has been for supervisors to attempt to organise themselves 'professionally', outside the boundaries of trade unions, but they nevertheless attempt to carry on with some traditional trade union activities.

It must be stressed that the above comments are generalisations and, for this country at least, there is little empirical evidence to substantiate them. However, Crozier's study (1964) of a French state-owned industry does indicate similar characteristics.

In the industrial monopoly studied by Crozier, the role of the supervisor was to 'act as time-keeper and accounting officer' (p. 66). The role is extremely limited. The supervisor has no powers of discipline and, although he handles the rules of seniority and is allowed some discretion in their interpretation, his decision is subject to ratification by the assistant director. Given this situation, then, the supervisor has little power or status (compared with the supervisor in the clerical agency studied by Crozier) and this gives rise to indifference in relationships between himself and the workers. The feelings of the shop-floor worker towards the supervisors can be summarised as follows: low personal involvement, tolerance and cordiality but no respect for the supervisor; any attempt by the supervisor to increase his power or to enlarge his role meets with the withholding of tolerance and a great lack of achievement (Crozier, 1964, p. 92). A situation of this nature is consistent with the general observations made above in terms of the rank-and-file organisation members increasing their power under nationalisation and in 'zero sum' terms the supervisor having relatively less power. Crozier points out that there is also increased pressure on the supervisor from individuals above him in the organisation hierarchy.

The supervisor's reaction to this relative lessening of power of the supervisor was not to become aggressive. Supervisors were passive in their reaction, their morale was extremely low and they lacked cohesiveness. They resigned themselves to blocked promotion opportunities and were uncritical of other groups within the organisation and of the organisation itself.

Given that this is only one case study and that it is French (that is there may be cultural differences), substantive conclusions are difficult to draw. However, the findings of Crozier's study are consistent with the *a priori* propositions made above and those of Chester and Forsyth. Given state ownership it would appear that the power of managers and operators is increased (although not necessarily rationally so) and the role of the supervisor is beset with new demands and his career possibilities are attenuated.

Turning to strictly capitalistic industries, there have been significant changes in this sector. Since, as stated above, most of the studies of supervisors and of industrial organisations are of this kind of industry, little needs to be said since the whole of the analysis indirectly refers to either the private or public company. One important shift which cannot be dealt with adequately elsewhere can be examined.

In the private sector of industry in this country (that is amongst strictly private and also public companies) there has been a continuous shift which shows no apparent signs of stopping. This shift is in the position of management, away from the entrepreneur-owner type of manager towards the professional-shareholder type of manager (Newcomber, 1955). In a sense this is part of the realisation of Burnham's Managerial Revolution (1962). The work of Berle and Means (1932) has discussed the changes apparent in ownership and control in private industry. The 'new' manager is responsible to the shareholder, not to himself, and the shareholder wishes invariably for maximum profit combined with minimum risk and a fair distribution. In other words, the economic autocracy of the single owner disappears, given the existence of shareholders. Gordon (1955) makes the point that the manager is holding the same position as he has traditionally held, except that now there are 'different stakes' (that is the shareholder has to be taken into account).

The relevance of such a change in management in private industry for the supervisor is without doubt an indirect one. It is possible to postulate, however, that the influence of shareholders produces different objectives and means for achieving these objectives from those organisations which do not have shareholders. The postulation is that in privately owned industrial organisations (such as the family firm) there are short-term profit-oriented pressures on the supervisor. In public companies (that is those with shareholders) there is a greater possibility of long-term customer-oriented pressures. Thus the ideology of the public company is consistent with having the minimum risk with the maximum profit.

Several conclusions can be drawn from this analysis of ownership of industrial organisations and the relevance it has for the supervisor. Any conclusions that are drawn are tentative because of the lack of hard empirical evidence on this question. Even where some evidence does exist there are doubts as to the validity of it (see, for example, Nichols (1969) for a re-analysis of the Berle and Means's evidence). Theoretical differences should exist in supervisor relationships and the style of supervision between state-owned and privately-owned organisations. In practice, these differences are probably negligible. General trends which can be noted are in the form of diminishing power for the foreman in the state-owned industry and the need to find mechanisms to accommodate latent conflict. In private industry, general organisational objectives vary with the existence of shareholders, and the way in which these objectives are filtered down to the level of the supervisor can have an influence both upon his functions and upon the relationships he has with other organisation members.

Market

The market of an organisation can be regarded as an organisation level input, but the influence that the market has upon the supervisor's role is a tentative one. In the same way in which, under the factor of ownership, unsubstantiated propositions were made, the same holds true for market considerations. Very few studies deal with the market of an organisation specifically, although there are oblique indirect references in several case study analyses. Despite this dearth of material on 'the market', the actual nature of the market would appear to be significant for supervisory roles. Particularly, as discussed below, the market would appear to determine, in part, the degree to which the supervisor's role is formally patterned.

Three features of the market can be distinguished which could be of significance for this analysis. Each of these three can be characterised by two polar or extreme types of situation which, in reality, are rarely to be found. Thus an organisation's market will usually lie somewhere between being:

1 Totally competitive———Totally monopolistic
2 Highly predictable—————Highly unpredictable
3 Completely static——————Completely dynamic

These three features can be examined by what case material exists.

McMurray's study of recruitment, dependency and morale in the banking industry (1958) presents the case of the highly stable organisation. The actual operations within the bank are highly routinised, banks themselves are 'unsinkable', the market is highly predictable and the opportunities for individual initiative are minimal. Such characteristics affect the roles of employees of a bank. McMurray makes the point that banks only employ the 'right type' of employee, that is the individual who will conform to the total ethos of the bank, who is willing to forego economic rewards for status rewards, and so on.

There are two principal characteristics of the supervisor's role in the banking industry—routine work role and job security. When employees are appointed to supervisory positions their role is undefined (McMurray, 1958, p. 96) and two alternatives present themselves. The supervisor may be *laissez-faire* by allowing subordinates to do what they want (Argyris, 1954, p. 65) or the supervisor may become authoritarian. It is suggested that the structuring of banks attracts individuals who are basically dependent and this makes it almost inevitable that the supervisor will adopt the authoritarian type of leadership. The effect of authoritarianism upon the work activities of employees is minimal because of the way in which tasks are so highly structured and routinised.

Although the isolated case of the banking industry has been taken, the observations made are applicable to other organisations with a highly predictable and highly static market. Such a model or organisation has been called a mechanistic type (Burns and Stalker, 1961). A mechanistic organisation and management structure corresponds very closely to the Weberian 'ideal type' of model bureaucracy (Weber, 1947). It is appropriate in stable conditions (that is stable external conditions such as the market) and is characterised by its formal character and its insistence upon rules and established procedures. Such a polar model can be compared to the organic type of organisation and management structure, which is appropriate in conditions of change, and characterised by its flexibility and spontaneity. Clearly, whichever polar extreme an organisation tends towards will have consequences for most organisational roles and not simply for supervisory ones. However, the supervisor has such a key position in the organisation, as Chapter 3 has suggested, that his role is likely to be more affected than others. Thus, the degree of predictability and/or static qualities in an organisation's market has effects upon the supervisor's role.

The third type of situation for the market is the degree of competitiveness or monopolism. The French industrial monopoly studied by Crozier and analysed above had a market which was both stable and predictable. Given this situation, which is not unlike that for the banking industry, foremen's roles were prescribed very precisely and there was a high degree of security for them in terms of future employment. It might be concluded that the monopolistic situation is far more likely to have stability in the market situation than is the highly competitive situation.

One further study by Emery and Marek (1962), which has already been discussed, is of some relevance. The industrial plant studied was in the process of change to automation and this changeover was brought about smoothly, partly by long-term stability in the internal and external environment. Given this change in internal characteristics, it was observed that operators were given an increased responsibility such that their role more closely approximated that of the supervisors. Parallel to this, the role of the supervisor altered such that he became responsible for technical advice for operators rather than strict supervision. In the context of the market factor, however, this study does demonstrate that the stability of the market can allow for easy changeover of technical conditions and that these, in turn, can lead to changing role definitions.

There are other aspects of the market situation which can have an effect upon the actual structure of an organisation, but the effect that they have upon the role of the supervisor is a tentative one. For example, Woodward (1965) observed organisational differences with the degree of specificity in the market and the actual size of the market. From the point of view of organisational analysis, these are important, but they have no direct relevance for the analysis of an organisational role.

For the purposes of this analysis, then, the three factors of competition, predictability and stability are taken as the important influencing factors on the supervisory role. In most cases the three factors are closely linked (for example an organisation with a monopoly on the market is both highly predictable and highly stable), but for the purposes of analysis it is useful to distinguish between them.

Trade unions

There are two ways in which the influence of trade unions on the supervisory role can be viewed. First, the effects that the unionisation of employees within the organisation have upon the role can be studied; and, second, the effects of the supervisor himself being (or not being) a trade union member can be analysed. At the moment, this analysis is dealing with structural factors at the organisational level and so only the first of these two interpretations will be analysed. The second is dealt with in another section.

The foreman's role is often interpreted as having undergone a considerable loss of power due to several changes in the supervisory environment. One such change is the growth of collective bargaining and the increasing power of the shop steward within industry. It is commonly said that the shop steward has taken away many of the traditional functions of the foreman and that this 'power loss' has not been replaced by any additional functions. In examining trade unions as a structural input to the organisation, considerations such as these need to be examined. In terms of the literature on the subject, this is difficult to do since this is one area that has little empirical backing, most of the writing is in the form of 'armchair theorising' which may well have particular relevance but cannot be taken as having generalised validity.

As early as 1949 Wray wrote that the difficulties and personal conflicts that are experienced by foremen could be explained by their essentially passive role. In particular, Wray saw this passive role being most evident in union–management relations. That is, to Wray, the foreman's job involved conforming with decisions that are settled between management and unions. The foreman then is a recipient, not a contributor, to union–management relations. If Wray's proposition is a correct one then the traditional image of the supervisor as a positive participant in negotiations needs to be changed.

It would appear that decisions that are made between management and trade unions are centred on a belief that it is necessary to centralise the industrial relations function (Baker and France, 1954). By 'centralise' in this context is meant the point in the authority structure where administrative decisions are taken. Baker and France carried out a longitudinal study and found that a consistent change in this matter of centralisation seemed common. Thus, from 1938 to 1948 there was a change in favour of decentralisation and also a very considerable discrepancy between 'the attitude and practice'. In addition, they found that trade union opinion, in contrast to that of management, was strongly in favour of a centralised function, as this would mean they were more powerful and hence more capable of redressing the power balance. Furthermore, it was noted that if supervisors were delegated to handle issues with trade unions then they usually had been specially trained to carry out this role.

Wray (1949) stated that it was important to compare unionised and non-unionised factories to discover differences in supervisory attitudes and practices. Where there is no union, the supervisor is in a key position for participating in labour relations. In a sense, given a situation such as this, the supervisor has, as part of his role, a personnel function. But, where there is trade union influence in an organisation, the foreman has a very minor role to play in the bargaining process, even though he may have some responsibility for routine personnel functions. Wray maintains that more and more it is wrong to regard foremen as having a key role to play in labour relations. Policies are usually decided without his involvement and he merely carries out policies that have been decided elsewhere. More and more, then, it is trade union officials and top management that make the decisions concerning labour relations and less and less does the foreman become involved in these decisions.

Halpern (1961) tested the hypothesis that 'union and non-union plants represent essentially different social contexts with different sets of constraints, communications patterns, decision-making processes, and authority structures, and that these differences will be reflected in foremen's attitudes' (p. 73). It is reasonable to assume that in unionised organisations there are fewer opportunities for the supervisor to exercise authority, to participate in decision-making and to gain recognition in terms of prestige. Also, it is reasonable to assume that there is less job satisfaction for supervisors in unionised plants than for supervisors in non-unionised plants.

The main findings from a large return on a postal questionnaire can be examined. Halpern found that in unionised plants there was less likelihood of supervisors feeling that they had adequate communication with management. This would suggest that if there is a trade union in an organisation this lessens the potential for a supervisor to participate in management and also that the supervisor does not have a central role as a communication link between management and operators. In terms of job satisfaction, Halpern found that supervisors in non-unionised plants experienced far greater satisfaction from their role than did those in unionised plants. This arose because a trade union lessened the supervisor's authority, power and prestige in the plant (and to some extent outside the plant as well). Halpern does point out, however, that the degree of job satisfaction can be related to the degree of identification that the foreman has with management. One final result was that Halpern shows that supervisors in non-union plants have a more positive orientation towards success values than do other foremen. Again, this is a reflection of the degree to which supervisors are constrained by the existence of a trade union.

2 Organisational conversion variables

Power and control

There is some confusion among social scientists as to the strict meanings of the terms 'power' and 'control'. Often the two concepts are treated synonymously with each other, and also with the related concepts of influence and authority. For the purposes of the present analysis it is necessary to define precisely the two concepts in order to distinguish between them, and also to distinguish between related concepts. Regardless of the way in which they are defined, it is somewhat arbitrary to place these variables under the heading of organisational conversions, especially since the concept of authority is listed as an output of the organisational level sub-system. In fact, power and control could just as easily be classified as organisational inputs or outputs. The discussion below will clarify some of the reasoning behind classifying them as conversions, particularly in terms of the way in which they are defined.

It is more logical to examine the concept of control first, since the variable of power includes that of control (as do the concepts of influence and authority). An observation of any organisation makes it clear that control in some form or another is a universal feature of all organisations. If the concept of organisation is taken to mean simply that there is planned and co-ordinated activity among a group of individuals, then, to paraphrase Michels, he who says organisation, says control. Organisational control ensures that the activities of organisation members are co-ordinated and orientated towards the achievement of organisation objectives. Because organisation members and organisational groups can have objectives which are at variance with the organisational objectives and because control mechanisms are instituted within the organisation to minimise this variance, the problem of control is central to any organisation. The phrase 'problem of control' is used because organisational effectiveness and individual adjustment are dependent upon the control variable.

Control is a pervasive variable in that not only the total organisation objective is dependent upon it, but, also, control determines the degree of decentralisation there is in an organisation, the shape of the organisation chart (in terms of tall or short) and, what is more relevant here, the nature of supervision in an organisation.

Most definitions of control are interchangeable, and one seems to be as exhaustive as another. Thus, Tannenbaum (1962) defines control 'to refer to any process in which a person or group of persons or organisation of persons determines, i.e. intentionally affects, what another person or group or organisation will do' (p. 239). The related variables can be defined as corollaries of this central definition. Thus power is ascribed to an individual 'to the extent that he is in a position to exercise control' (ibid., p. 239). Or, power is 'the probability that one actor within a social relationship will be in a position to carry out his own will despite resistance, regardless of the basis on which this probability rests (Weber, 1947, p. 152). On the basis of a review article, Van Doorn (1963) concludes that a definition of power should be adequately restricted, sociological, relational and nominal. Taking these factors into account, he defines power as 'the possibility, on the part of a person or group, to restrict other persons or groups in the choice of their behaviour, in pursuance of his or its purposes' (ibid., p. 12).

Summarising the definitions of control and power, it can be said that power (as a feature of an organisation position) is the degree to which a behaviour pattern is initiated and the outcome delimited for those held accountable to those positions. Power can be distinguished from influence in that the latter does not necessarily refer to components of action or just to those who are accountable to a position (cf. Cartwright, 1965, p. 38). From a positional point of view, then, control is the variable of the total number of behaviour patterns subject to power compared with the total number of behaviour patterns enacted by a subordinate.

Blauner takes powerlessness to be a primary indicator of alienation in his comparative analysis of industrial organisations. Four types of powerlessness are delimited which impinge upon the manual worker: first, separation from ownership of the means of production; second, inability to influence managerial policies; third, lack of control over the conditions of employment; and fourth, lack of control over the immediate work process (Blauner, 1964, p. 16).

These modes of powerlessness impinge upon the industrial foreman as well as upon the manual worker. When the variable of technology is isolated, and alienation is measured on the basis of the nature of technological process, Blauner found that power, of all the dimensions of alienation, was the one most affected and influenced. The actual means of production (that is the technology in this sense) lay down what the pace of work is to be, the actual pressure on work and the freedom of movement of both manual workers and supervisors. In the printing industry, the degree of control was highest for the worker as compared with all the other industries. 'The craftsman's high degree of personal control implies a complementary freedom from external supervisory control' (Blauner, 1964, p. 43). There is, in fact, little need for control because of the nature of craft, self and group discipline. With individual worker control being high, there is consequently a low measure of powerlessness. In line with a zero-sum argument, it might be assumed that in an industry where the supervisor has little control over the work group, he himself might suffer from feelings of powerlessness. This does not occur in the printing industry because the foreman is, in fact, a member of the work group—'often the oldest and most experienced journeyman' (ibid., p. 43). In fact, the nature of the work process does tend to give the supervisor rather more power than in other industries, since he is able to control the kinds of factors that Blauner delineated above.

The other extreme to the printing industry is the motor industry. Here, the control functions of the supervisor are taken over by the assembly line. Factors such as control over quantity, control over quality, predetermination of techniques and control over physical movement are all determined by the technology. The assembly-line worker is relatively free of supervision from foremen because of this.

The chemical and textile industries studied by Blauner represent intermediate stages in the degree of control and power that the supervisor has. The important conclusion to be drawn from Blauner's work is that power is most influenced by technology, when positional power is being referred to.

The foreman, like any individual in a position of authority, may not always exert a unitary form of power and control. In some circumstances, he may exercise power over an individual or group who are in other subordinate positions. This may take the form of dual control or an even greater amount. One example of this can be taken from Strauss's study of the 'set-up' man (1954). This study shows the effect of dual control by a supervisor and the complexity and variability of the power relationship as a result of this feature.

As a result of organisational changes in the plant analysed by Strauss, the chief mechanic of the department being considered had to report to the departmental foreman instead of to the master mechanic, as had been the case previously. This change for the chief mechanic had ramifications for his subordinates in terms of their roles. In particular, it was the set-up man who was most affected. Basically, the role of the set-up man involved ensuring that the lines were in good working order and making adjustments to them where necessary. Also, the set-up man was in complete control of his crew (helpers and operators) and he made the decision as to which line should be set up first when more than one line was in need of repair. The chief mechanic was regarded as the head of the department and the set-up man reported to him. In fact, the foreman was the nominal head of the department. With the organisational changes, the changes shown in Table 4.1 were made to the role of the set-up man (adapted from Strauss, 1954, p. 19).

TABLE 4.1

Before	After
Supervises operators and helpers	Foreman does this now
Reports to chief mechanic	Reports to foreman
Opportunity to rise in management	Promotion blocked by requirement of college degree
Freedom to decide which line to set up	Freedom reduced

The position after the introduction of organisational change led naturally to a great many strains in the organisation. In particular, the two main areas of strain were that the set-up man lost some of his previous power, control and status, and, second, the supervisor was put into a position of dual control. In order to reduce these strains, the supervisor voluntarily relinquished some of his control and this brought the organisation into a state of greater equilibrium.

In one of a series of articles, Tannenbaum reviews the literature on control in organisations. He concludes that increased control exercised by all levels of the industrial hierarchy is associated with increased organisational effectiveness. There are two implications of every act of control: these are pragmatic and symbolic (Tannenbaum, 1962, p. 240). By this is meant that control dictates what an individual can and cannot do in a particular situation (the pragmatic sense) and also that control has an emotional function for the individual exercising control (say, in terms of superiority or dominance). Tannenbaum concludes from his survey of the literature that control is desired by all groups in the industrial setting. Nobody will ever say that he has too much power and yet will frequently admit that groups either above or below him have too much. Thus, control and power are desired commodities and they may be desired for pragmatic and/or symbolic reasons. Control is a key factor in leading to increased job satisfaction and, in this sense, control may take many forms. Blauner, for example, found that control over freedom of movement, control of the pace of work, and general control of the near environment all led to increased job satisfaction (Blauner, 1964).

Since control is a variable (that is there can be varying amounts of control in an organisation or exercised by one individual) it is possible to plot control curves for the organisational hierarchy. To produce a control curve, organisation members are asked questions relating to the amount of control which they and various other members of the organisation possess and are able to exercise. Two curves are possible—one relating to how members themselves see how much power they have and the other relating to the pattern of control they desire. Thus one may be labelled the 'actual' and the other the 'ideal' curve. The reproduction of control curves is shown in Figure 4.2 and demonstrates that both in the actual and in the ideal setting control decreases as we progress down the organisational hierarchy. The ideal, it is interesting to note, is at a higher level than the actual position. Also, there are differences in terms of the position in the hierarchy of the person reporting the amount of control.

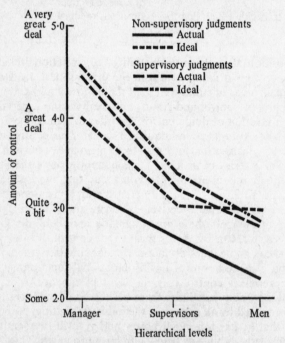

FIGURE 4.2 *Average control curves for thirty-two stations of a delivery company: actual and desired control—non-supervisors and supervisors*

The value of being able to analyse control quantitatively in the way Tannenbaum demonstrates is that different control patterns in different organisations (and for that matter in the same organisation) can produce different behavioural consequences. For example, the amount of influence exercised by three levels as perceived by the men in two industrial plants studied by Mann and Hoffman (1960) was as shown in Table 4.2.

TABLE 4.2

Level	Old plant	New plant
Men	2·64	3·12
Foremen	2·42	3·51
Front office	4·56	4·48

It can be seen that in the new plant foremen were seen to have more influence than those in the old plant. Associated with this, 66 per cent of the men in the new plant and 36 per cent of the men in the old plant felt very satisfied with their foremen. With the foremen having more influence at the new plant a far more integrated structure arose than in the old plant. The degree of interdependence between foremen and their work groups increased in the new plant.

Tannenbaum concludes that increased control exercised by all levels in the organisation hierarchy is associated with organisational effectiveness. Furthermore, a 'relatively high level of total control may reflect increased participation and mutual influence throughout the organisation and a greater degree of integration of all members' (Tannenbaum, 1962, p. 250). This in turn enhances members' ego-involvement, identification, motivation and job satisfaction. And taking Blauner's findings it could be suggested that technological factors may account for variations in the minimum parameters.

Other factors account for variations in the maximum parameters of supervisory control, but these are characterised under different headings from the present one. In particular, managerial ideology and environmental factors might possibly be the most important of these.

Professionalism and professionalisation

In the sense in which this particular organisational conversion is being dealt with here, there are several studies which relate to it. Before turning to these, it is important for the concepts of professionalism and professionalisation to be understood. It is not being suggested that the occupation of foreman, or rather, in more precise terms, the position of foreman (Taylor, 1965), is a professional occupation or position, as the following analysis will show. Rather, it is being suggested that there are aspects of the supervisory role which can be taken as measures of professionalism and that perhaps the role is undergoing a process of professionalisation due to certain organisational characteristics.

71

It is possible to separate certain characteristics of professions which distinguish these occupations from other (non-professional) occupations. What is given here is a summary of the points that are made by Wilensky (1964), Caplow (1954) and Millerson (1964). Only when all of these characteristics are present can we meaningfully talk of a profession, since several of the characteristics are shared by some non-professional occupations.

1 There must be a socially required activity carried out by a group of people and this activity must be distinct from other activities.
2 There must be an organised occupational association and certain criteria have to be met for any individual to be admitted to that association.
3 For a profession, the criteria of admission must be developed such that admission is only allowed after the successful passing of an examination. The latter requires a high level of intelligence. Often, the examination is linked with university qualifications.
4 An ethical code has to develop within the occupation which will guide members and form the basis of a mandate for the occupation. The code of ethics also ensures that the 'public' is being served to its best interests.
5 There must be public support for an occupational mandate (Hughes, 1959).

These characteristics deal with the process of professionalisation for a particular occupation. Turning from these general considerations, it is necessary to see how the 'occupation' of foreman fits into the schema.

First of all it is necessary to see how far we are justified in calling 'supervision' an occupation. If the definition given by Salz in *The Encyclopaedia of the Social Sciences* (1933, p. 424) is taken, then there is some claim for calling supervision an occupation, viz.: 'That specific activity with a market value which an individual continually pursues for the purpose of obtaining a steady flow of income; this activity also determines the social position of the individual.' But does this definition go far enough?

The verb form of occupation, 'to occupy', is basic and generic in the sense that the word 'work' is basic and generic. But from a sociological point of view a far more precise and specific meaning is required. Occupation involves the notion of solidarity amongst members of the occupation and it implies a degree of corporateness, consciousness and reciprocity. There must be both an ideology and an identity for occupational members. Whether supervisors exhibit these key characteristics is a matter of some dispute.

The term 'supervisor' indicates a position title more than it does an occupation, if the specific meaning of occupation is taken. After all, a supervisor may work in any kind of industry; all the term tells us about is the work area, it tells nothing of the specific content of the work.

However, if the more general meaning of the word 'occupation' is taken, it can be seen that supervision can constitute an occupation. The definition given by Salz, for example, would ensure this. So also would that given by Hughes (1959, p. 452) as a 'bundle of activities, but it is not some particular set of activities: it is the part of the individual in any ongoing system of activities'. The emphasis here, then, is that occupation is something involved in a system of human relationships, and this, by no stretch of the imagination, is precisely what the supervisor or foreman is involved in.

Thus, taking supervision to be an occupation, rather than more precisely a position title, it is possible to turn to the question of whether this occupation is undergoing a process of professionalisation as a result of organisational characteristics (hence the conversion variable) and whether the occupation exhibits any of the characteristics of professionalism. It has to be remembered that this question is being looked at from an organisational point of view and not from the point of view of other variables. Thus, the question of an occupational association or of an occupational ideology is dealt with elsewhere.

Three studies of professionalisation are selected here as they relate to professionalism and professionalisation to both inputs and outputs. The first of these studies makes the point that technological factors make technical knowledge important in the organisation. Brown (1953) studied 400 employees in a Naval research and development department. The aim was to discover the extent to which the professional nature of the tasks was related to outputs at variance with the demands of bureaucratic procedures. He found that different levels had been grouped according to a number of variables, including components of equipment, the phases through which they must pass the special training required, the location of objects used by the groupings and the problems they had to consider. Because of these factors Brown found that precise, close and impersonal supervision was made extremely difficult. In effect, the supervisors were individuals who had the most knowledge and thereby the most respect of the sub-groups.

The second study by Weiss (1956) analyses a similar situation and he shows that informality and leadership implied that the supervisor protected his group by 'liaising' with the management that provided the objectives.

The third study relates to a laboratory experiment carried out to see if subordinates differentiated between technical knowledge and administrative knowledge as types of supervisory authority (Evan and Zelditch, 1961). A research organisation was simulated for the purposes of the experiment, with three main hierarchical positions—project director, coding supervisor and coders. In terms of the goals of the organisation, they had a professional character, but the coders used in the experiment were not in any sense professionally orientated, even though some attempt at inducing this feature was made in the training sessions.

Three main hypotheses were tested (Evan and Zelditch, 1961, p. 891):

1 If an official held office without the commensurate knowledge, subordinates would not accord legitimacy to the official's authority.
2 This erosion of the superordinates authority would have negative effects both on subordinates performance and on their conformity to technical rules and commands.
3 That conformity to the administrative rules and commands would not be affected by treatment differences.

In general, these hypotheses were confirmed, and this raised some important issues. It does, for example, demonstrate the important role of professionalisation of both the task and of the supervisor. Also, the experiment does confirm what happens in reality when there is either office without knowledge or knowledge without office. Evan and Zelditch make the point that unless there are socially structured accommodations for these discrepancies, there are bound to be further problems for complex organisations.

3 Organisational output variables

Structure

The concept of structure has a great many meanings and a great many uses. For the present purposes, structure is used to refer to the patterning of positions in an organisation. This approach is, of course, the most simple of the meanings and uses the concept can have. From the point of view of studying foremen, the structure is the level they occupy in the organisation and what span of control they have as compared with the total organisation. Both of these have to be objectively stated rather than subjectively perceived. For this reason, and for the reasons of simplicity, the more complex variables of formal-flexible continua (for example, Whyte, 1944) and adjectival uses (for example, communication structure and authority structure) will not be used.

It has been shown that the level and the span of control of first-line supervisors have been related to the organisational technology (Woodward, 1958). The supervisor in mass production industries has a large number of subordinates compared with the supervisor in the unit or process industries. Haire's empirical study of the histories of growth in organisations once again indicates that span of control of supervisors is a variable that appears to stabilise after a considerable number of years (Haire, 1959).

In addition to these generalised findings related to the individual supervisor, there is growing evidence to suggest that if the span of control is shared by a number of supervisors rather than by one, the group decisions shift towards those of a more risky nature (Stoner, 1961; Marquis, 1962). This is an interesting finding since it is often assumed that group decisions, such as those of a committee, tend to be conservative in nature, are cautious and are even compromising. Rim (1965) examines this kind of proposition further in terms of Fleishman's consideration and structure (Fleishman, 1951) and confirmed the finding that group decisions are riskier than individual decisions.

Halpern's study of employee unionisation and foremen's attitudes shows that, by taking levels of control and the context of unionisation, the closer a foreman felt his position to be with the rank-and-file, the lower his job satisfaction, and vice versa (Halpern, 1961).

Halpern's finding is particularly interesting since it does indicate the need to relate the objective and subjective aspects of structural variables. The previous findings also illustrate ways of establishing the degree to which the supervisor is, in fact, the 'man in the middle' (Wray, 1949).

Job activities

In looking at the work entailed for any organisational role, there are at least two strategies that can be pursued. In the first place, the work could be described simply in terms of job characteristics. Using this strategy would emphasise the technological aspects of the work or emphasise what was being accomplished in the job. The second approach involves looking at organisational roles to see what it is that incumbents actually do when performing the role. These two strategies can be called 'job-oriented' and 'worker-oriented' descriptions of work respectively (Palmer and McCormick, 1961). Under this particular heading of organisational outputs, the emphasis will be placed upon the second of these approaches—worker-oriented descriptions. That is, the analysis will be a description of what the individual actually does and how the technological factors are used to achieve the desired results, instead of looking at the conditions of work and even the results of work.

75

Several studies delimit the activities of supervisors in the work situation, and of these a selection of the important findings will be examined below. Of the British studies, the work of Thurley and Hamblin (1963) presents the most systematic attempt to look at what supervisors actually do and the way in which these activities are constrained by the influence of various organisational characteristics.

Thurley and Hamblin studied five firms, which they called Packaging Ltd, Engineering Ltd, Footwear Ltd, Electronics Ltd and Brewing Ltd; these five were broken down into the technological classifications used by Woodward (1958). That is, the first two were examples of small batch production industries, Footwear was large batch, Electronics was mass production and Brewing was labelled process-batch production. The numbers of supervisors studied in each of the five firms were 43, 14, 7, 22, and 51 respectively. All of them were first-line supervisors.

Various functions were performed by the supervisors at each of the five firms, and these functions can be examined sequentially.

1 *Planning production* 'The amount of planning by the shop-floor supervisor varied according to the degree of planned variation in the operation in his department or section' (Thurley and Hamblin, 1963, p. 8). The engineering firm had the greatest degree of variability mainly due to the diverse nature of the product. The packaging firm was similar to this. At the other extreme was the electronics firm where there was little in the way of day-to-day planning and what there was was carried out by higher management. The supervisor was, however, responsible for planning of labour when there was high absenteeism.

2 *Planning the use of labour* '[This] was common to all supervisory systems studied' (ibid., p. 10). As mentioned above, this function became more important for the supervisor when there was a high level of absenteeism, but in the normal course of events it represented a small amount of the supervisor's time.

3 *Preparing for implementation of plant* Under this heading, the amount of work carried out by supervisors varied with the nature of the shop-floor operations. Thus, the greatest amount of work was involved in those organisations having high variability in operations. Again, the engineering shop constituted the greatest amount of work and brewing had the least.

4 *Routine distribution and transfer of work* Supervisors were found to allocate work in three of the five firms on a regular basis (this means that allocation due to absenteeism was not carried out).

5 *Performing operative functions* Supervisors carried out manual work frequently in two of the firms. For the remaining three firms supervisors never carried out manual work, even when absenteeism was high.

6 *Supervising operatives at work* This function only took up a significant amount of time in two of the firms, though even here it never exceeded 8 per cent of the working time. The amount of supervision for skilled manual workers was negligible, and at Brewing Ltd the nature of the operative task meant that there was no need for direct supervision.

7 *Checking the product* This function appeared in most cases to be a more effective means of control than supervising the operatives. This was the way in which the performance of operatives was checked in three of the firms.

8 *Checking the machinery* In firms with complex machines and more advanced technology, this was an important function for the supervisor. For example, in Electronics Ltd this accounted for 16 per cent of the time of the first-line supervisors. Thurley and Hamblin point out, however, that supervisors varied a lot in the amount of time they spent in this function and there appeared to be no differences in production or efficiency figures.

9 *Dealing with contingencies* In all the firms this was an important function for the supervisors. Two major types of contingency were noted: technical and human. The two most common technical contingencies which occurred in all of the firms were variations in product or raw material and shortages of raw material.

10 *Variations or breakdowns* This caused problems for all of the supervisors, but the nature of the technology determined the extent of this. Thus, the engineering firm had the most breakdowns and supervisors spent a lot of time making alterations to the machinery.

11 *Absenteeism* This was the major human contingency in all the firms studied. It assumed the least important factor in the brewing firm since the operatives had a minor role in the work process.

12 *Disputes and disciplinary matters* These are human contingencies but took up little of the supervisors' time in any of the firms.

13 *Personnel matters* Although most of the supervisors had the responsibility of teaming up with the personnel department in

matters relating to selection and training, this took up little of their time. At two of the firms supervisors were responsible for working out bonus and piece rates. There was some consultation with shop stewards but this was an unimportant function.

14 *Acting as a communication link* The widely-held view that the supervisor acts as a communication link between management and operatives was not borne out by the Thurley and Hamblin study. This was not due to lethargy on the part of the supervisors, but because they themselves were, in general, uninformed by management. Again, this did tend to vary with the amount of variability of operations.

Using the methods of work-sampling, Thurley and Hamblin were able to look at the work activities of supervisors. Figure 4.3 (reproduced from pp. 8–16 of their study) summarises the main results of this activity analysis. What is shown by the diagrams is that there are large variations in the activities of supervisors, even within the same firm.

In terms of the amount of time spent, communication was the major activity of the supervisors. Three basic types of communication were delineated: first, acting as a link between management and operatives; second, communicating as a means of carrying out other functions; third, personal conversation. In most cases, the second type of communication occupied the most time (Thurley and Hamblin, 1963, p. 17).

Another major British study concerning the activities of supervisors was carried out by the National Institute for Industrial Psychology (1957). The study is, in effect, a series of seven case studies of widely differing firms. These can be examined by looking at the differences in the activities of supervisors in the different firms, and then some general conclusions can be drawn concerning these.

1 An electrical engineering works

In this firm, the activities of the supervisors were, in general, three-fold, viz. technical, administrative and supervisory. Many of the traditional technical functions of the supervisors had been taken over by the progress department and the planning department. With the existence of these departments, there was a re-distribution in the nature of the labour force. As a result, the supervisor was in charge of far more semi-skilled and unskilled workers. There was less planning, but still some training of new operatives.

Again, with the administrative duties, the new department had taken away many of the traditional supervisory functions. A new

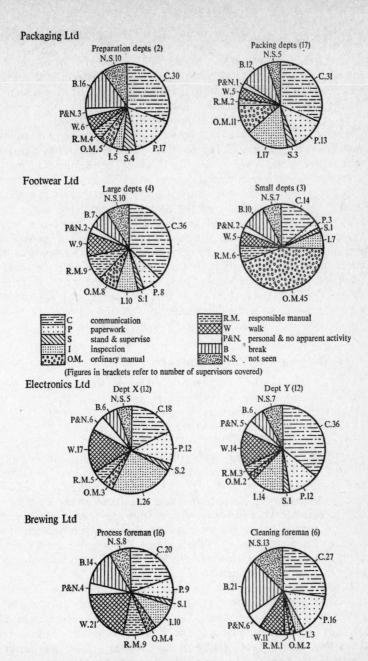

FIGURE 4.3   *Activity patterns of first-line supervisors (percentage of total working hours)*

production control system meant that the foreman was involved in much more paper work than previously, and much of this was of a routine nature. The keeping of records and returns constituted an important part of the supervisory role. The increase in the number of operatives supervised multiplied the amount of routine administrative work of the supervisor. The role of the supervisor, in effect, became one of supplying information to other departments.

Under the heading of supervisory duties, the function of discipline was the most important. The position of the foreman has changed with regard to this function since the threat of the ultimate sanction—dismissal—is no longer a major threat to employees. The personnel department has taken away many of the traditional areas of activity in this region. In the case of the electrical engineering works, the only sanctions which could be imposed by the supervisor were suspension and variation in the pay rate. The sanction of suspension was, in fact, no longer used by the company; and pay rate variation could now only be carried out in consultation with the works manager. Due to this absence of penalties available for the supervisor to use, the NIIP researchers found that the supervisor had to adopt a new approach to leadership which involved the supervisor reasoning with his men, rather than merely threatening them.

2 A firm of light vehicle manufacturers

This firm is divided into several departments, the number of men for whom supervisors are responsible varying from department to department (in fact, from seventy-five to four). The supervisors in all departments are involved in the production processes because of the smallness of the working groups. Manual work constitutes an integral part of the supervisor's role. There are definite supervisory functions to perform such as responsibility for the work produced and discipline. The tasks of organising and allocating the labour is also a supervisory activity. In this firm, the foremen are what have been called 'working foremen'. Apart from the nature of the production process producing this, another factor which accounts for working foremen is the age of the foremen. The average age was very high, and the NIIP researchers conclude that this characteristic led to 'abnormal' working patterns.

Five other firms are studied in relation to the supervision activities, but these tend to discuss the supervisor's attitudes to the work rather than to analyse the actual activities the supervisor is engaged on. The NIIP researchers conclude from their studies of the seven firms that the technical nature of the foreman's tasks was an extremely important feature. In all the firms it was necessary for the foreman to be concerned with the actual job operations and, even though some of the firms had specialist departments such as quality or production control, administration and general supervision were not seen as the chief requirements of the job. The researchers stress that it was necessary for foremen to have considerable knowledge about the firm, and usually this knowledge was technical in nature. Practical experience on the job was also emphasised. In some of the firms, management was having to reconsider its procedures for supervisor selection because of the technical complexity of the position. Theoretical knowledge was stressed in a few of the firms, but really this prerequisite tended to depend upon the technological structure of the firm. For some firms it was of paramount importance that supervisors had a theoretical knowledge, whereas in others (particularly mass production plants) it had little significance. The nature of the product, also, influenced the degree of theoretical knowledge necessary for the job.

Dubin (1962) has made the observation that little is known about managerial and supervisory behaviour. The actual activities and time distributions amongst supervisors is a subject that has been under-researched. Dubin assembles what material there is on activities and role behaviour in an attempt to redress the balance. From his analysis on managers and executives two important conclusions are drawn which have relevance to understanding the activities of supervisors (Dubin, 1962, p. 15):

> First, as we go downward in rank, the proportion of time spent with superiors markedly increases, and, correspondingly, the proportion of time spent with subordinates decreases. . . . Second, we observe that there is a very substantial increase in the proportion of time spent in interaction that is devoted to peers as we move downward in the rank system. This reaches half the total interacting time for the senior and junior staff men under the departmental manager.

The literature reviewed suggests that whereas managers spend a considerable amount of their time in verbal communication, foremen are 'more likely to be doers than talkers' (ibid., p. 20). Taking a selection of studies from which information is available, this proposition is borne out. For example, Ponder (1958), in his study on supervisors, divides them into two categories—'high effective' and 'low effective'. The high effective foremen spent 56 per cent of their time talking, while the low effective foremen spent 45 per cent of their time in such activity. Guest (1962) has shown that his motor car supervisors spent 46·6 per cent of their time talking.

Turning to the first of these two conclusions from managerial data, Dubin found that the further down the organisational hierarchy we go, the greater the amount of time that is spent with superiors relative to the time spent with subordinates. Table 4.3 would suggest that the foreman represents a deviant case to this general conclusion.

TABLE 4.3 *Percentage of foreman's total interaction time spent with people of various ranks*

Rank of person	'High effective' (Ponder)	'Low effective' (Ponder)	Motor (Guest)	Production (Piersol)
Superiors	Not given	Not given	10	30
Subordinates	34	39	46	60
Peers	Not given	Not given	12	10
Others	66	61	32	0

What emerges from Table 4.3 is the suggestion that foremen do spend more time with their subordinates than do managers (at least, that is, more time talking to them). Dubin, in discussing this point, makes two suggestions (1962, pp. 22–3):

Direct supervisory responsibility forces downward orientation for a boss, whether he is a department manager or a first-line foreman. On the other hand, it may be that line supervisors without a direct rank-and-file command or who perform both line and staff functions must spend more time interacting with the boss to find out what is expected and/or to be one of his informational sources and advisors.

Peer communication appears to be extremely important for the foreman. Of the three hundred contacts made by the foreman in the Guest study, three-quarters of them were with foremen preceding the foreman in question on the assembly line or with foremen immediately following the one in question. Again, Simpson (1959) found from his study of foremen that between 43 and 76 per cent of all contacts were peer contacts. This would suggest that horizontal

TABLE 4.4 *Subjects of foreman-to-foreman interaction*

Subject	Interaction time (per cent)
Production	27·1
Personnel administration	13·7
Equipment and methods	3·1
Quality	35·8
Personal, non-work	9·7
Other	10·6

communication is important for the supervisor and, as pointed out by Dubin, does give some kind of clue as to the nature and volume of non-formal relations. This area of activity can be looked at further by considering Table 4.4, adapted from Jasinski (1956).

The interesting point which emerges from Table 4.4 is that peer interaction among foremen is almost exclusively devoted to work and, further, that almost 80 per cent of peer interaction time was devoted to four work-oriented subjects—production, personnel administration, equipment and methods, and quality.

As far as what Dubin calls 'functional behaviour' is concerned, results are not as available as for other areas of activity. Getting information from subordinates appeared to be an important part of the foreman role. Dubin makes the point that the power the rank-and-file member of the organisation has is quite considerable, particularly in relation to this information-giving. The supervisor is very dependent upon lower-level participants for the receipt of this information and for the effectiveness of his own position.

An important finding is made by Dubin: 'The overwhelming content of the interaction of foremen with all other people was devoted to the close details of work' (1962, p. 24). The four important functional areas delimited with regard to peer interaction are examined in terms of their interactions from three different studies (see Table 4.5).

TABLE 4.5 *Percentage of total time of foremen spent in areas of operating responsibility*

Areas of operating responsibility	'High effective' (Ponder)	'Low effective' (Ponder)	Motor (Guest)	RCA (Zinck)
Production	20	40	34·5	
Personnel administration	23	12	13·2	
Equipment and methods	14	8	16·3	78
Quality	6	6	18·2	
Other	37	34	17·8	22

Summarising Dubin's data, it can be seen that some of the prevalent observations relating to supervisors are in need of redefinition. It is usually thought that supervisors mainly work with subordinates and that they transmit managerial decisions: these assumptions are now questionable. The classical functions of managers in terms of decision-making and giving instructions do not appear to be of primary importance. This also applies to supervisory practices. Information-gathering and -seeking seems to be a dominant part of the activities of supervisors. The high level of interaction with peers is a further interesting point from the analysis.

A more recent discussion bears out the points made by Dubin (Dunkerley, 1969). A sample of six foremen in a medium-sized steel plant were continuously observed for two weeks each and the results given in Table 4.6 were obtained. There was a very high level of communication, particularly verbal communication, which was sub-divided into talking, discussing (that is with more than one person), time spent in formal meetings, telephoning and dictating. Other communication—that is reading and writing—made up a small part of the total working time.

TABLE 4.6   *Media of activity (percentage of total observed time)*

	PFA	*PFB*	*PFC*	*PFD*	*EFA*	*EFB*
Talking	27·31	25·87	31·58	23·73	37·62	41·60
Discussing	9·47	18·92	25·62	19·61	7·97	24·16
Formal meeting	13·02	—	24·02	31·29	11·08	—
Phoning	4·66	8·88	2·69	3·77	8·12	8·82
Dictating	—	—	—	—	—	—
Total communication	54·46	53·67	83·91	78·40	64·79	74·58
Reading	11·13	3·86	2·75	2·49	5·16	2·94
Writing	10·73	0·77	2·82	3·28	9·67	0·63
Total communication	76·32	58·30	89·58	84·17	79·62	78·15
Moving	17·05	7·72	—	5·06	9·34	6·72
Inspecting	4·89	31·27	6·92	3·70	7·96	5·67
Reflecting	—	—	—	1·23	—	5·56
Manual	1·74	2·70	—	5·13	4·12	3·89
Personal	—	—	—	0·71	—	—

(Dunkerley, 1969, p. 109)

As for the direction of communication in this study (Table 4.7), the peer interaction rates were not as high as Dubin found in other studies. For some of the foremen in the study, the amount of interaction with superiors appears to be extremely high, although it should be pointed out that the nature of the technology did demand this in some cases.

The work of Palmer and McCormick (1961) stresses that the interaction process is a central feature of job activities analysis. This feature of interaction is stressed in both of the orientations discussed earlier—that is in 'job-oriented' and 'worker-oriented' approaches to work. They are more concerned with the worker-oriented approach and they use this as a basis for factor analysis. Their results

TABLE 4.7 *Direction of communication*

	Superiors	Peers	Sub-ordinates	Others
Production foreman A	8·35	15·14	31·27	1·49
Production foreman B	5·30	10·93	74·83	—
Production foreman C	13·91	27·67	13·91	—
Production foreman D	17·89	26·32	17·89	—
Engineering foreman A	36·72	1·30	23·49	5·31
Engineering foreman B	14·12	6·80	36·82	17·15

(Dunkerley, 1969, p. 110)

show that a 'large number of job activities for rather a wide range of jobs can be organised meaningfully in terms of a small number of independent dimensions' (p. 289). One of their factors was supervisory decisions which covered in all thirty-three items relative to the broad dimensions of responsibility for supervision; oral, written and signal communications; and interpersonal contacts in these activities. This was only a pilot study, but it does suggest a large number of possibilities for supervisory job analysis—possibilities which do not yet appear to have been exploited.

Authority

Power and control have been analysed as being organisational conversions, whilst authority is being used as an output variable. There is a significant difference between authority and power and control, even though in everyday language the distinction between them tends to get blurred. Power was used as being concerned with means–ends control. Authority is the legitimised right to exercise power. Authority, then, is viewed as a special kind of power relationship, but one in which the person exerting power feels he has a right to do so and the persons over whom power is being exerted feel that it is their duty to obey (Weber, 1947).

In the writings of the social psychologists examining the nature of the small group, the supervisor is taken as a good example of an 'agent' exerting influence. That is, one having authority over others because of the dual legitimacy of the relationship (see, for example, Cartwright, 1965). The concept of an 'agent' exerting authority and influence is used because it is not always a person who is in this power relationship; sometimes it is a group or even an organisation. Authority can be seen to stem from an organisational position, as in the case of the foreman. Thus, Barnard (1938) talks of the authority of position and the authority of leadership, as authority deriving from a particular organisational position regardless of the individual who is occupying that position at any particular time. This is in contrast to Barnard's concept of personal power where it is the personality of the individual that enables him to exert authority (in a sense this can be equated with Weber's concept of charismatic authority).

Cartwright (1965) points out that in the 'classical' writings on organisations the concept of an office or position exerting authority prevailed. This is true if we examine the writings of the formal theorists of organisation, particularly Weber (Gerth and Mills, 1949). In writings such as these, the personality characteristics of the individual occupying a particular position were regarded as being irrelevant to the nature of the power relationship. The 'same amount' of authority would be wielded no matter who held the position in question.

Barnard's distinction between power of position and personal power was and is important in that this was a break from the classical treatment of authority in organisations. It is a distinction which has considerable relevance for the analysis of supervisory authority. Today, it is recognised that an influence attempt has a problematic success rate. The success rate depends as much upon personal traits as upon positional authority. In treating authority as an organisational output, this analysis is concerned, for the time being at least, with positional authority and not with personal authority. This latter is dealt with under the personal characteristics of the individual level sub-system.

Whether we are dealing with positional power and authority or personal authority, the ability of successfully exerting authority depends to a large extent on the resources available. Dahl (1957) uses the term 'the base of power' to describe the resources available to carry out an influence attempt. The reward system available to an individual often constitutes this base of power. The amount of authority of a supervisor has been shown to vary with the amount of resources and rewards available to him (Bennis et al., 1958). Bennis points out that where the legitimised right to means–end control (that is authority) diverges, the ability to influence the behaviour of subordinates may be seriously impaired. The effectiveness of reward systems in hospitals was compared to test this hypothesis. Ninety nurses were studied in six out-patient departments. Measures were taken of the rewards each nurse wanted from her job and of the rewards that were likely to be received. Rewards included wage increases, promotion, praise and educational opportunities. The influence of the supervisor was measured by comparing the amount of time each nurse spent on certain activities and the amount of time her supervisor wanted her to spend.

The study by Bennis found two limitations on the supervisor's authority. First, the supervisors did not perceive correctly what rewards the nurses wanted. Second, the supervisors were not able either to increase or withdraw these rewards. Where the limitations were less extreme, it appeared that supervisors were able to exert a greater degree of authority. Thus the legitimation of the supervisor's power was greater when there was a congruency between expectations and receipt, and when the supervisor had the institutional means to dispense the rewards. These findings are significant because there is an indication here that authority is dependent not simply upon the authorisers but also upon the role and power of the supervisors.

Other findings show that the amount of control over rewards is a determinant of authority. Occupational psychologists and the neo-human relations researchers have shown that rewards are not merely economic in nature. Also, it has been proved that the supervisor is in a position to satisfy or frustrate subordinates by the use of non-economic rewards and thereby to alter his authority. This, however, depends upon the personal power of the supervisor and is dealt with later.

The study by Bennis focuses the analysis on the role and the power of the supervisor. If this focus is maintained, an interesting distinction can be made between rational and legal authority (Evan and Zelditch, 1961). In the simulated research laboratory established by Evan and Zelditch and referred to earlier in the study, it was found that subordinates do discriminate between rational and legal authority. The 'superordinate degree of technical knowledge affects his subordinates legitimation of his task authority, but not his authority on administrative tasks' (p. 885).

In a major research study carried out by Michigan University (Patten, 1968) 1,457 supervisors in nine plants were systematically studied, examining in particular their responsibilities and authority. Three degrees of authority were de-limited (p. 71):

a Full authority: exercised in compliance with assigned position responsibilities
b None: authority that is exercised by the superior and/or staff
c Some authority: this covers all other degrees of authority

Using the technique of activity analysis, a profile of the degrees of authority of foremen was constructed. This was based on a total of 2,698 incidents. Full authority was observed in 86·2 per cent of the activities; some authority in 9·6 per cent; and 4·2 per cent of the activities represented no authority. By taking different grades of foremen, this picture changed. The figures for general foremen and superintendents are given in Table 4.8.

Incentives

Incentives (or motivators) are included under the heading of organisational level outputs because they can be dealt with as the tangible output of the interaction of role and of power and control. Incentives are reward systems and, as such, they entail expectations and receipts intended to support the power and to maintain or to extend the span of control of the supervisor. Whyte (1944) has pointed out that incentives can be used as a lifebelt for a drowning productive organisation, but the focus here is the system that is implied between supervisors and subordinates.

TABLE 4.8

	General foreman	Superintendents
Full authority	80·3	85·3
Some authority	15·5	10·9
None	4·2	3·8

In order to understand the nature of incentives for the foreman, it is necessary to digress to discuss some of the important findings in the area of motivational research and then to relate these to the context of the foreman.

Vroom and Decci (1970) have noted that there are three general strategies open to management in an organisation in order to motivate employees. These strategies derive from the fact that different people have different performances on the same job. These differences in performance can be accounted for in a variety of ways. For example, there are individual differences in skill and differences in adaptability on the part of the individual. Vroom prefers to account for differences in people's performance by the differences that are extant in individual motivation, and this is where the three general strategies for motivation come in. The total amount of skill or ability of an individual can be stated as:

Performance $= f$ (ability . motivation)

For the present discussion, the individual ability can be disregarded. The three approaches which are delineated by Vroom are the paternalistic, the scientific and the participative strategies. Each of these can be discussed in turn.

The paternalistic strategy is based on the assumption that the more people are rewarded the harder they will work. If needs are satisfied in the work situation then this will produce individual job satisfaction which will in turn produce motivation and hence higher output or performance. Using this strategy, the organisation in which the individual is employed becomes the source of satisfaction. Everyone within the organisation receives the rewards no matter how he performs on the job—that is, rewards are unconditional. The only requirement for receiving rewards is that the individual is a member of the organisation. Organisational rewards would include most of the features usually expressed as 'fringe benefits', such as pension plans, comfortable working conditions, and so on. If this approach to motivation is used then the primary objective of the supervisory role (and, for that matter, of the managerial role) would be to ensure that individuals within the organisation had all their demands met. This strategy assumes that if all demands are met, then the individual will assume organisational loyalty and display enthusiasm in the work situation.

Some research has been carried out to test the validity of this approach, but there is very little evidence to suggest that unconditional rewards and paternalism either motivate or satisfy people on the shop-floor. It has been shown that a degree of satisfaction has been produced by this approach for the individual and this can, in turn, influence his decision of whether to stay in the organisation or not. Beyond that, there is little to prove the effectiveness of the approach.

The paternalistic approach does have implications for the foreman. If an organisation decides to adopt this strategy then the role of the supervisor, as the immediate link with the shop-floor, becomes one of a human relations specialist. The supervisor has to become employee-centred rather than production-centred, a situation which most supervisors would tend to reject.

The second general approach or strategy which can be used in order to motivate people and hence improve their performance is the 'scientific' approach. This strategy assumes that if performance is related to the rewards or penalties, then this will produce motivation. Here rewards are made conditional—the harder one works, the more money (or other reward) one will receive. Wage incentive schemes provide good examples of this approach, as are promotion systems based on merit ratings.

The role of the supervisor under this particular strategy differs from that in the previous, paternalistic, approach. The supervisor becomes primarily an inspector: he checks that standards are being maintained, he continually monitors the behaviour of the individual and performance is continually checked. The supervisor becomes the personification for the man on the shop-floor of an external control system. In a sense, rewards are conditional upon the appraisal of the supervisor and there is not always total objectivity.

There are strict limitations to this approach for motivation, of which two seriously weaken the validity of the approach. First, reference has to be made to the work of Maslow (1943). Maslow's model of motivation hypothesises five broad classes of needs which are arranged in hierarchical order of potency so that when one level is satisfied the next level is activated. The levels are:

1 Physiological needs
2 Security or safety needs
3 Social, belonging or membership needs
4 Esteem needs, further divided into esteem of others and self-esteem
5 Self-actualisation or self-fulfillment needs

If Maslow's model of a hierarchy of needs can be taken as generally valid, under the 'scientific' strategy of motivation there are going to be a lot of unsatisfied needs for each individual. If the supervisory task is to be an inspector of work and performance, it is impossible for the higher level needs of the individual to be satisfied. A control system which is externally contrived (to the individual, that is) cannot meet the needs of esteem or self-actualisation, for example. Similarly, research going back as far as the Hawthorne Experiments has shown that the informal work group satisfies many needs of the individual. Under this type of strategy, in which there is strict control and in which the supervisor is seen as being the main instrument of control (due to visibility), then the informal group is unlikely to develop. Without the existence of an informal group, many of the needs cannot be satisfied satisfactorily.

The second major limitation of the scientific approach is that it does rely heavily upon objective methods of measurement of performance. Clearly this can be done for many routine repetitive tasks particularly low in the organisation, but for any skilled or craft work measurement becomes a real problem. Also, if measurement is required of personnel higher in the organisation, it becomes increasingly difficult, the higher in the organisational hierarchy one progresses. The main impediment to effective measurement is that tasks are so interdependent that results cannot be pin-pointed to any one individual.

The third general strategy is the participative approach. This is an approach which has gained contemporary popularity. The basic assumption is that individuals derive satisfaction from doing an effective job *per se*. The approach attempts to get people involved in their work, to be emotionally committed, to take pride in doing an effective job, and so on.

A process of job enlargement takes place under this approach. People are encouraged to use their discretion on the job, in fact the discretionary element in the task is enlarged and the amount of programmed content is minimised. The individual himself determines how the objectives he has been set are to be achieved. The objective of all this is that if there is individual control concerning how the job is to be carried out, then the individual will look upon the task as a challenge, or certainly more of a challenge than if he is simply told what to do.

The amount of power, control and authority that could be exerted is reduced under this strategy. The role of the supervisor changes radically. Instead of having an authoritative role, the supervisor has a helping role. Shop-floor workers should view the supervisor as a resource, rather than as an agent of authority. The role of consultant or even colleague would be more appropriate. Indeed, the supervisor is not seen as being the head of the work group, but rather as an integrated member of it. The work group itself becomes the source for decision-making rather than the supervisor authoritatively imposing decisions upon the work group. The supervisor meets with the work group, problems are shared and he encourages participation within the work group in solving the problems and taking the decisions. All of this is supposed to lead to commitment on the part of the individual and to lead to an identification with the objectives of the organisation by all organisation members.

Of course, participation of this kind cannot be applied in every organisation. In mass production assembly-line work, for example, there is minimal opportunity for group decision-making and problem-solving because of the technological constraints.

Taking these three strategies for motivation and incentives—paternalistic, scientific and participative—all have implications for the role of the foreman. Under paternalistic motivation, the supervisor is viewed as an aid—as the person to see when difficulties arise. With the scientific approach, the supervisor has an autocratic authoritative role; he makes the decisions and continually checks and controls the performance of subordinates. The participative strategy has the supervisor as a working member of the group; he does participate in the making of decisions, but not in any autocratic sense.

In addition to the treatment of motivation and incentives by psychologists, there have been attempts to place this question within a sociological framework. Thus Blauner (1964) has noted that there are occupational differences in motivation and job satisfaction. He notes that the greatest degree of satisfaction is to be obtained amongst professionals and businessmen; greater amounts amongst clerical workers than manual workers; and greater amounts amongst skilled than unskilled workers. There are several sociological and situational variables that account for these differences, many of which can be regarded as 'organisational outputs'.

The amount of prestige that an occupation has accounts for some of the differences and to some extent this is determined by organisational factors. Prestige is dependent upon the skill level, the amount of control and responsibility, and income. Different organisations will give different amounts of these variables to their supervisors.

The amount of control over the work is an important determinant of satisfaction, and it has been stressed that this factor is determined mainly by the technological structure of the organisation. The more control of time, movement and the environment, the greater the satisfaction.

Another characteristic accounting for differences is the degree to which there is an integrated work group—the greater the integration, the greater the satisfaction. Again, this factor is often technologically determined.

One further variable accounting for satisfaction differences is the degree to which the occupation can be said to be a part of an occupational community. The classic example is that of mining, in which there is no strict boundary between the work and non-work situations. Usually, the occupational community is likely to develop in isolated occupations, isolated on the basis of space or on the basis of hours of work. As Blauner points out, the occupation becomes the reference group for all people employed in it. Gouldner (1954) found that supervisors were themselves a source of satisfaction and a source of incentives for subordinates. They themselves were motivated by the 'indulgency pattern' to be found in the gypsum mining community. Indulgency patterns, then, become implicit reward systems. Indeed, one way in which the supervisor might attempt to gain more rewards for and from his subordinates is through such a system.

A study of hospitals by Bennis *et al.* (1958) was concerned with relating the amount of supervision and influence with the relative effectiveness of reward systems. The actual incentive content is neglected in favour of standard measurement systems of the variables. Two general 'types' of reward were outlined: first, 'psychological'—the importance of the reward as defined by the congruency of hoped for and likely rewards, the frequency of rewards and the accurate perception of rewards by the rewarder; and, second, the 'sociological' type, with which these subordinate factors have to be balanced. The rewards have not only to be through institutional means, but capable of being manipulated by the supervisors themselves.

It is clear that incentives are much more complicated than 'carrots' or 'sticks' from supervisors to subordinates. For the supervisor it has been seen that it is of importance what his goals are, what the subordinates expect, the means at his disposal and, possibly, what extra efforts he makes to provide positive rewards. In addition, the supervisor's use of rewards will be closely related to his style of supervision, about which more is detailed below.

Conclusions

From the above analysis, it is clear that organisational variables greatly affect the supervisory role—perhaps more so than is generally recognised. If the notion of role is taken, as discussed earlier, to be a system or set of expectations associated with a particular position, the effect of organisational variables is seen even more clearly. There is remarkably little information relating the exact effect of structural variables upon expectations, but at a common-sense level is it true to say that a factor such as automation is bound to change expectations. After all, with the example of automation, this not only changes the technical expectations of the foremen themselves but also allows more responsibility for operators. The consequences of such changes might be that management's expectations of foremen are of greater technical competence and that operators' expectations of them are of greater assistance. It would correspond to the 'supply functions' and the 'supervisory functions' discussed by Goldthorpe (1959).

Other 'behavioural' consequences of organisational variables are evident. For example, the nature and quality of interpersonal relationships are closely related to the extent of formalisation and control of subordinate tasks, as determined by the technology as already seen. Again, it has been shown that increasing levels of technology increase the control of the subordinates on the shop-floor and the control of the foremen who encourage participation (Tannenbaum, 1962).

In terms of the general comments about role conflict and marginality made in the previous chapter, the relevance of organisational characteristics is evident. As the discussion in the previous chapter has pointed out, role conflict is dependent upon the centrality of the role. If, as writers such as Wray (1949) suggest, the role of the foreman is a peripheral one (that is that it is not a part of the decision-making process), then the experienced role conflict will be a 'personal' conflict within the foreman himself—it might be what Kahn *et al.* (1964) call 'intra-role conflict'. Either way, there is some doubt about whether role conflict can be seen purely in structural terms.

As far as the system concept being employed in this study is concerned, the organisation level sub-system can be represented diagrammatically as shown in Figure 4.4. At the moment, then, the sub-system is represented as being relatively closed in nature because, of course, there is little system synthesis—that is, linking this sub-system to others in order to complete the total system. This exercise

93

cannot be completed until the other two major sub-systems have been analysed in detail.

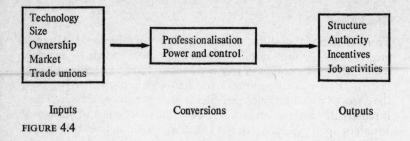

Technology Size Ownership Market Trade unions	→	Professionalisation Power and control.	→	Structure Authority Incentives Job activities
Inputs		Conversions		Outputs

FIGURE 4.4

5   The foreman and the group

Introduction

Compared with the previous chapter, the analysis in this chapter narrows and focuses upon the foreman as a group member. A different approach is taken from the previous chapter because of the difficulties in distinguishing the exact variables affecting the foreman role. Instead, the analysis focuses upon the foreman, not merely as a member of a group but as the leader of a work group. In order to do this successfully, the concept of leadership is thoroughly described before any attempt is made to apply the concept to the foreman role.

Also, there is some overlap with the previous chapter in that foreman leadership is seen in the organisational setting as well as in the setting of the small group. This is entirely consistent with the overall approach being taken in that the task and structural components of each aspect of the role are seen as having importance. It becomes clear in the text that only emphasising the small group in relative isolation is inadequate since new properties emerge at higher levels of analysis that are not present at the lower levels.

Leadership as a concept

Leadership is a concept that has interested social scientists for a long time. The 'founding fathers' in sociology analysed leadership at a macroscopic level of analysis—albeit as derivations of their main theses. Weber, for example, in his theory of power and domination, distinguished between charismatic, traditional and legal-rational wielders of authority—or leaders. Marx, in analysing the nature of the class system, talked of the potential leadership of the proletariat in juxtaposition to the leadership role of the capitalists. As shown elsewhere (Dunkerley, 1972), the macroscopic level of analysis in sociology was overtaken by the microscopic level. When a shift such as this occurred in analysing leadership, social psychologists appeared to carry out much of the fundamental research and only comparatively recently have sociologists re-asserted their interest in the concept (cf. Etzioni, 1965).

Before examining the more recent developments in leadership theory, it is necessary to be able to distinguish leadership from other behaviour patterns. As with most concepts in behavioural science, there is a lack of univocality concerning this concept. There are, however, several common elements to be found in most of the writings on the subject, and, having distinguished these, an attempt at a synthesis will be made.

The concern here is with the problems of equating the supervisor with a leader. In a sense, this makes the analysis simpler than it might otherwise have been. In the first place, there must be a recognition that 'foremanship' only takes place in an organisational setting. By accepting this premise, there is no need, here at least, to be concerned with the 'great man' theories of leadership. Foreman leadership, then, has an organisational basis.

Taking this organisational basis, there are two perspectives that can be taken—theory and practice. Organisation theory has long assumed that the effectiveness of an organisation is, in part, dependent on the nature of leadership within the organisation. In a more extreme sense, some writers have gone so far as to say that the survival of the organisation is dependent on leader behaviour. McGregor's assumptions in Theory Y (1960) and Likert's System Four (1961) would suggest this close relationship between the organisation and leadership. Other writers, however, give the concept no importance at all. For example, neither Thompson (1967) nor March and Simon (1958) really mention leadership in their analyses of formal organisations. The examples given do represent the polar extremities of the nature of leadership behaviour. This analysis, in its concern with the supervisor as leader, takes a middle-range viewpoint. Thus, there is some link between the nature of leader behaviour and the effective functioning of organisations, but this is not to say it is the only determinant of effectiveness.

The other perspective mentioned is that of organisation practice. Here there is also some ambivalence in the significance of leader behaviour. On the one hand, management ensures that tasks are so routinised and standardised that leadership becomes an irrelevance to effective operation. Despite this view, which has a degree of following or is essential due to the nature of the technology, the majority of organisations have formal positions of leadership. Thus foremen, by whatever title they may have, exist in all organisations. On the other hand, management and the organisation place enormous emphasis on the formally designated positions of leadership.

This is the way in which foremen have traditionally been viewed—as marginal men of industry (Wray, 1949). If the organisation achieves a certain level of success then the formally designated leaders are rewarded; if there is failure, then the leaders are punished or at least reprimanded. In practice, it is recognised that organisations must, to some extent, be adaptive structures, and as such there have to be systems or structures within the organisation to allow for changes, for improving established methods of working, and so on. Managers generally recognise that positions of leadership can contribute to this flexibility and organic nature, and as such place some importance on them.

In attempting any definition of any concept, cognisance must be made of previous writings. Traditionally, there have been two main streams of thought in leadership studies—the 'great man' theorists and the 'cultural determinist' theorists. As suggested earlier, the former approach sees history in terms of great figures. In narrowing their analysis, the great man theorists would look at ICI in terms of Sir Paul Chambers; the British motor industry in terms of Lord Stokes; or the educational system by referring to Newsom, Clegg, Albermarle and Robbins.

The second main stream of thought concerning leadership— cultural determinist theory—looks at the history of society or any particular sphere of society in terms of social and cultural patterns, which may or may not include the analysis of particular leaders.

Clearly, these two approaches are unsatisfactory, at least for the present analysis. Few people would doubt that the industrial supervisor has a leadership position and yet, on the one hand, he would be unrecognised by the great man theorists and, on the other, any of his achievements would be subordinate to an investigation of social and cultural patterns. Having said this, patterns of leader behaviour can be examined 'microscopically' as a phenomenon of formal organisations.

In addition to the two main streams of thought in the general literature, there are varying approaches to leadership used by behavioural scientists. It is usual to distinguish between two ideas of leadership, although a third is equally important. Leadership can be taken to be a personal quality (similar to Weber's concept of charismatic authority) or it may be an organisational function. The third is the idea that leadership can be viewed as a category of behaviour. Each of these ideas of leadership inevitably leads to different strategies on the part of the researcher. Thus, leadership as a characteristic of a person refers, by definition, to a certain pattern and combination of personal characteristics. Sometimes, these characteristics are seen as being unique to the individual—the particular combination cannot be replicated by anyone else. Taking this view

97

of leadership would involve an examination of these individually unique characteristics. As another example, leadership as an organisational function refers to the attributes of an organisational position. Adherence to this approach would involve an analysis of the power, the authority and the status characteristics of the position. And beyond this, the patterns of power and authority in the organisation would become relevant. The organisational strategy for the third notion of leadership—as a category of behaviour—would again be different to the other two notions.

The three main ideas of leadership can be illustrated by recognising that, for example, a foreman because of his organisational position, is assigned a leadership position. The general manager of the organisation is also assigned a leadership position. Nobody would doubt that, in this positional sense, the general manager has a greater leadership role than the foreman, but because of personal qualities the foreman may, in fact, be exercising far greater leadership than the general manager.

Whichever conception of leadership is taken, there is one area of basic agreement. Leadership has to be regarded as a relational concept. It is relational in the sense that it implies two basic terms—the person actually leading and the person or group actually being led. Cartwright (1965) uses the term 'agent' so that one can refer to either person, group or institution. A recognition that leadership is a relational concept has at least one important implication—that without followers (or agents being led) there can be no leader. By assigning leadership to an organisational function, there is an awareness of this because of the nature of organisation hierarchies. Leadership as an ability, however, does depend a lot upon situational factors and upon the individuals who are being influenced by the leadership act.

Leadership is often seen as being somehow involved with influence and control (Cartwright, 1965). This approach has to recognise, however, that influence is not an absolute quality. More accurately, then, leadership can be viewed as the differential exercise of influence. The term 'differential exercise' is used since a leader must be able to exercise more influence than other members of the group. This can be said almost by definition. If all group members were able to exercise equal amounts of influence, then the concept of leadership becomes meaningless (unless of course there is a 'rotating' leadership dependent upon who is performing the act of influence at the time).

Again, in everyday speech, if an individual exercises influence and this influence derives wholly from the position he holds then this is rarely called an act of leadership. An act of leadership involves the special use of the position that the individual occupies. Confusion is likely here, for it may be thought that leadership acts are only those that go beyond the formal structure—that is only informal acts. This is not the case since this would deny the existence of 'institutionalised leadership' (Selznick, 1957). Leadership, then, can be a property of formal organisations and of formal positions within organisations.

This distinction between formal and informal leadership is essentially a difference between leadership and routine or formal role performance. This is a useful kind of distinction to make since it enables us to examine the kind of behaviour which goes beyond the formally defined behaviour. This also enables a deeper understanding of the nature of interpersonal influence. An argument such as this is consistent with the definition Katz and Kahn (1966) give of leadership: 'The influential increment over and above mechanical compliance with the routine directives of the organisation.' By 'influential increment' Katz and Kahn mean the greater ability one person in a group has to influence the behaviour of other members of the group. This definition also accounts for the fact that the exercise of leadership must also involve the use of power and authority.

The notion of 'influential increment' is a useful one. It can be used as a springboard for the analysis of leadership derivatives. The question can be asked, for example, 'Why is it that all foremen at a given level in an organisation are not equal in their leadership attempts?' After all, the exponents of the idea of leadership as an organisational function would argue that all foremen in this organisation and at the same hierarchical level are assigned the same amounts of power; they are formally given the same status; the rewards and penalties at their disposal are similar; and so on. And yet, it is a common observation that different foremen exercise different degrees of leadership.

The answer to a question such as this lies in the concept of power. Elsewhere in this study, the power of the foreman role is examined in terms of it being an organisational variable. There is almost an assumption that power is an 'either–or' concept or that it has a unitary meaning. At least one study has discussed the fallaciousness of this approach and pleaded the need to observe five types of social power. French and Raven (1959) distinguish the following bases of power:

1 Reward power: this is based on the belief that the agent exerting power has the ability to give rewards (and negative rewards or penalties) to the agent over whom power is being exerted. The strength of this kind of power is dependent upon how much the resources used as rewards are valued and upon the intensity of the belief that rewards will actually be mediated.

2 Coercive power: this is similar to reward power in that it is based on the belief that punishments can be used against the agent over whom there is influence. The strength of this power base is the product of the estimated magnitude of the punishment and the probability that punishment can be avoided by conformity.

3 Referent power: this is based on an identification of the agent over whom influence is being exerted with the influencer. Identification can mean either an actual feeling of identification or a desire for it. Using this perspective, the ability to exercise power need not involve any attempt to do so. Here the usefulness of the term 'agent' is demonstrated since the power of a group over its members increases with the attractiveness of the group. This ought to be qualified by recognising that French and Raven are unable to isolate referent power as the sole cause of this. They suggest that reward and coercive power may operate in any combination.

4 Legitimate power: this stems from a belief that the influencer has a right to use his influence and that the influenced have an obligation to accept it. There is here a dual notion of legitimacy. Legitimate power can be an extremely strong form of power. An experiment by Raven and French (1958) demonstrated the strength of legitimate power by examining two work situations which were identical except that in one the supervisor had been elected and in the other the supervisor merely assumed the position. It was found that an influence attempt was more effective when made by the elected supervisor than by the other, that is when legitimate power was being used.

5 Expert power: this is based on the belief that the influencer has relevant technical knowledge or expertness. Elsewhere this has been called informational power (Deutch and Gerard, 1958).

Having briefly examined the five bases of power described by French and Raven, we can refer them back to the discussion of leadership. It will be recalled that the proposition was made that differential leadership for individuals having the same organisational position may be a product of the nature of power.

With regard to legitimate power it is clear that all individuals in similar positions are allocated the same amount. Also, they have the same opportunities for using the rewards and punishments that the organisation defines as legitimate. If the position of the foreman is taken here, given that there are equal amounts of legitimate power for each foreman in the organisation, a differential can be established by the way in which the individual foreman uses his power to maximise the influence. Deriving from this, of course, is the fact that the actual use that the foreman makes of his legitimate power and his actions beyond formal power can produce differential referent power.

Referent power is not given by the organisation, nor is expert power. Both of these depend upon the use the position-incumbent makes of his legitimate power and upon his personal characteristics. Although the organisation has no say in the amount of referent or expert power an individual has, these are both important in the functioning of the organisation. It is even said (Katz and Kahn, 1966) that legitimate power cannot be 'spelled out' for more senior personnel in a formal organisation.

As shown below, many explanations and descriptions of leadership are made in terms of how it (leadership) produces organisational effectiveness. If Katz and Kahn's notion of leadership involving influential increment is accepted, then by linking this to the bases of power, organisational effectiveness does have a lot of relevance and can be seen as, in part at least, being derived from acts of leadership. Since referent power and expert power are not conferred by the organisation, they can be viewed as additions to the available 'stock' of power in the organisation. There is then an increase in the amount of control that can theoretically be exerted in the organisation. The work of Tannenbaum (1962) on organisational control shows that there is often a causal relationship between an increment in control and an increment in organisational effectiveness.

The existence of referent and expert power can also mean that in some cases they can substitute for legitimate and coercive power. It is said that the latter can lead to organisational dysfunctioning; that there can be unintended consequences for the organisation; and that they do not in some circumstances produce organisational effectiveness. The writers of the Human Relations School (McGregor, 1960; Likert, 1961; Argyris, 1962; and others) have suggested (by a different route) that an organisation will be more effective the more that referent and expert power can be substituted for legitimate and coercive power.

Another way in which organisations can be made more effective is that, in addition to referent and expert power increasing the total stock of power available, they can be used by individuals who are not assigned formal positions of leadership. This is where the notion of peer influence can be valuable for improving procedures and communications, and ultimately for improving organisational effectiveness.

Summarising, then, the view being taken here is that leadership involves the use of influential increment (this is consistent with the view of Katz and Kahn). This view necessarily involves examining the concept of power and influence, and, as a derivative, the concept of organisational effectiveness can be examined.

A distinction for leadership theory was made earlier between leadership as a personal attribute of an individual and leadership as an organisational function. Now that the concept of leadership has been described, this distinction can be examined more fully. Usually, the two approaches are signified by the terms 'leadership traits' and 'organisational leadership'.

It would appear from examining the history of the analysis of many concepts in social science that analysis passes through different phases. For example, the concept of formal organisation was initially analysed in terms of its relationship to the major spheres of society such as the economic or political spheres. Then, the next phase was the systematic analysis of human relationships in the organisation. Next, the environment of the organisation was studied. Finally, the position today is that comparative studies of organisations predominate. The history of the concept of leadership has passed through different phases in the same way, although, it must be stressed, not the same phases. Basically, there are three phases that can be observed: first, the search for leadership traits in which psychologists dominated the analysis; second, a 'human relations' phase in which leadership was seen as a function of a group; and finally, the analysis of leadership in which attention focuses on the tasks of the leader. Logically, it is to the first of these phases that attention must first be drawn.

Leadership traits

There has been comparatively little research into the personal qualities of leaders, and one of the reasons for this may be the early days in which research of this nature was 'in vogue'. Leadership was initially equated with the possession of special powers which non-leaders did not possess. Early attempts at discovering leadership traits went on beyond the notion of charisma (with the implication of great works and abilities). Bavelas (1960) notes that some early approaches attributed to leaders powers such as the ability 'to tell the future' and 'to compel obedience hypnotically' (p. 491). Cartwright and Zander (1968) observe that early attempts at understanding the trait approach reported that leaders 'tend to be bigger (but not much bigger) and brighter (but not too much brighter) than the rest of the members' (p. 302). Traits or qualities such as piety, honesty, courage, perseverance, intelligence and imagination were 'discovered' in leaders. Attempts actually to define these qualities and objectively to measure them led to failure. The main reason for this failure was that leadership traits were merely expressions of what the researcher felt leaders ought to be like, rather than statements of what they actually were. Bird (1940) examined much of the early work on trait analysis and found that only 5 per cent of the traits to be found in the studies were common to four or more of them. Stogdill's review (1948) of the literature does not produce much better results. From this survey of over one hundred studies, the main conclusions are that (p. 64):

a. The average person who occupies a position of leadership exceeds the average member of his group in the following respects: (1) intelligence; (2) scholarship; (3) dependability in exercising responsibilities; (4) activity and social participation; and (5) socio-economic status.

b. The qualities, characteristics and skills required in a leader are determined to a large extent by the demands of the situation in which he is to function as a leader.

The study of leadership traits has developed somewhat since the rather disappointing beginnings. Traits are examined as a result of tests which are 'scientifically' derived and administered. In general, trait studies have concentrated on the intellectual, social and physical characteristics of leaders, and these have led to rather more guarded statements about leadership. For example, 'On various tests, persons who are leaders tend to be brighter, tend to be better adjusted psychologically, and tend to display better judgement' (Bavelas, 1960, p. 492).

Trait studies have been criticised a great deal. Cartwright and Zander (1968) suggest that the poorly conceived nature of personality traits and their unreliable measurement has led to much of the criticism. They keep an open mind and note that, as tests improve, it might be the case that distinctive traits will emerge. Another criticism of the trait approach, and one which has a long history, is that personality or physical determinants that elevate an individual into a leadership position may be different from those that result in effective leadership.

The problem of values invariably creeps into leadership research. There is an extant qualitative connotation attached to the term 'good leader'. Even the concept 'leader' has a value notion, implying something 'better' than a non-leader. This might appear to be a pseudo-problem unless it is understood that the values of the researcher enter into an evaluation of what is a 'good leader'.

A situational view

It has been suggested that the failings of the trait approach to leadership has given rise to a related view—the situational approach. What this approach says is that each leadership act and each leader should be looked at by defining the particular situation. Thus, the situational approach is almost the antithesis of the trait approach: one particularises, the other generalises. Each organisation has a unique pattern of relationships and a unique structure, so that leadership in the context of a particular organisation will also be unique.

Although the word 'antipathy' can be used in comparing the trait and situational approaches, there is a sense in which a combination of the two leads to a more complete picture of the concept of leadership. In the first place, there are similarities between organisations in terms of their structure and function which do enable generalisations to be made, both about the organisations and about the individuals who are potential leaders. Second, the unique characteristics of a particular organisation have to be comprehended before a particular leadership style can be delineated.

Organisational leadership

The combination of leadership traits and a situational approach to leadership focuses upon the organisation, and in this respect the earlier discussed notion of leadership as an organisational function can be returned to. When leadership is viewed in this way, a different foundation is required from that of leadership as a personal quality. Leadership as an organisational function requires an answer to the question, 'How are the leadership functions distributed in this organisation?' (Bavelas, 1960). Clearly, in the large-scale complex organisation the leadership functions are distributed throughout the organisation (or, minimally, to supervisory levels).

Selznick (1957) was partly concerned with leadership as an organisational function; his main concern was 'leadership in administration'. He lists three premises which, for him, underlie the whole notion of 'institutionalised' leadership (pp. 22-5):

1 Leadership is a kind of work done to meet the needs of a social situation. A theory of leadership is dependent on a theory of social organisation.
2 Leadership is not equal or equivalent to office-holding, high prestige, authority or decision-making.
3 Leadership is dispensable—that is, it is not equally necessary in all organisations.

Having looked at these premises, it is logical to ask what the functions of organisational leadership are. A long list could be constructed so long as Selznick's premise of non-equivalence is noted. Functions such as planning work, rewarding, punishing, information and advice-giving come readily to mind. Whatever the 'list' looks like and however many items are included in it, the basic function of leadership runs through all of them—that is enabling organisations, groups or persons to achieve objectives. Again, Selznick narrows all leadership functions down to four (1957, p. 61):

1 Definition of institutionalised mission and role. That is, the actual setting of objectives.
2 Institutional embodiment of purpose. That is, building the set objectives into the structure of the organisation.
3 Defense of institutional integrity. That is, the striving for a distinctive reality for the organisation and maintaining the values of the organisation.
4 Ordering of internal conflict. Here, the operational function is of a dual nature: to maintain the balance of power and to maximise voluntary co-operation.

There is a lot of agreement concerning these functions. Bavelas (1960) says that 'leadership consists of the continuous choice-making process that permits the organisation as a whole to proceed toward its objective despite all sorts of internal and external perturbations' (p. 497).

At the supervisory level, there are problems that can arise from examining the functions of organisational leadership in this way. Selznick states that the first function is the definition of objectives. Manifestly, this is not a supervisory function—goals are set and defined at a higher level in the organisation. March and Simon's notion of a hierarchy of objectives (1958) may mean that sub-goals in the organisation can be set by supervisors and attribute to the overall goal of the organisation. Only in that sense can supervisors be involved in this definitional function.

It was said that using this approach to leadership meant that the concepts of leadership and organisation were closely intertwined. This is clearly the case and can be shown by recognising that in all organisations there is a need for leadership for a number of reasons. Even though 'top leadership' sets objectives and produces an 'embodiment of purpose', no organisation can be so constructed that the need for leadership at lower levels in the organisation declines. To take a simple example, the formal theorists of organisation have suggested that abstract rules and procedures exist to cover every contingency (Weber, 1947). And yet, given the reality of organisations, occasions are bound to occur when rules and procedures do not cover the problem in question. The individual organisation member then has several strategies open to him, one of which would be to refer the problem to his superior. The superior (in the role of leader) would then have the function of exercising discretion in providing a solution to the problem. A simple example such as this provides several reasons why it is necessary to have leadership in organisations.

First, one of the key components of organisations is fallible human beings. Mann (1965) has noted that a feature of mass society is that role relationships are segmental (while they can be regarded as total in folk society). The relevance of this is that individuals have multiple roles, only one of which is a work role (at least for the majority of the occupied population). As a consequence, the behaviour of individuals is to a large extent determined by roles outside the organisation in which they are employed. Performance of the organisational role, then, is in part a function of extra-organisational roles. Variations in non-work roles is common, and these produce changes in behaviour patterns. As a result, organisational roles may be changed or varied because of the extra-organisational changes. One of the functions of the leader in the organisation must be to re-define the organisational role in the light of extra-organisational roles, and to the extent that the objectives of the organisation are still striven after and achieved. The supervisor as leader in this context comes to have an extremely valuable role since he comes into contact with the problems and changes that the individual brings to the organisation. Further, this influence from the outside gives a reason why it is generally operationally impossible for an organisation to have a 'working blue-print'.

Second, and closely related to the first reason for leadership, the dynamics of organisation have to allow for labour turnover and recruitment. Since it has been established that each organisation is unique, it follows that new organisation members have to be 'organisationally socialised'—they have to be taught the value systems, the rights, duties and obligations associated with their role, and so on. There is a continual movement of people being recruited and people leaving any organisation, and an effective leader can ensure that these changes in the human component are assimilated as smoothly as possible.

Third, individual needs and requirements change over time. For example, the problems of the ageing worker are well known (Blum and Naylor, 1968). Physiological, psychological and social changes in the individual over time have to be accommodated, and here again a leadership function in the organisation becomes an absolute necessity.

Fourth, the actual workings of an organisation demand that changes be made in the internal structure. Organisations are not self-contained, isolated or vacuumed from the outside world. There is a continual interaction between an organisation and its environment. It has been shown that external factors can influence the internal structure of an organisation, whether these events be other organisations (Blau and Scott, 1963), technology (Woodward, 1958; Harvey, 1965), market considerations (Burns and Stalker, 1961)

106

or trade unions (Vroom and Decci, 1970). There are, of course, other external determinants of internal organisation change (Dunkerley, 1972). Anyone with a leadership role in an organisation consequently has a key role in effecting a smooth pattern of change in the organisation. The supervisor, by being close to the workaday problems, has an important role in this.

A final need for leadership in complex organisations lies in the fact that there might be what Katz and Kahn (1966) call the 'incompleteness of organisational design'. The work of Blau (1959) demonstrates quite clearly that no organisation functions in the manner in which, say, the organisation chart lays down that it should. The informal organisation, 'discovered' as a result of the Hawthorne Experiments (Roethlisberger and Dickson, 1939), is superimposed on the formal organisation. The problems which arise when workers 'work-to-rule' again shows the incompleteness of the design of the organisation. In reconciling the formal organisation with the informal, a leadership function becomes absolutely necessary. Again, the supervisor as leader is important because of his physical and, to some extent, social proximity to the rank-and-file organisation members.

There are other important reasons why any organisation has a need for leadership. In a sense, the five factors listed here can be regarded as five key functions of organisational leadership; they lead back, in any case, to the principles of leadership as seen by Selznick.

In talking about organisational leadership, it has so far been assumed that it is possible to discuss it as a unitary concept. This is not the case, since different types of leadership occur at different levels in the organisation. In explaining behaviour, psychologists have recognised that both personality variables and environmental variables have to be examined. Thus, Lewin (1951, p. 239) says that 'behaviour (B) is a function (F) of the person (P) and of his environment (E)', or:

$$B = F(P.E)$$

Similarly, social psychologists have explained behaviour in these kinds of term, except that structural variables are given greater emphasis because of the different focus. In explaining leadership as a function of an organisation, Katz and Kahn (1966) have said that it is 'always a combined function of social structural factors and of the particular characteristics of the individuals making up the structure' (p. 305). Symbolically:

$$L = F(S.P)$$

where L=leadership, S=social structural factors and P=personal characteristics.

Katz and Kahn make the observation that researchers have tended to neglect the setting in which leadership acts occur—what they define as the social structural factors. They propose a typology of leadership behaviour to be found in complex organisations (Katz and Kahn, 1966, p. 308):

1 the introduction of structural change, or policy formulation.
2 the interpolation of structure, i.e. piecing out the incompleteness of existing formal structure, or improvisation.
3 the use of structure formally provided to keep the organisation in motion and in effective operation, or administration.

The first type of leadership behaviour has been described above. The external influences on an organisation often demand continual internal structural changes. The second type involves the interpretation of the general objectives stated by the organisation. Although the formal structure of the organisation dictates the general guide-lines, they have often to be made operational, and this involves a different pattern of leadership behaviour.

Following the argument proposed by Katz and Kahn, leadership behaviour of the kinds distinguished above can be ordered systematically. It has already been established that organisational roles or positions always have expectations associated with them. Furthermore, leadership positions have rewards and punishments associated with them that facilitate the exercise of leadership (cf. French and Raven, 1959). Katz and Kahn maintain that their typology of leadership behaviour can be examined in relation to an organisational hierarchy. The first type of behaviour is exercised by senior members of an organisation. Typically, goal-setting, objectives-formulation and structural changes are made as a result of boardroom decisions. The second type of leadership behaviour—the interpretation of structure—is typically carried out by middle organisation levels. And, lastly, the actual use of structure is the leadership behaviour of most supervisory levels in an organisation. The distribution of leadership behaviour in a typical organisation could look like Table 5.1. Clearly, there is a considerable blurring of the boundaries between each of these types and levels, such that it is to be expected that managers can be involved in Type I behaviour as well as Type III. Similarly, supervisor's behaviour is not solely concerned with Type III, as is shown below.

Since the concern in this analysis is with the supervisor as a leader, Type I of leadership behaviour need not be examined in any great depth. It is worth discussing because supervisors are at times responsible for the setting of sub-goals which might be due to structural changes, in turn caused by external influences of the organisation.

TABLE 5.1

Leadership behaviour	Level of organisation
Type I	Directors
Type II	Managers
Type III	Supervisors

For each of these three patterns of leadership behaviour there are appropriate cognitive styles and affective characteristics. Because of these, Katz and Kahn (1966) maintain that 'leadership skills appropriate to one level of the organisation may be irrelevant or even dysfunctional at another level' (p. 311). The cognitive and affective requirements of leadership behaviour can be represented diagrammatically as shown in Table 5.2.

From the paradigm it can be seen that the cognitive and affective requirements for the first type of leadership behaviour are 'systemic perspective' and 'charisma' respectively. Since it has been established that this type of leadership behaviour is only really appropriate to the upper echelons of the organisation, it need not be a matter for present concern.

Type II leadership behaviour can be of some relevance to an understanding of supervisory leadership. Cognitively, interpolation involves internal perspective in the sense of having knowledge regarding the sub-systems of the organisation, both in terms of the nature of the work and the interdependency between them. Cognitively also, the role incumbent with leadership behaviour of this nature has what Katz and Kahn call a 'two-way orientation'. That is, he has to take cognizance of both superiors and subordinates in exercising leadership.

The affective requirement of Type II leadership behaviour is the integration of primary and secondary relationships—this is known in another context as practising human relations skills. This aspect of the role is discussed below in some detail.

At the third 'level' of leadership behaviour—the use of the existing structure—the cognitive and affective aspects are technical knowledge and concern with equity respectively. Again, these are discussed fully below.

There is one further comment to be made on the analysis of leadership as presented by Katz and Kahn. The implicit assumption of the three types of leadership behaviour is that they are mutually exclusive. This, however, is not the case, given the dynamics of organisational functioning. In some situations it is necessary for different

TABLE 5.2 *Leadership patterns, their locus in the organisation and their skill requirements*

Type of leadership process	Appropriate organisational level	Cognitive	Affective
			Abilities and skills
Origination: change, creation and elimination of structure	Top echelons	Systemic perspective	Charisma
Interpolation: supplementing and piecing out of structure	Intermediate levels: pivotal roles	Sub-system perspective: two-way orientation	Integration of primary and secondary relations: human relations skills
Administration: use of existing structure	Lower levels	Technical knowledge and understanding of system of rules	Concern with equity in use of rewards and sanctions

(Adapted from Katz and Kahn, 1966, p.312)

hierarchical groups and levels to employ different patterns of leadership behaviour. A study of leadership in hospitals (Mann, 1964) suggests that there is a need for 'skill-mix' according to the level in the organisation. The departmental heads studied were either satisfied or dissatisfied depending on the 'co-ordinative' and 'integrative' abilities of their superiors. These abilities that Mann talks of can be equated with Katz and Kahn's systemic perspective and origination of structure. The feature of skill-mix mentioned above is important since Mann found that if there were a period of rapid and major change, the effects of this move through the organisation very quickly. So quickly, in fact, that although theoretically the directors of an organisation should be responsible for formulating policy, this can in practice be left to lower level participants in the organisation. So, in certain circumstances, several different types of leadership behaviour may be exercised by different levels in the organisation.

There are other issues which can be discussed under the heading of organisational leadership, but these can only be referred to after an analysis of leadership as a group function. This is a logical step since an analysis of group integration and leadership in a complex organisation has potential for reductionism, and this can be largely reduced by examining group processes first of all.

Group leadership

The study of leadership has primarily been the interest of social psychologists. This proposition is partially supported by the plethora of research studies in the area of group leadership. Historically, the development of group leadership study arose from the unsatisfactory results of the trait approach to leadership. The aim of group leadership analysis is to examine the characteristics of small groups and to understand the social situation in which the groups operate. Moving away from the trait approach, this analysis, by having the group as the primary focus of concern, looks at the attempts made by groups at goal achievement and links these attempts to the necessary actions that are required of a leader. As a derivative of this, many writers have discussed the roles of group members in actions performed by the group. Leadership in this context can be defined as 'the performance of those acts which help the group achieve its preferred outcomes' (Cartwright and Zander, 1968, p. 304).

The 'acts' which Cartwright and Zander refer to are several, the chief ones being the definition of the aims or goals of the group; manipulating group members in pursuit of these aims; promoting interpersonal relationships within the group, and so on. There has to be a recognition, then, that a leadership function may be per-

111

formed by any and all members of the group. Having established this, it is logical to ask what leadership functions are performed at the group level and how these differ from institutional leadership functions.

Leadership functions

In many cases, leadership and acts of leadership are discussed as being synonymous with influence and attempts at influence (see, for example, Cartwright, 1965). If this kind of synonym can be accepted, then a leader can be viewed as an individual who is in a position to exercise rather more influence than any other group member. A strict meaning of the concept of leadership has to be made if this reasoning is followed. It is not good enough, for example, to say as Cattell (1951) does that a leader is any member of a group who is able to modify the properties of the group merely by his presence. The main drawback to this approach is that, in the extreme, all group activities are leadership activities. However, as Cartwright and Zander (1968) point out, this approach has merits in that leadership and group performance are related to one another; that leadership is not dichotomous (that is one does not either have or not have the quality of leadership); and that not only the individual occupying the formal position of influence need be the sole leader of the group.

Many writers have attempted to classify the functions of leaders, both widely and narrowly. At the most extreme of narrowness, leadership functions could be expressed as planning, decision-making and co-ordinating. At the most wide level, or extreme, the functions could be listed as executive, planner, policy-maker, expert, group representative, controller of internal relationships, purveyor of rewards and punishments, arbitrator, exemplar, group symbol, surrogate for individual responsibility, ideologist, father figure and scape-goat (Krech and Crutchfield, 1948). Clearly, we could add to and subtract from this list at random.

A recognition of the problems involved in delineating leadership functions at a group level has led to agreement that functions can be listed under two general headings. These two headings relate to the objectives to which leadership functions attempt to relate, and are, first, the objectives of the achievement of some specific group goal and, second, the maintenance or strengthening of the group itself. When a leader is formally appointed, he is given the responsibility for achieving both of these objectives. Research has shown, however, that placed in a laboratory setting, these two tasks are usually split between two or more individuals (see, for example, Bales and Slater, 1955).

112

The two generalised leadership functions distinguished above are usually labelled as 'consideration' and 'initiating structure'. These two leadership patterns or dimensions were first focused upon as a result of the Ohio State University Leadership Studies (Fleishman, Harris and Burtt, 1955). Factor analysis showed that the two dimensions represented 83 per cent of the common variance in the behaviour of leaders. The two patterns correspond to the goal achievement and group maintenance functions as described above. Specifically, they can be defined as follows (Fleishman and Harris, 1962, pp. 43–4):

Consideration includes behaviour indicating mutual trust, respect and a certain warmth and rapport between the supervisor and his group. This does not mean that this dimension reflects a superficial 'pat-on-the-back', 'first name calling' kind of human relations behaviour. This dimension appears to emphasise a deeper concern for group members' needs and includes such behaviour as allowing subordinates more participation in decision making and encouraging more two-way communication.
Structure includes behaviour in which the supervisor organises and defines activities and his relations with the group. Thus, he defines the role he expects each member to assume, assigns tasks, plans ahead, establishes ways of getting things done, and pushes for production. This dimension seems to emphasise overt attempts to achieve organisational goals.

These two dimensions arose from the Supervisory Behaviour Description Questionnaire which was completed by the subordinates describing the behaviour of superiors. It might be expected that the two dimensions are negatively correlated—particularly in the light of the work by Bales and Slater—but this has been shown not to be the case. The dimensions are both uncorrelated and relatively independent. Because of this feature of relative independence, a supervisor may in fact be characterised by any combination of them —viz. high on both, low on both, or high on one and low on the other.

Using the framework of consideration and initiating structure, Fleishman and Harris (1962) investigated the relationships between supervisory behaviour and group member behaviour. The form of the relationship between the two was analysed, and the effects of different combinations of consideration and structure. Two particular aspects of behaviour were investigated—labour grievances and employee turnover. The sample was composed of fifty-seven supervisors and their work groups in a motor truck manufacturing plant. The scores obtained for consideration and structure were related to the grievance rates and turnover rates of the supervisors' departments. The more important results arising are shown in Figure 5.1.

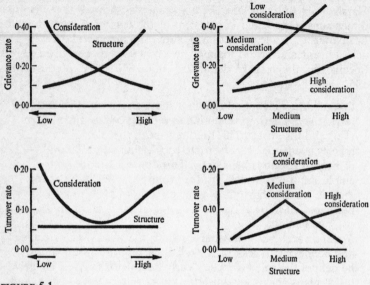

FIGURE 5.1

Several important conclusions arise from these results. A significant relationship is to be found between supervisory behaviour and grievances and turnover; this relationship can be expressed as 'low consideration and high structure go with high grievances and turnover'. After a certain point, no effects were noticed on grievances and turnover with increased consideration or decreased structure. The relationship would appear then to be curvilinear and not parabolic, linear or hyperbolic, as had been suggested in other previous studies.

In general, subordinates preferred supervisors to be high in consideration and disliked working under supervisors who scored high on initiating structure. Nevertheless, those supervisors with the highest proficiency ratings were those that scored highest on the structure items. In non-production departments the reverse was true—those supervisors having the highest proficiency ratings scored highest on consideration scores. As found elsewhere many times, absenteeism in production departments was related to structure and negatively related to consideration.

Many different dimensions of leadership behaviour have been suggested. The analysis of Halpern and Winer (1957) is similar to

TABLE 5.3 Correspondence of leadership concepts of different investigators

Bowers & Seashore (1966)	Hemphill & Coons (1957)	Halpern & Winer (1957)	Katz, et al. (1950)	Katz & Kahn (1951)	Kahn (1958)	Likert (1961)	Cartwright & Zander (1968)
Support	Maintenance of membership character	Consideration	Employee orientation	Employee orientation; closeness of supervision	Providing direct need satisfaction	Supportive relationships	Group maintenance functions
Interaction facilitation	Group interaction	Sensitivity		Group relationships		Group methods	
Goal emphasis	Objective attainment behaviour	Production emphasis	Production orientation		Structuring path to goal / Modifying employee goals	High performance goals	
Work facilitation		Initiating structure		Differentiation of supervisory role; closeness of supervision	Enabling goal achievement	Technical knowledge, planning, scheduling	Goal achievement functions

From Gibb (1969), p. 369.

the one of Fleishman and Harris (1962). Data was collected from air-force crews, using 130 items. When the items were factor-analysed, four orthogonal factors resulted: consideration, initiating structure, production emphasis and sensitivity or social awareness. The interesting point is, as Cartwright and Zander (1968) point out, that the last two dimensions take the analysis back to dividing leadership functions into goal achievement and group maintenance respectively.

Instead of laboriously listing the different dimensions which have been used by different researchers, these can be tabulated as shown in Table 5.3. It is clear from this table that there is quite a large degree of correspondence between the various classificatory attempts. It is also important to recognise that the classification used by both Bowers and Seashore (1966) and Likert (1961) would appear to be the most comprehensive. Thus, with Bowers and Seashore the following factors comprise the leadership structure:

1 Support: behaviour enhancing someone else's feeling of worth and importance.
2 Interaction facilitation: encouraging the development of close relationships.
3 Goal emphasis: stimulating enthusiasm to group goal achievement.
4 Work facilitation: behaviour instrumental in goal achievement.

Turning now to look at the work of Likert, his *New Patterns of Management* (1961) contains a great many useful insights into leadership functions, behaviour and performance. Initially it is necessary to look at the leadership functions. The first function centres around the question of whether a supervisor should be employee-centred or job-centred. Reviewing the literature on this subject leads to the conclusion that the more work-orientated a supervisor is the less the work group will 'produce', and vice versa. This can be illustrated diagrammatically as shown in Figure 5.2 (from Likert, 1961, p. 7).

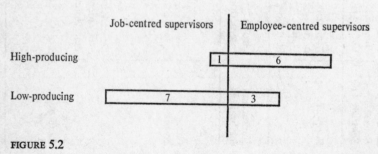

FIGURE 5.2

116

Only a partial picture is given here, however. A high level of performance does not result purely from a supervisor being employee centred. Kahn (1956) has shown that, in addition to being employee-centred, a supervisor must be seen by his employees as feeling that achieving high output was a major job component. This leads Likert (1961) to state his first function for leaders: 'If a high level of performance is to be achieved, it appears to be necessary for a supervisor to be employee-centred and at the same time to have high performance goals and a contiguous enthusiasm as to the importance of achieving these goals' (p. 8). In terms of Table 5.3 as constructed above (p. 115), there has to be the condition of *high performance goals*.

Associated with the above condition is the amount of pressure by the supervisor for better performance from his subordinates. As might be expected, research has shown that more trust and confidence will be felt by subordinates towards their supervisor if there is reasonable pressure from him for improving performance. Pressure can increase to such a stage that it 'turns' into manifest conflict. Once again, research has demonstrated much that would be expected. Georgopolous (1957) has shown that the greater the conflict between a supervisor and his subordinates, the lower the level of production.

The second condition for effective leadership (and, simultaneously, effective supervision) is what Likert (1961) calls the *principle of supportive relationships* (p. 103). This principle states that

The leadership and other processes of the organisation must be such as to ensure a maximum probability that in all interactions and all relationships with the organisation each member will, in the light of his background, values and expectations, view the experience as supportive and one which builds and maintains his sense of personal worth and importance.

It would appear that the principle of supportive relationships uses the role set as its conceptual base, although this is not suggested by Likert. In role theory terminology, the 'focal person' (in this case, the supervisor) has his expectations concerning the operation of his role. The members of his role set (subordinates comprising the work group, in this case) have their own expectations of what the focal person should do in that position. Likert is saying that the supervisor has to undergo a kind of role-playing exercise in order to fully understand the expectations of his subordinates. The developments of group relationships is an important way in which the supervisor can 'measure' the felt needs and expectations of his subordinates. This proposition leads to the third condition for effective leadership— *group methods of supervision*.

117

Likert maintains that it is only in the work group that effective supportive relationships can be developed: 'management will make full use of the potential capacities of the human resources only when each person in an organisation is a member of one or more effectively functioning work groups that have a high degree of group loyalty, effective skills of interaction, and high performance goals' (p. 104).

The last of Likert's leadership functions is *technical knowledge*. A supervisor will only be truly effective when he possesses technical knowledge: 'The leader [in a highly effective group] has adequate competence to handle the technical problems faced by his group or sees that access to this technical knowledge is fully provided' (p. 171).

Supervisory leadership and productivity

A great many studies have recognised that there is a link between the nature of supervision (that is both the supervisor himself and the 'leadership climate') and the performance and productivity of the work group. In analysing this relationship, it is often the case that other variables are introduced, such as the attitudes of subordinates towards their supervisor. A study carried out by Katz, MacCoby and Morse (1950) was one of the first, and remains one of the most important in examining this relationship by means of an intervening variable. From this study, it was possible to identify certain 'high'-producing sections and certain 'low'-producing sections. All sections were doing similar work. From the morale point of view, four attitudinal variables were developed—pride in the work, intrinsic job satisfaction, involvement in the company and financial and job status. 'Scoring' these variables meant that they could be compared to the high- and low-producing sections. It was found that 'pride in the work' had a significant relationship to the work performance, and that the other three areas appeared to have no relationship at all.

In addition to looking at morale, Katz, MacCoby and Morse determined a description of supervisory behaviour and attitudes towards the job and company policies by interviewing all of the supervisors in the high- and low-performance sections. Supervisors were classified under the heading of 'employee-centred' or 'production-centred'; 'democratic' or 'authoritarian'; 'high or average judgment' or 'poor judgment'. It was found that the supervision of the high-performance sections were employee-centred, democratic and had high or average judgment. The supervisors of low-performance sections were production-centred, authoritarian and had poor judgment.

Likert (1961), merely by using a different terminology, comes to the same conclusion: 'General rather than close supervision is more often associated with a high rather than a low level of productivity' (p. 9). This relationship has been found in many studies, but as Tiffin and McCormick (1966) point out, it cannot definitely be said that these characteristics are the sole cause of the differential performance in similar work groups. Some of the research carried out by Likert shows, however, that if 'high performance' supervisors are transferred to 'low performance' departments, productivity can be radically altered. It would appear that more weight is lent to the argument concerning supervisory style and group performance.

As a derivative of this relationship found above, more recent research has found that the employee-centred, democratic and high or average judgment supervisor produces favourable attitudes to a whole series of work variables. These include not only supervision itself but also working conditions, compensation and the work itself. Table 5.4, adapted from Katz (1949) and Likert (1961), shows these relationships.

TABLE 5.4 *Behaviour of supervisors as reported by subordinates in forty high-morale and forty low-morale groups*

Supervisory behaviour	% in high-morale groups	% in low-morale groups
Makes work assignments	67	69
Enforces rules	54	54
Supplies materials, tools	36	41
Keeps men informed	47	11
Tells men how they are doing	47	12
Recommends promotions, etc.	61	22
Encourages ideas	62	17
Hears complaints	65	32
Takes interest in men	81	29
Stands up for men	87	30
Treats men as human beings	97	33

Many more studies can be quoted in examining the relationship between supervisory style and the performance of the work group. There is still a great deal of contradictory evidence concerning the kinds of relationships which have been discussed here. For example, on logical grounds there ought to be a relationship between productivity and job satisfaction, and yet no consistency has been found here. Many obvious relationships of this kind have not been consistently proven. But when the role of the supervisor is examined, something rather more 'concrete' does emerge. Perrow (1970, p. 7) quotes from a recent unpublished study by Tannenbaum and Seashore:

Supervisors of high-producing groups seem in the worker's view to behave differently than supervisors of low-producing groups, they seem to be different kinds of people. In many cases, the high-producing supervisor was less punitive towards his subordinates, he supervised in general ways rather than closely, he was more likely to be concerned about his subordinates as human beings, as individuals, rather than as a means for turning out a product.

In other words, a general conclusion for this section would be that it does not matter whether the subordinates are satisfied with their work, but the manner in which supervisors behave is the determining factor. Given a conclusion such as this, the role of supervisory training becomes very important, and is discussed in a subsequent chapter.

The organisational context

There is little doubt that the studies of leadership and supervision examined above have greatly increased our knowledge of the subject in general. More recently, studies of this nature have been criticised in line with the general developments in the study of complex organisations. Some of the studies, more than being criticised, have been disproved by expanding the analysis to take account of the organisational context.

Current thought in management and organisation theory recognises the need to account for the *context* in which management and supervision takes place, the *nature of the work* being managed and supervised, and the *nature of the personnel* involved. Brown (1960), for example, proposes the task approach to management. He says (p. 42): 'Effective organisation is a function of the work to be done and the resources and techniques available to do it. . . . Failure to make explicit acknowledgement of this relationship between work and organisation gives rise to non-valid assumptions.' The work of the Tavistock Institute researchers also suggests that the nature of the task has to be accounted for. Pugh, Hickson and Inkson (1970) have stressed the necessity for examining the context in which organisational operations are conducted.

In applying the task and contextual approaches to the study of supervisory leadership, some of the main recent studies can be examined to illustrate the point. The complexity of this approach is, in part, demonstrated by the very few studies of leadership and supervision in complex organisations.

Pelz (1951) criticises many of the leadership studies on the grounds of reductionism. It is clear that work groups do not operate in isolation in the sense that several of the above studies suggested. Work groups are always couched in an organisational context, and Pelz sees the necessity to examine the interaction between these two levels. Pelz's study was of first-line supervisors in a large electrical company and revealed some interesting points.

1 No overall difference was found in 'styles of supervision' between highly satisfied and low-satisfied work groups.
2 Supervisors who were willing to take the side of their men in the cases of dispute with their own superiors had highly-satisfied work groups. This was particularly so when the groups were small and mainly on the shop-floor. Large work groups preferred a supervisor who was a 'management man', particularly in clerical and administrative departments.
3 Those supervisors who were willing to take the side of the men in their work groups to help them with their problems and to put them forward for promotion were preferred only if they were successful. Therefore, only if the supervisors had the power to carry out their policies were they viewed as successful.

A more recent work by Fiedler (1965a) has attempted to classify the effectiveness of 'styles of leadership' according to the conditions under which they are operating. The aim of Fiedler's work is to get away from the rather naïve generalisations such as 'the more democratic the supervisor, the more . . .'. Fiedler attempts to specify the kind of situation in which leadership attempts operate, to specify factors which affect leader influence and to integrate these into a coherent theory. Three major factors or dimensions are delineated that determine the kind of leadership style called for by different situations.

1 *Leader–member relations* These involve the degree to which the leader is personally accepted and liked—that is members' liking or respect. If the leader has the loyalty and confidence of his group, he needs little else to influence the group: it is easier to lead a group in which you are liked or accepted than it is to lead one in which you are disliked or rejected. The personal power of the leader *vis-à-vis* his group can be measured either by averaging member feelings toward a leader or leader ratings of his group along several dimensions. This gives rise to Fiedler's Least Preferred Coworker scores.

2 *Task structure* The most obvious dimension of assessment of the task is in terms of its degree of structure—the degree to which the task is defined. When the task is highly structured, the group leader can control how well the task is performed, he can describe each step in the process and, if the group follows instructions, it will complete

121

the task. Any person who fails to perform his job, or who performs it in the wrong sequence, can immediately be spotted and corrected. This is not possible, however, when the task is vague and unstructured. For example, developing a new policy or a new product is very different from implementing a given policy. Here, the leader neither knows nor can control the steps that are necessary to achieve a successful result. In fact, frequently, the leader cannot even spell out exactly what a successful product should look like. In such a situation, the leader could not, for example, punish a man for failing to be maximally creative or for misjudging a difficult problem. The unstructured task, therefore, presents a much more difficult task for the leader. Task structure is measured by Fiedler by rating on four aspects: decision verifiability; goal clarity (the degree to which the goal is clearly stated); goal path multiplicity; and solution specificity (the degree to which there is more than one correct solution).

3 *Power of position* The leader who can hire or fire, promote or demote, can obtain compliance under conditions which might be impossible for a leader in a relatively powerless position, such as the

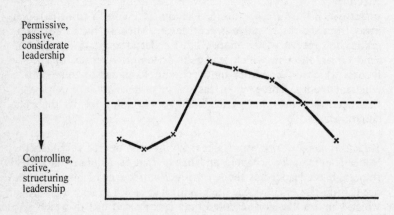

Leader - member relations	Good	Good	Good	Good	Poor	Poor	Poor	Poor
Task structure	Structured		Unstructured		Structured		Unstructured	
Leader - position power	Strong	Weak	Strong	Weak	Strong	Weak	Strong	Weak

FIGURE 5.3 *How the style of effective leadership varies with the situation*

chairman of a volunteer group whose members are at liberty to walk out at any time; this kind of leader has high positional power. Power of position can be measured by means of a simple check-list, which includes such items as the ability of the leader to promote or demote, and his special rank or title.

These three dimensions, when they have been measured or judged, can each be dichotomised. This leads to eight possible types which can be expressed as in Figure 5.3. The horizontal axis shows the different situations in which groups worked. The vertical axis shows the leadership style which was most effective in each situation, as shown by the correlation coefficient between the leader's Least Preferred Coworkers Score (LPC) and his group's performance.

Correlations between the leader's LPC scores and the groups' performance suggest that managing, directive leaders are usually effective in situations which are favourable for them, or relatively unfavourable. Permissive, considerate leaders are best suited to intermediate situations. In other words, when the group backs the leader and the task is clear, the leader is expected to give clear directions and orders. In fact, the leader who under these conditions becomes non-directive and passive frequently loses the esteem of the group. Similarly, when the task is confused, when the leader has little power or when he is disliked, it is better to do almost anything rather than to stand helplessly by. The permissive, non-directive, human relations oriented approach is most appropriate in two types of situation. In one, the leader deals with a group which is engaged in a highly unstructured task, such as one requiring problem-solving, decision-making or creativity, where he must not be too threatening, directive or critical. The second type of situation is one in which the not-too-well accepted leader has a structured job. Even though his position may hold power, the leader may have to stop carefully and to be diplomatic to avoid being completely rejected by members of his group. The leader with a good rating from his group and who is permissive and group-oriented is likely to perform better under these circumstances.

Further verification at the common-sense level might be possible from this model. It can be seen particularly in crisis situations or research groups. By definition, crisis implies a situation which provides no guide-lines for behaviour. The typical pattern is such a case; the organisation returns to routine and fairly well structured tasks which require directive, managing, controlling leadership. Similarly, in a new research team, there is great confusion until the project is decided upon, duties are assigned, and so on.

Other recent work has important implications for the understanding of the concept of supervisory leadership, particularly since it is discussed in terms of the situational variables. Etzioni's 'Dual

123

Leadership in Complex Organisations' (1965) is a good example of this approach. Etzioni recognises that the early work of Lewin and Mayo on small groups has resulted in the pair of concepts of formal and informal organisation (and of formal and informal leadership). Etzioni attempts to take their analysis a step further by using the Bales–Parsons model of small groups in the theory of formal organisations. Etzioni, then, is concerned with the organisation as it affects the fulfilment of the functional needs of small groups and the way these functions are served affecting the operation of the organisation itself.

Basically, the Bales–Parsons model suggests that if small task-oriented groups are to operate efficiently, two kinds of leadership are required. These two should be mutually supportive. One is the expressive or social-emotional leader, who ranks higher than other individuals in such interaction as 'showing solidarity' and 'asking for suggestions'; the other—the instrumental or task-oriented leader—ranks higher than the other individuals in such categories as 'giving suggestions' and 'showing disagreement'. From this, it is possible to regard all role clusters in any group as being oriented around either of these two functions, and all individuals have the potential to occupy either of these two fields. The Bales–Parsons analysis suggests that task-oriented groups will be more effective in terms of task achievement and members' satisfaction when the group commands both instrumental and expressive leaders. It suggests that while both these functions could be embodied in one man ('The Great Man Theory') usually they are not. When two individuals carry out the two leadership roles, mutual support is required for effective leadership and for the group to perform maximally.

Organisations differ in many ways from the small group situation, and one of these ways is to see the dual nature of power in terms of either organisation position or of personal power. These two give rise to differing conceptions of leadership, as Figure 5.4 shows (Etzioni, 1965, p. 691).

Positional power

	+	−
+	Formal leader	Informal leader
−	Official	Follower

Personal power

FIGURE 5.4

Thus, in the organisational context, several issues become critical, of which one, as seen above, is how and to what extent the leadership is backed by organisational power. Arising from this, Etzioni sees the organisational location of expressive and instrumental leadership affecting, first, the degree of organisational control over the group—generally, the control is weaker over the informal leader and, hence, an organisation that provides both kinds of leadership will have more control over its participants than an organisation in which both kinds of activities are controlled by informal leaders; second, the degree of collaboration between the two kinds of leaders—generally, it is more likely when both kinds of leader are provided by the organisation, or neither does; third, the power relations between the two kinds of leader—this is dependent on organisational positions, which in turn affect and reflect the goals and compliance structure of the organisation. Clearly, whichever type of leader is accorded the greater power by the organisation, that leader will have more power than the other over his group. In other words, to maximise the effectiveness of control over the group, the organisation must not only control its leaders but also allocate power so as to establish the superiority of the desired kind of leadership over the other.

From this type of analysis, it is possible to classify organisations according to their goals and the corresponding needs to gain high, low or medium commitment from the participants. This analysis is useful for the comparative analysis of organisations. For example, in organisations that have either a high or a low socialisation role, like prisons, voluntary associations, schools, and so on, it is essential for the organisation to provide leadership of the small groups or to gain the leader's support. Again, those organisations concerned with the production or exchange of goods or services require commitment from their members (though perhaps not as much as from socialising organisations). Production organisations will operate more efficiently in terms of Etzioni's model, if leadership is accepted by the small groups within them. Even if such leadership is rejected, production organisations can still operate effectively on the principle of reciprocity (for example, a fair day's pay for a fair day's work).

Etzioni's analysis of leadership appears to be a development of his more general compliance theory (Etzioni, 1960). A number of specific propositions can be gleaned from the text—propositions about the relationship between the level of commitment of an organisation and the kind of leadership that will be effective. Put in another way, these propositions can be listed as:

1 Organisations vary in the degree to which effective operation requires them to gain the control and the loyalty of the small groups that function in them.

2   The degree to which labour commitment is a crucial variable for an organisation will determine the extent to which expressive leadership will be effective.
3   If an organisation requires little or no commitment from its constituent groups to function effectively (for example, prisons and mental hospitals), the most effective leadership will be informal and expressive.
4   If an organisation requires moderate commitment from its constituent groups (for example, production and service organisations), the most effective leadership will be formal and instrumental.
5   If a high level of commitment is required (for example, religious organisations), the most effective form of leadership will be formal and expressive.

The crux of Etzioni's argument is, therefore, that the general characteristics of organisations set limits on the kinds of leadership that emerge. In looking at the position of the industrial supervisor, the analysis has to be specially focused on production organisations. If organisational characteristics do in fact determine, in part, the type of leadership, for production organisations two levels of organisational phenomena can be distinguished. First, there are technical arrangements that influence the degree to which negative work attitudes can adversely affect the final product. The greater the individual's control over the quality and the quantity of the product and the more work done in groups rather than individually, the higher the required labour commitment. Second, there is the relationship between the organisation and its environment. In certain circumstances, the maintenance of high commitment can be crucial for an organisation. If the organisation is having difficulty in surviving in its environment, its failure to maintain high commitment on the part of the labour force can mean the difference between survival and failure. Organisational adaptability, the ability of an organisation to survive in its environment, is therefore an important determinant of required labour commitment. Also, of course, Etzioni suggests that the higher the required labour commitment, the more the formal leadership roles tend to be expressive.

A study by Rossel (1970) investigates the instrumental and expressive leadership orientations among managers and supervisors in eight production organisations that had varying labour commitment. Respondents in the study were classified as top management, middle management (line heads of major operating procedures), top supervision (general foremen, departmental heads) and front-line foremen (foremen and lower supervisors). The main results to the study are shown in Figure 5.5. Rossel found that, for some supervisors, their leadership style affected the quality of the product and the amount produced. Where this occurred, the supervisor tended to use expressive leadership. It is the lower supervisors who paradoxically feel the style of top management leadership the most. If top management has an instrumental orientation, the lower supervisor is also expected to adopt this form of orientation even though he may in fact be an expressive leader. Rossel suggests that the supervisor attempts to reconcile this by alternating between the two poles of expressiveness and instrumentality. A consequence of this is that his subordinates view him as inconsistent and arbitrary. This only occurs when labour commitment is high; when it is low, he is relatively free of demands from above and can assist in the production process.

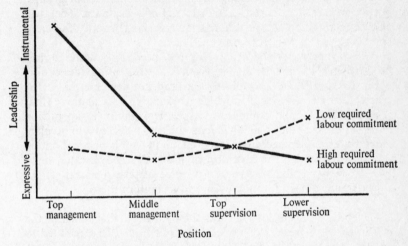

FIGURE 5.5 *Means within leadership orientations, position and required labour commitment*

Conclusions

In the light of the studies taking account of the organisational context, and from other research findings, some specific generalisations can be put forward.

1 The effect of 'style' of supervision is much greater in work groups where there are not any incentive schemes or other independent motivators (Argyle, Gardner, Cioffi, 1958).

2 Much of the effect of any particular 'style of supervision' is very dependent on both the amount of formal or informal power of the supervisor within the broader organisation (Fiedler, 1965a; Etzioni, 1965; Pelz, 1951) and upon the type or purpose of the organisation. In some organisations, such as the school, the voluntary organisation

and the religious association, ability to capture the affections and loyalties of the group is crucial. On the other hand, production organisations can afford to fail to capture these qualities and rely upon commitments and acceptable performance levels by other means (for example job security, financial incentives, etc.) (Etzioni, 1965).

3 The democratic, employee-oriented style of leadership relies heavily for its success on work that necessitates some degree of creativity, innovation, and the like. The best example of this is to be found in Morse and Reimer (1956) in their study of the Prudential Assurance Offices.

4 Authoritarian leaders tend not to be accepted in small groups, but in large groups there is a higher level of acceptance. They will also be more accepted by authoritarian workers (Vroom, 1964) and those high in self-esteem (Korman, 1966).

5 Close supervision by itself will not necessarily lead to low productivity; it may be dissatisfying and frustrating (depending upon the kind of work involved) but need not decrease output. A crucial factor is the extent to which workers see it as punitive (that is as deliberately and consciously aggressive). Punitive supervision increases the frustration and will lead either to a decrease in involvement, for example, mentally opting out, and possible physical opting out, manifesting itself in absenteeism and high turnover rates, or to retaliatory aggression—aggression directed against productivity. In some circumstances, it might even lead to both of these.

Generalised conclusions such as these do show that much of the confusion in the results of some of the studies can be attributed to certain definite factors such as:

1 How the 'style of leadership' is measured. If employees describe the supervisor's behaviour they may well be biased. If they are satisfied or high producers they might describe the supervisor as 'considerate' when he may not be.

2 The type of work performed.

3 The nature of the relationship between style and effects. It may be one-way and causal or it may be co-varying due to the influence of a third factor.

4 Particular organisational constraints. The size of the work group, the positional power of the supervisor and the type of organisation all affect this.

5 The relationship between particular 'performance criteria'. For example, Fleishman and Harris (1962) found that low consideration on the part of a supervisor will 'cause' high dissatisfaction and grievances long before it affects the turnover rate.

Arising from all of this, there is one note of caution. The ability of any particular supervisor to change his 'style' is very limited. The fact that the supervisor operates within an organisational framework means that he cannot simply choose to behave towards his subordinates as he would like. He is frequently under great pressure and closer supervision than his own subordinates, and this hardly contributes to his taking a supportive/considerate approach with them. And, furthermore, his own immediate subordinates may distrust him simply because they distrust the company. In other words, changes in supervisory practices cannot be made effective without thorough and profound changes in the organisation structure. Or as Tannenbaum and Seashore put it (1964, p. 83):

> The best way of getting supervisors to respect their men is to make their men respectable; that is to change the organisation in ways to give them some authority, responsibility, influence, control over significant parts of their work life; to give them respectability.

6 The individual characteristics of foremen

Introduction

The third important sub-system distinguished as being of significance for an analysis of the foreman role is at the individual level. Again, the same pattern emerges in terms of system inputs, conversions and outputs. In each of these it is shown that very little is known about the individual characteristics of foremen, notwithstanding the methodological problems of generalisations. A basic social psychological tenet is confirmed in that foremen attitudes and behaviour are largely determined by individual characteristics such as personality and background. These, in their turn, as the previous chapter has demonstrated, act as some of the inputs into the group level sub-system.

Foremen attitudes

The attitudes an individual has towards work are important for at least two reasons. In the first place, attitudes do represent a kind of blue-print for behaviour. The importance of these attitudes can further be seen in that they can be used as a means of evaluating observed behaviour. They enable comparisons to be made between one individual or group of individuals and another. As well as comparison, attitudes can be used to measure change. For example, on a human relations course for foremen the effectiveness of student-centred and instructor-centred approaches have been compared with attitude measurement scales. In fact, the comparison showed that there did not appear to be any significant difference between the two approaches. Attitudes are also a useful guide to an understanding of an individual or group since they are changeable as well as being measurements of change. It has been shown on many different occasions that when supervisors are exposed to human relations courses there is likely (in the short-run at least) to be a significant shift towards 'consideration' and away from 'initiation'. Further amplification of this premise is given by Carter (1951).

A study of the variability in the knowledge that employees have of the attitudes of 'others' has noted that the accuracy of the average answer and the spread about the average appeared to depend slightly upon the status of the respondents. In general, then, the information given by supervisors tends to be less variable (though only slightly so) than the information given by operators (Fagg *et al.*, 1958).

One reason that is often given for this observed increase in the accuracy of job knowledge can, in part, be attributable to increased identification of foremen with management. Dalton (1951) has indicated the possible benefits that this would accrue for the organisation and more particularly for supervisors themselves. A further study discussed the extent of identification. It appears from the work of Dalton that factors such as age, length of tenure, educational standard and sex are all correlated. By this is meant that as these individual factors increase so identification increases (in the case of sex, this is dichotomous, and Dalton found that identification increased if the respondent was male). The closeness to management has been found to be associated with job satisfaction. Halpern (1961) found that as unionisation of the plant places the foreman closer to the rank-and-file membership of the organisation (in terms of status), it frustrated the foreman's identification with management and this in turn decreased his job satisfaction.

On the question of job satisfaction, this is a configuration of attitudes that has received a good deal of attention, as later stages of this analysis show. One central study factor-analysed the sources and correlates of job satisfaction (Friedlander, 1963). The sources that emerged were social and technical environment, self-actualising aspects of the position and the opportunities for advancement. Taking each of these in turn, foremen have been found to have a higher job satisfaction associated with technical environment. There is a need for this association to be placed on a comparative basis. This is because technologies vary and when grouped in terms of unit, mass and process production, the first and last types have a higher supervisor satisfaction rate (cf. Woodward, 1958, 1965; Blauner, 1964; Goldthorpe, 1959; Gouldner, 1955; Walker and Guest, 1952). The routine supervisory tasks in mass production might be compared to those in the banking industry, where there has been found to be very low supervisory morale (McMurray, 1958).

In the same study of the banking industry, low supervisor morale was found to be related to the absence of clear channels of communication. This did, in fact, appear to be involved in the second factor found by Friedlander (1963) when he noted that this factor was more important for the younger foremen than for older ones. A clear perception of management's role has also been found to be necessary for self-actualisation for foremen. Sykes (1962) has shown that when this perception has been aided by a human relations course and not satisfied by management, dissatisfaction is likely to occur. This was found among supervisors in the construction industry, dissatisfaction increasing to the measurable extent of 45 per cent of the foremen leaving or attempting to leave the company.

Another factor in the opportunity for advancement has been expressed as 'a belief, or lack of belief, in the ability to use the occupational hierarchy' (Form and Geschwender, 1962). This particular study also related job satisfaction to the social reference group of supervisors—their family and parents.

Clearly, then, job satisfaction is an important variable with a complex of causal factors. The studies cited here appear to support Friedlander's factors and indicate that more research is needed in this area, particularly comparing the variation within the factors and relating them to hypothetical differences in the actual job performance of foremen.

Performance

The point is repeatedly made in this study that the measurement of the performance of foremen is extremely difficult. This has been put forward, for instance, as an example of the difficulty of applying the advantages of productivity bargaining to supervisory grades and of the problems in evaluating the effectiveness of training programmes for foremen. There is agreement that performance is difficult to measure for foremen. Dubin (1962) states that the actual measures of real performance for foremen are rare. There appears to be a complete lack of standard measures for performance as there are indeed for role definition. Despite this, it can be shown that performance can be related to a number of individual characteristics of supervisors and, if only because of this, it is worth considering some of the attempts that have been made to understand and to measure performance.

In the study of Swedish school superintendents, Carlson (1951) found that performance of the superintendents could be associated with whether they were 'insiders' or 'outsiders'—that is whether they were stabilisers or innovators respectively. The particular cluster of factors used in this study to measure performance was similar to that used in a study by Rim (1965) in looking at leadership attitudes and decisions involving risk. It is shown elsewhere that studies of risk-taking in the role performance of supervisors offers an analytical cluster of relevant personality factors. Those supervisors who were at the risky end of decision-making were found to be high on extroversion, achievement-need and tolerance of ambiguity. In addition, it was found that sex and consideration in supervisors are important for the degree to which they take more risky decisions in group situations.

To be able to talk realistically about performance, certain prerequisites have to be understood. If a manager is to employ certain criteria which measure performance, this means that he must have some preconceived idea about what he expects from the foreman. In a sense, the performance can be viewed as an exercise in matching the expectations of an 'other' to the actual playing of a role by the 'actor'. If the two match more or less equally, then the manager would define the performance of the supervisor as being satisfactory. However, as shown elsewhere, the foreman rarely knows what the expectations and intentions of the manager are beyond rather general limits. Also, of course, if managerial expectations and objectives can be operationalised, it is unlikely that the foreman has the necessary discretion to carry these out. Organisational constraints may mean that the foreman is unable to carry out his role in the 'defined' way (the definition may be his own or the manager's); he may thus be carrying out duties which are not strictly supervisory and which would then be seen as poor supervisory performance.

It might be suggested that there are indirect ways of measuring supervisory performance. The productivity of the foreman's work group is one such indirect method of assessing performance. The previous chapter has discussed this issue in some depth and it was shown that the particular 'leadership style' that the foreman adopts is in many cases related to the productivity of the work group. Again, an indirect measurement could be certain visible manifestations in the work group. It can be assumed that absenteeism rates, labour turnover rates, accident rates, and so on, are all reflections, in part, of the effectiveness of the foreman. If data could be collected relating to all these factors, a composite index could be arrived at which would give comparative measurement of a foreman's performance. However, it is very rare for all this kind of information to be collected, and, even if it is, it would be even rarer for it to be used in the way suggested here. There are, of course, serious difficulties in this since absenteeism, turnover, and so on, can be caused by so many factors which may have nothing at all to do with the leadership style of the supervisor. In other words, the foreman of a group with a bad record on all measurements may be reprimanded although the bad record has little to do with his performance.

Again, when taking measurements of factors in the work group, there need not be the subjective measurement that might be expected. Different appraisers are bound to come to different conclusions about the same factors. Quantification in this area, therefore, is very difficult to achieve on an objective basis. Many writers have drawn up lists of what they consider to be the important requirements for a foreman to have. The fact that there is little agreement at all concerning what these requirements should be shows the problems of 'objective' statements about performance. Beyond this question of separating the subjective from the objective assessment is the whole question of isolating these qualities of the foreman from all the structural conditions of the work group itself that have little to do with the particular supervisory style being used. A highly effective supervisor in one group may turn out to be a low-effective supervisor in a different group, even though his particular leadership or supervisory style has not changed.

Individually, it is possible to assess the performance of foremen. To do this would involve taking data that related to a particular foreman, take into account the peculiar characteristics of his work group, and note the special work situation. An assessment in these circumstances could then be made on factual and qualitative data. An individual assessment of this nature is rarely possible because of the constraints of time and resources. Also, individual assessment such as this is of little use since it is difficult to compare 'like with like'.

Psychologists have attempted to answer certain questions relating to the performance of personnel in the industrial situation. For example, Westerlund and Stromberg (1965) in a research study measuring the performance and appraisal of foremen ask whether it is possible to find factors in the work situation that enable comparison between one foreman and another, whether these factors are mutually independent, whether they can be ranked in any way, and whether these factors are relevant in all leadership positions. The generalised issues arising from all of these considerations are therefore whether the measurements that are made of performance are sufficient to make wide generalisations.

Performance of foremen in the sample was measured 'by way of his department's achievement or the "productivity of the department"' (ibid., p. 349). Three types of measures were used: first, those relating to a managerial frame of reference using data that was of interest to management; second, measures that were methodologically reliable; and, third, measuring those variables that had 'vital importance'. The following hypotheses were formulated for the study (p. 351):

1   concerning the relationship between various measures of performance and behaviour of the employees in their departments.

2   concerning the possibility of agreement among rankings of different categories of judges with reference to the foreman's style or way of carrying out the duties.

3   concerning the relationship between superior's ranking of how well the foreman carried out specified tasks, and of the measures of performance and behaviour of the employees in the foreman's department.

4   concerning the relationship between characteristics of the foreman and the measures of performance and behaviour of the employees in the foreman's department.

5   concerning the relationship between the frequency of the foreman's contacts with superiors and peers, and the measures of performance and behaviour of the employees in the foreman's department.

6   concerning the relationship between the superior's ranking of how they consider that the foremen carry out their duties and the foreman's ranking of how important they consider the corresponding duties to be.

7   concerning the relationship between superiors' ranking of how they consider the foremen carry out the duties and the foreman's ranking of how important they believe their immediate superior considers the corresponding duty to be.

It is not considered necessary to analyse the results of all of these hypotheses. This is because, in general, the data provided by Westerlund and Stromberg concerning the performance and behaviour of their foremen was found to be quite unreliable. No correlation could be found between performance and actual behaviour, nor was there a correlation between the assessments made by superiors of the foremen and the characteristics of the foremen. A conclusion that can be drawn from all of this is that, as yet, the possibility of measuring the performance of foremen beyond very simple measures is very small. As techniques become more refined the possibility is bound to increase.

Trade union membership

It was shown earlier that current thinking regarding the role of industrial supervisors is to regard them as the first rung of the management ladder in most organisations. Arising from this is one of the inconsistencies in the supervisory role. Traditionally, managerial grades in British industry have not been unionised, and yet there are claims that today the supervisory group is taking such action.

135

The inconsistency, however, arises in the form of an ideology more than anything else—the ideology that foremen are part of the management team and that management is not unionised. If we break away from the ideology and look at the structural conditions, then the inconsistency referred to no longer holds.

It has been established that supervisory personnel have lost much of their former status, power and authority both within the plant and outside of it. They have variously been described as marginal men of industry (Wray, 1949), as the master and victim of double-talk (Roethlisberger, 1951), and so on. There is little doubt, as the present analysis has shown, that the foreman does suffer from role conflict. The power of the manual worker trade unions, of personnel departments, of various specialised functions in industry, and so on, have all contributed to the loss of power and prestige of the foreman. Given all this, it is only psychologically normal for foremen to attempt to win back some of their former strength. And the traditional way of doing just this is to engage in collective action—that is to become unionised.

All of this represents a logical argument, but the argument is difficult to demonstrate by reference to empirical data. Industrial organisations seem loathe to disclose the extent to which their supervisors are unionised. It becomes difficult to talk meaningfully about this issue when there is lack of evidence.

Some figures are available. The Government Social Survey on *Workshop Industrial Relations* (1968) sampled 598 foremen from 319 organisations and found that overall 32 per cent of all foremen were members of a trade union, and that they had been members of trade unions for an average of seventeen years. The 32 per cent figure was broken down as follows:

Construction 24%
Metal handling 33%
Other manufacturing 24%

The actual unions that the foremen in this sample belonged to were: TGWU (11 per cent), AEU (24 per cent), NUGMW (7 per cent), ETU (2 per cent), AUBTW (5 per cent) and others (51 per cent).

Clearly, these figures are quite high if a managerial grade is being dealt with. They are consistent with the figures that can be abstracted from the 1961 Census of Population and from the analysis by Bain (1967) in a research paper for the Royal Commission on Trade Unions and Employers' Associations (see Table 6.1).

From the figures given by Bain in his research paper, it would appear that three trade unions are most concerned with supervisory membership. First, there is ASSET (now ASTMS), which has roughly half of its membership composed of foremen. In 1964, it

TABLE 6.1

Chemical	Metal manufacturing	Metal NES	Engineering electrical	Ship ME	Vehicles	Textiles	Leather and fur
1·6	8·3	3·2	13·6	2·9	10·8	28·2	1·1

Clothing and footwear	Bricks, etc.	Timber, furnishing, etc.	Paper and printing	Other manufacturing	All manufacturing
—	2·0	3·8	n/a*	4·7	8·8

* None of the unions in this industry keeps their membership figures in such a way that it is possible to determine the number of foremen in membership. It is generally known that a relatively large number of employees in this industry retain their membership when promoted to a supervisory position.

had a total membership of 30,000, all of whom were white-collar workers and 81 per cent of whom were employed in manufacturing industries, particularly engineering and electrical goods, vehicles, metal manufacture, rubber and plastics. The second major union is ISTC, in which foremen compose 16 per cent of the total white-collar membership of 7,520. Metal manufacture is the major industry in which ISTC members are to be found. Lastly, there is a special section of the TGWU (NACSS) which comprises 4 per cent of the total membership of the TGWU. Of this 4 per cent, 55 per cent of the membership is found in manufacturing industries and is composed of clerical and supervisory grades.

Besides these overall figures that are available, the first report of the Commission on Industrial Relations published at the end of 1969 provides some clues to attitudes of industry towards supervisory unionisation. The report comes out in favour of supervisors joining trade unions in very precise terms. It is interesting that when the report was published there was very little comment made on it within industry itself—it might well be that management now accepts that foremen ought to become unionised. An editorial in the journal the *Supervisor* (March 1970) makes the point that if the report had been published ten years ago it would have been a 'veritable bombshell'—'The cat has been put among the pigeons, but it looks as though the pigeons have already flown' (p. 50).

In no uncertain terms the report of the Commission favours trade unions for foremen. For example, it says (pp. 1–16):

There is no evidence that trade union recognition for supervisors . . . would adversely affect good relations between men and the company.

The supervisors are in a vulnerable position which gives them a strong motive to bargain collectively.

The main negotiating demand of the supervisors will probably be for information on how their pay and incremental scales are determined—this demand [is] reasonable.

The supervisors seemed satisfied in some respects, but dissatisfied with a system which isolates each man in his discussions with the company.

The inquiry on which the report is based arose from a claim by ASTMS that the Associated Octel Company had refused to give it recognition, despite the fact that the union had organised the majority of foremen at the plant. In fact, 54 per cent of the foremen were ASTMS members. There had been employer resistance to the foreman becoming unionised, but the membership figures had reached this level from nothing in only six years, and it looked as though membership was still increasing.

The argument used by the employers, and one of the stated reasons for their resistance was that collective bargaining for staff employees was not the best way of conducting industrial relations at the company's Ellesmere Port plant. The employers felt that if foremen and staff in general became unionised this would mean a deterioration in the personal nature of labour relations at the plant: 'If an employee cannot reach an agreement with the management he can always leave the company.'

In reply to the employers' view, the CIR report said: 'The CIR does not believe that there is a special relationship between the employer and staff workers which is incompatible with representation by a trade union.' One of the aims of the CIR, in fact, was to avoid inter-union strife due to the developments of white-collar unions.

This report is being dealt with at some length because several important questions are raised by it. This is the first 'policy' statement that the present writer has seen relating to the unionisation of foremen. The Associated Octel Company case is almost a 'test' case on this issue in this country. It should be that in the USA the problem for industry of organised supervisors is being dealt with, but in this country this is a new problem (Sturmthal, 1966).

The evidence in the CIR report implies that all company managements should allow foremen to become unionised if they so desire. This must surely represent a *volte-face* for management who have been pleading the case for supervisors to be a part of management. The emphatic recommendation of the inquiry is that 'the commission considers the firm's supervisors and method improvement officers are a viable negotiating unit. The company has already recognised the common bond by establishing a "Supervisory Forum" for the two grades.' This statement produced an almost desperate counter-statement from the editor of the journal the *Supervisor* (March, 1970, p. 50):

> Will this cause other companies to look with concern at their supervisory associations or foremen's clubs? Will foremen's canteens be opened up to other employees and the supervisors told not to gather in any number greater than two? Can we now expect to see a dismantling of such groups in an effort to avoid guilt by association?

Despite this 'straw-clutching' statement from the Institute of Supervisory Management, there does appear to be a great deal of truth in the findings of the CIR inquiry. On the basis of a small survey at the plant and the result of formal and informal interviews, the inquiry believed that unionisation of foremen will lead to 'an improved relationship between these men and the company'. Many of the arguments used by the inquiry are inevitable. It is a fact that

139

white-collar unionism is increasing—it is short-sighted of management in any company not to recognise this fact and to compromise their situation. Nevertheless, the inquiry believed that 'a multi-union situation should be avoided' or, to put it differently, foremen tend to see themselves as being a fairly homogeneous group and have no desire to 'split their ranks' by inter-union disputes.

In the public sector of British industry, supervisors have been members of trade unions for a long time and there have been no discernible ill-effects. Also, in Sweden, there has been almost total unionisation of supervisors with no apparent adverse results (Lennerlöf, 1968). If management accepts supervisory unionisation as a fact at the moment, this is likely to avoid any long-term struggles for recognition and the corollaries to this. Without unionisation the position of the foreman is likely to get worse rather than better, despite the pleas that he is a member of the management team. The differential in pay, for example, between supervisory grades and manual grades has been drastically reduced in recent years. Many supervisors see trade unionism as the opportunity for regaining the *status quo* of twenty or thirty years ago.

Training

Few people today would deny that training of personnel in any industrial role is a matter of the utmost concern for industry as a whole. Similarly, the training of foremen has come to be an area of great concern to industry, particularly since the passing of the 1963 Industrial Training Act. In this analysis, no attempt can possibly be made at providing an exhaustive study in itself. Instead, the aim is to examine some of the current thinking surrounding the training of supervisors, the way in which training needs can be identified, the various methods available for training, the evaluation of training and the implications for industry of such training.

Although it has been asserted that training is an extremely important consideration of supervisory roles and that there is at present a voluminous literature surrounding this consideration, there appears to be little consistency in methods of training or even in the reasons for training. Hesseling (1966), for example, has said that (p. 4):

> the science of supervisory training is poorly developed. . . .
> Every trainer has his theory to explain the facts which he
> observes before, during and after training. This 'theory' is based
> upon his need to find rational considerations for his approach.
> But a well-knit conceptual scheme inter-relating these various
> 'theories' has not yet been developed.

Demands for industrial training for supervisors and others have arisen for several reasons. The pressure for increased productivity in industry has certainly demanded that supervisors and others are adequately trained. If current trends towards larger and larger organisations continues (Florence, 1961), then the supervisor's role is likely to become more and more specialised, and with this is the need for increased training in particular specialisms. An economy with a high rate of employment has also been seen to contribute to the need for increased training of supervisors (Armstrong, 1961). Supervisors have to be seen as 'personal leaders' concerned with the 'human understanding of the individual'. The Institute of Supervisory Management regards training as one of the ways in which the supervisor can maintain his status when the structural conditions tend away from this. On this issue of supervisory status, Meade and Grieg (1966, p. 2) see supervisory training as a way in which the supervisor can change from being a 'boss' to being a 'diplomat'. Changes in structural conditions which are discussed earlier, such as the influence of trade unions, the greater complexity of the production process, and the increasing complexity of managerial functions, all indicate that there is a need for supervisors to change their traditional 'image' if they are not to undergo losses of status both within the plant and outside it. Training can be seen as one of the ways in which management can 'lubricate' this evolved change.

In talking about supervisory training, as when talking about practically anything to do with supervisors, it is almost impossible to make any kind of generalisation because the heterogeneity of foremen. Thus, what may be effective training for a production foreman may have the opposite effects on an engineering foreman; what may be effective training for a young supervisor may have no relevance for the older supervisor; and so on. Having said this, however, it has to be recognised that general points for consideration can be made in relation to supervisory training, particularly with regard to the identification of training needs, the relevance of different types of training for different types of foremen, and the current appraisal systems of training. This can be said with a degree of confidence since this study has already shown that there are 'constants' in the role of all supervisors. The fact that a definition has been agreed upon, that the layman knows roughly what functions the supervisor undertakes, and so on, all show that there are these constants. Armstrong (1961, p. 9) sees both structural and non-structural arrangements here:

> Firstly, every supervisor must, by definition, control and deal with subordinates. Secondly, if he is to be effective in his job, he must establish proper relations not only with his superiors, but also with his equals in related departments or sections.

141

Thirdly, he must be articulate enough to give clear instructions and communicate his thoughts effectively. Finally, he must bear at least some responsibility for the training of his subordinates.

Given these conditions and that they hold for all supervisors, it is clear that despite the heterogeneity of the role, training can be talked about in general terms, as can the corollaries of training.

In talking about training in general, there are also certain 'constants' whether one is dealing with the training of supervisors or managing directors. In the first place, the traditional approach to training has been to focus upon the individual. Second, what the individual learns as a result of training needs to be applied to the work situation in which he finds himself. In talking about the evaluation of training needs, Meigniez has said (1963, p. 30):

Organisational action attempts to affect the general factors in the organisational situation. In training, on the other hand, a direct attack is made on the trainee, with a view to changing his outlook or his level of knowledge, on the assumption that these changes will be transformed to his environment and to his professional activity. We may say then that the basic hypothesis of training is this transfer, that is, the transmissibility of what is learned in training to actual work life situations. This approach assumes that the major effort will be made through the individual, who is the only common denominator linking the training situation with the actual job situation.

As Meade and Grieg (1966) see it, the concept of supervisory training has a distinct history which can be viewed in three stages. This history is similar to the history of leadership studies already described. Originally, say before the Second World War, there was the notion that it was the intrinsic qualities of the individual that either made or marred him as a supervisor. Thus, the ideology of the time was 'supervisors are born not made'. Training never entered into the question since selection of supervisors was made on the basis of finding consistencies between a supervisor's personal qualities and the actual demands of the job. Since the war, most industrialists have come to recognise that they can do something to improve the quality of their supervisors and that this is not merely a question of innate traits. The second stage in the development of supervisory training, then, is the recognition that supervisors can, in fact, be trained. This involves a recognition that the work of supervisors involves the use of certain skills and knowledge, and that these can be developed through training.

Meade and Grieg recognised that this was an important step forward, but it was not until comparatively recently that it was recognised that training means more than 'armchair theorising' about the knowledge and skills associated with supervisory roles. It also meant a recognition that supervisors do not constitute a homogeneous group of individuals, and that what is relevant in one industry or even one company may not be relevant in another. It was at this second stage of supervisory training that there was a great interest in the human relations approach. The argument used by the trainers was that supervision is essentially a question of controlling people and that they can be controlled more effectively through a human relations perspective.

It has come to be recognised today that a third stage has to be rigorously pursued and that this involves training through an analysis of the job itself. This might be called the 'task' approach to training, in the sense that Brown (1960) was able to talk about the task approach to management. One of the first to see the need to train 'on the job' was a Ministry of Labour report in 1962—the Barnes Committee report—which among other things said that 'as training should fit the needs of a particular job, the major part should be undertaken by and within the firm' (p. 17).

Even though there is a fairly high level of agreement today that training should be based on an analysis of the job and that it is preferable to have company-based training rather than any other kind, there is still a great deal of confusion about which components of the job should be analysed, and even if there is agreement on this, there is confusion about what to do with the analysis once it has been obtained. One possible way of avoiding this problem can be suggested by the use of the argument that first, supervisors need training; second, superiors should train supervisors; and third, superiors' behaviour influences supervisors' performances. This is a similar argument to the one actually used by Meade and Grieg (1966, p. 5):

> Almost more important than the variations in job content is the fact that how the supervisor gets his work done is affected greatly by the methods, personality and style of his managerial superiors. This leads us to the conclusion that not only must supervisory training be job-centred and done mainly inside the firm, but most importantly, parts of the training must be done by line managers themselves rather than by personnel or training specialists.

Identification of training needs

Before any training exercise can even be contemplated, it has to be recognised that a series of logical steps have to be undertaken. The

143

first of these is to see if there is even the possibility of personnel wanting training in a particular organisation. It seems possible that at a time when training levies are imposed on industrial organisations, and when the more training that is carried out the more the organisation can get back in the form of cash payments (relative to what has been paid in), then the primary objective of training may be lost sight of. In the first instance, then, the training needs of personnel have to be determined objectively.

There is some agreement concerning the ways in which training needs may be assessed. Usually the needs of supervisors can be determined by analysing what supervisors actually do in their jobs. The jobs of individual supervisors in individual organisations need to be analysed, rather than taking a general overview of what supervisors are expected to be doing in any organisation. This, of course, refers back to the earlier discussion concerning the notion of company-based training. Analysis of supervisors' skills and knowledge necessarily become known as a result of such analysis; the possible differing expectations of members of the supervisor's role set may become meaningful; standards may become known for future selection, and so on. It is clear that analysis of jobs has many uses.

Elsewhere it is made clear that it is difficult to talk meaningfully about what foremen do in the work situation and that there are significant differences not only between different organisations but also between foremen in the same organisation. This surely demonstrates the necessity of job analysis in assessing training needs. The actual problems that different foremen experience are also likely to differ due to a variety of reasons (see, for example, Warr and Bird, 1967).

Once the need for job analysis is established, there are a number of purely practical issues that arise. There is, for example, the problem of deciding who is to carry out the analysis. Meade and Grieg (1966) suggest that it is probably as well for the foreman's superior to be excluded from this stage of the exercise because of his emotional involvement with the foremen. There should, however, be some involvement of line managers, and this involvement should increase as the exercise progresses. The analysis is best carried out by specialists in the particular area who are emotionally detached from the supervisors in question. Armstrong (1961) makes the suggestion that line managers must be involved from the outset and that they have a very important role to play in this since they have their own perceptions of what their foremen's training needs actually are.

The next practical problem that arises is what actually is going to be analysed. Job descriptions need to be written, if they have not been already. These give a broad outline of what the supervisor's main tasks are. It must be stressed that these are broad in nature and give no indication of the day-to-day problems that arise in the foreman's work. Meade and Grieg, from their analysis, indicate that job descriptions usually list the foreman's tasks under three headings: technical, administrative and social.

A more precise way of analysing the foreman's job is to undertake an exercise in activity analysis. Some of the results of such analysis have already been discussed, and they do give a fairly accurate measure of the actual tasks undertaken and the problems encountered by the foreman. Activity analysis can take several forms such as diary keeping, observation or activity sampling. The method which any particular organisation might choose is really dependent upon the resources available to that organisation. The use of interview techniques and questionnaires gives a fuller picture of the total situation, and if time and resources are available to a particular organisation, it is likely that these will be employed in addition to activity analysis.

The next problem that arises (in fact, as a result of job analysis) is that there is almost inevitably an inconsistency between the supervisor's 'perceived' role (as he sees it), his manifest role (what activity analysis shows he actually does with his time) and the 'expected role' (what his superiors expect him to do). It would seem to the present writer that inconsistencies such as these are almost universal (Dunkerley, 1969). It is necessary to minimise these inconsistencies somehow and, if possible, to make each 'role' consistent with each other 'role'. This is the stage in the training exercise when the line manager becomes involved. It is the stage when his perceptions of the supervisory role must be made consistent with the supervisor's perceptions of his own role. As Meade and Grieg put it (1966, p. 15):

> Management is compelled to do some fundamental thinking about the role of the supervisor in the company, and about the working of the organisation as a whole. The supervisor benefits from this by getting a clearer idea of where he fits in, and a better understanding between him and his superior should be created.

Once this stage has been reached, the actual assessment of training needs can be undertaken. This stage in the process is a continuous process in itself. It involves taking the objective results of job analysis and comparing these with the desired state of affairs, and then devising strategies for moving towards this desired state. Armstrong (1961) suggests that the following areas are most likely to be the ones for development: technical competence; competence in administrative matters; leadership abilities; and the ability to establish proper relations with equals and superiors in both line management

145

and service functions. Whatever the actual areas for discussion, the training needs identified will invariably take the form of objectives to be met. These objectives give the supervisor the idea that there is something to which he should strive to attain. The idea of objective setting arises from this appraisal. In turn, appraisal may be either managerial appraisal or self-appraisal. With the former, the performance of the foreman is considered by a line manager, this appraisal is made known to the foreman and then action is decided upon by both the manager and the foreman to remedy any weaknesses or shortcomings which might be visible in the foreman's role. The second type of appraisal—self-appraisal—involves the foreman himself recognising his own weaknesses and shortcomings. Self-appraisal is a basic part of the philosophy of McGregor (1960) and as yet there are not really enough conclusive research studies to be able to say how effective a means of appraisal this actually is.

Meade and Grieg give a kind of 'cook-book' approach to appraisal systems. They say that the following points should be observed (1966, pp. 23-4):

1 The appraisal should be based on a study of the individual's performance, not his character.
2 Its results should be expressed as far as possible in terms of objectives, not weaknesses.
3 Any rating form used should be based on the above two criteria.
4 Although the appraisal interview is conducted by the manager, he should provide as much encouragement as possible for the individual to express his own training needs. The manager may feel it necessary to specify in certain areas of difficulty where improvement can be made, but even in these cases he should encourage the supervisor to provide solutions, i.e. suggestions on what can be done to overcome the difficulties. The appraisal interview should not be a 'trial' with the supervisor in the role of the 'accused'.
5 Too much should not be attempted at any one interview. Whenever a manager feels that the supervisor has got 'enough on his plate', the interview should be terminated by agreeing on the action to be taken, and resumed later.

The training programme

It is clear by now that to talk of training of supervisors in general is difficult to do. To talk about an actual training programme is more difficult, and almost impossible if it is to be in any sense meaningful. There are very many variables involved in drawing up such a programme, for example. The personal characteristics of the foreman such as age and sex will involve different types of training. Warr and Bird, for example, found that 'several older foremen told us that it was "like going back to school" ' (1967, p. 349). The particular local technical demands of an organisation necessitate different types of training programme, and so on. Despite the difficulties involved here, a few general points can be made.

Training can take a great many forms. Initially, the choice might be between internal and external courses. Here there are obvious guide-lines that need to be followed, usually relating to the relevance of the courses for the individual foreman. What might be called job-specific training appears to be the currently accepted form of training. By this, the training needs identified by the kind of process described above can be specifically met. The point has already been emphasised that many training needs relate to individuals only, and job-specific training can ensure that these needs are met. General training, however, does have an important role to play in any training programme. The problems of leadership, of motivation and of relationships with the work group are all general problems experienced at some time or another by all foremen. What form this general training takes will vary according to the time and resources available. For example, role-playing has been seen to be effective in dealing with particular problems (*Supervisor*, October 1969); human relations training has been used in other circumstances (Scott and McGivering, 1953; Castle, 1952); and general management training elsewhere (Sykes, 1962).

The above discussion assumes that training need only be given to established supervisors. This is a distortion since the new supervisor or even the potential future supervisor is in need of as much, if not more, training than his established counterpart. Warr and Bird, for example, say that 'If a little more training attention was given to the new foreman it could greatly ease his lot and might well be rewarded in terms of his increased effectiveness' (1967, p. 251).

Evaluation of training

As shown elsewhere the assessment of supervisory work is a difficult operation, compared with shop-floor work. Assessment of role performance in organisations becomes increasingly difficult as we progress up the organisation hierarchy. While this is true of ordinary role performance, it is also true of the assessment of the effectiveness of training. The training of personnel on the shop-floor is not particularly difficult, in so far as it is measurable; for supervisors it is more difficult to measure; and for managers, the direct effect of training becomes almost impossible to assess, at least in the short term.

Meade and Grieg (1966) suggest that two factors need to be known for the assessment of the effectiveness of training: first, information gained as a result of job analysis; and, second, a measure of the extent to which existing supervisors already possess the skills and knowledge defined as being necessary from the first factor. They give two examples to illustrate their point (p. 34):

1 Technical knowledge: The provision of information about some new process or machine by means of a programme in a simple teaching machine gives us an immediate feed-back. Reductions in number of machine breakdowns, better overall utilisation of machines, better quality work and less scrap may be indices of long-term improvement in technical knowhow.
2 Cost control: Additional information on costs and how to control them given to a supervisor will only be worth giving if it can be shown to have improved his ability to control those costs in his own section or department which he is expected to influence.

The form of evaluation suggested by Meade and Grieg is not particularly 'scientific'. The suggestion here is that more quantitative methods of assessment are needed. For example, the use of attitude tests on a before-and-after basis might provide some measurement of the course or training in question. An immediate change is to be expected, but this might wear off once the foreman has been back 'on the job' for some time. (A good illustration of the short-term training effects is given by Fleishman, 1956.) To be rigorous in measuring attitude change a control group would have to be measured 'before' and 'after', even though they were not being exposed to the training programme.

It may be, of course, that the aim of the training programme for a particular group of supervisors is not to change attitudes towards the job, their subordinates, and so on, in which case the Meade and Grieg suggestions might be the only viable solutions.

Task relevance

A study in 1956 by Baumgartel into the concepts of leadership and motivation led to the emergence of a 'new' concept—task relevance. By this, Baumgartel meant the degree of conformity between the individual's job skills and motivations and the locally perceived aims of the organisation. With reference to industrial organisations, the aims of the organisation can be described in economic terms (for example the quantity and quality of production, absence rates, labour turnover, and so on). Baumgartel found that if a supervisor had a high task relevance, then he also had high job skill and a concern with performing his function adequately.

In a previous chapter, supervisory performance has been analysed in terms of leadership qualities and it was shown that there is some relation between the two general factors, or at least that certain configurations of them are related. Studies are beginning to emerge that suggest that task-relevant variables are at least as important as the so-called 'human relations' variables discussed earlier. As yet there is little evidence in this area, and the findings that are in existence may well be adapted or disproved by later research. In other words, since there is little corroboration in the findings they ought to be treated with a degree of caution.

The most important study in this area is one by Cooper (1966) in which he explores the importance of supervisor's task relevance in relation to subordinate behaviour. Cooper is specifically concerned with the variables of intelligence, job knowledge and motivation. A pilot study suggested that these variables were the most important in relation to the effectiveness of supervisors. It was found that operatives with a supervisor of high task relevance made fewer errors in the work process compared with operatives working under a low task-relevant supervisor. There also appeared to be differences in absenteeism.

Cooper's explanation for these phenomena was that workers set their behaviour to match that of their supervisor. This explanation is derived from the social-psychological theory that an individual has a drive to evaluate his abilities by comparing himself with other people. If abilities are below those of the compared person(s) he will attempt to reduce the discrepancy by increased performance. In addition to this, it was asserted that only those individuals who 'placed a positive value on work proficiency would perceive and respond to this in a work leader' (p. 79). Thus, those people who were not concerned with proficiency would not respond to the high task relevance of the supervisor.

Propositions such as these were tested in a larger study in an oil-processing plant. One of the characteristics of the plant was the close, intimate contact of supervisors with their subordinates. Job performances were found to be related to the proficiency levels of the supervisors. Thus, high subordinate performance was associated with high leader performance. The hypothesis concerning the differential value of work proficiency was substantiated—there was no relation between individuals who did not value work proficiency and the task relevance of the supervisor, and vice versa. There was also some evidence from Cooper's study that absenteeism and lateness were less for those with high task-relevant leaders.

Basically, Cooper's work is the only study to explore systematically relationships of this nature, and the caution mentioned at the beginning ought to be stressed. The factor of a supervisor's task relevance has as yet to be defined and tested rigorously, but it does appear to offer a bridge between personality factors and supervisory and subordinate behaviour.

Foremen's social background

The term 'background' is being used here to describe two character-istics of supervisors that are related, but the relationship between them will not be systematically explored here. They are the factors of family and education. It is also possible to add to these two the factor of individual training, but this has already been dealt with at some length earlier in the present chapter.

Occupational sociologists generally accept that the family is an important source of influence over a particular occupational role incumbent (Parker et al., 1967). The importance arises since the family is one of the chief socialisation agents of the child and thus 'moulds' the individual's future values, norms and expectations. Later in life the family can still be important in that it can act as a reference group for the individual. In applying this to supervisors, a hypothesis can be derived which is worthy of consideration. Again, this is an under-researched area, but one study by Form and Gesch-wender (1962) examines the social reference basis of job satisfaction. This is an important study since personal evaluations of the 'life situation' are seen as being relative to the precise social locations which people occupy and the specific groups to which they commit their identities.

Arising from a study of social mobility by Lipset and Bendix (1959) in which it was shown that changes in social position force changes in the aspiration levels of individuals, rather than the other way around, Form and Geschwender formulate the following hypothesis: job evaluations are not so much a function of the individual's aspirations or of the aspirations of their parents, but a response to the occupational position that their parents and brothers occupy. Thus, if they occupy superior positions, they should feel more satisfied; if they occupy lower positions than parents and brothers, they should feel dissatisfied. This is an interesting hypo-thesis since it has been established for some time that parents usually want their children to 'achieve' higher occupational positions than they themselves have done.

The findings of the study do indicate in some way the relationship between family aspirations and the present job attitudes of an indivi-dual; 80 per cent of the respondents said that their parents had no occupational aspirations for them. Although this finding is inconsistent with some of the British findings (for example Dennis *et al.*, 1956), there is some consistency with the results that Lipset and Bendix (1959) came up with. Belief in occupational mobility appears to be largely irrelevant in the life situation. Upwardly mobile people were found to exhibit higher job satisfaction scores than downwardly mobile individuals. This is to be expected. Beyond this, however, it was found that if an individual achieved the same occupational level as his father, there would be high satisfaction; achieving a higher occupational level did not significantly increase the satisfaction experienced by the individual. When a similar test was applied to brothers, it was found that if the individual achieved a higher occupational level than his brother, then he experienced greater satisfaction than being at the same level. Overall, there was a relationship between generational mobility and satisfaction which suggests that 'family' is used for social reference purposes, particularly for evaluating occupational achievements.

This study by Form and Geschwender (1962) also indicates some other 'background' material. Married men were more satisfied than single men; those with two children were more satisfied than those with one child or none; men over age forty were more satisfied; and so on. Only one factor did not correlate positively—that of education.

A general conclusion to be drawn from the study is (Form and Geschwender, 1962, p. 237) that

> the relationship between occupational mobility and job
> satisfaction is mediated by the belief in opportunities or lack
> of them for individuals to rise in the occupational hierarchy.
> And that such beliefs are largely structurally determined by
> past experience, rather than arising randomly or as a product
> of ideology.

Of the studies that deal with the foreman's pre-employment education, it would appear that this is a minimal factor in determining role behaviour. The study by Vroom (1959), discussed above, held educational attainment constant and found that the needs for independence and authoritarianism are independent and are much more important determinants of attitudes to participation.

Dalton (1951) studied the career patterns of 226 individuals as they were selected and promoted through managerial hierarchies. He was concerned to see what factors were operative in the advancement of individuals through an industrial hierarchy. The respondents were distributed as follows:

93 first-line foremen
61 general foremen

36 superintendents
36 staff heads' assistants and specialists

Dalton adopted the stance of participant observer at the plant and collected data on age at appointment, years of service, years of education and current age. In addition, specific observations were made on such designated informal factors as members of group organisations, religion, ethnic background, and so on.

Dalton found that most Protestant non-Masons and Catholics agreed that being a Mason was a prerequisite to advancement in the plant. At one point, the younger Catholics indicated '95 per cent of management belong to the Masons' and, again, 'Masons are getting too strong in the plant' (p. 411).

Ethnic origin was another informal factor asserted to be a major consideration in career advancement. Analysis of the situation did reveal that a disproportionate number of top positions were given to Anglo-Saxon and German ethnic types. Scandinavian, Italian, Polish, French, Serbo-Croation, Negro and Spanish were found in the universal sample, but rarely were they in the highest positions.

It was further asserted that membership in the local yacht club provided connections essential to promotion. Objective analysis did reveal that 114 people from the plant were yacht club members. The proportion of club membership was not high enough to be 'alarming', yet interviews and casual comments revealed that efforts to maintain the club's physical plant did tend to win the favour of higher management.

Political party affiliation suggested that all members of the top management were Republicans. The evidence for this came from four sources: overt statements favouring the Republicans; a universal reading of Republican newspapers; discussion favouring the Democrats was covert and then was chiefly among the first-line foremen; and where managers had stood for political office it had always been for the Republicans (p. 414).

The importance of Dalton's study was made clear by these observations. It demonstrates the reality of informal factors in the selection and advancement in an organisation. Dalton is at pains to point out that formal factors did operate as much as the informal ones at this particular plant.

In discussing the effects of educational background on foremen, a crude distinction ought to be made between the 'old-style' and 'new-style' foremen. The old-style was and still is recruited from the 'ranks', his educational attainment being unlikely to be high. The position of foreman is probably the highest point in his career pattern; at this point, his career curve reaches a plateau. For the new-style foreman, this particular position may only be the starting point of his career. He may be a graduate, or at least will have technical paper qualifications. He enters employment at the foreman level and moves up the organisational hierarchy from there. Unfortunately, there is no data available comparing the two types of foreman to enable a comparison in terms of educational achievement. Nevertheless, the distinction between the two broad types is seen as being significant and is explored in more detail later.

Foremen and forewomen

There are few studies that deal with sex as a variable in the role of the supervisor. What studies do exist show that this attribute is relevant to an understanding of both personality characteristics and leadership style. Of the seven plants studied by the NIIP (1957), two analysed the special position of women supervisors. Most studies of supervisors assume that the role incumbent is male (and, of course, in terms of numbers they are correct in making such an assumption) and thence make no allowance for a differential based upon sex. Because of the comparative value of the NIIP study, this is analysed in some detail.

The two studies relevant to female supervisors showed that their position in the organisation was different from that of male supervisors. The differences between the sexes will be examined, rather than looking at the common elements to both, since this latter feature has already been discussed.

Both of the firms had difficulty in recruiting female supervisors. Operators who were offered a supervisory position were reluctant to take it, since they regarded it as strenuous and thankless. Also, no added status was seen to accompany the promotion. The NIIP researchers hasten to point out that this is not a universal problem, but was certainly in evidence in the firms they studied.

In the two firms, the supervisor still had a predominantly manual task. Her job was different from the rank-and-file operators, but still had a high manual component. Management in the two firms saw the activities of female supervisors as being primarily manual operations, but, in addition to this, management felt that the supervisor should also be concerned with giving advice to operators, maintaining discipline, and having concern for the quality of the product. All of these activities, it should be stressed, were seen as being necessary and yet were secondary to the main function of manual work.

One consequence of the role of the female supervisors was that they themselves saw responsibility as being strictly limited. This led to organisational problems since the supervisor is responsible for direct control of the work and yet has little responsibility for the quality of the work. There appeared to be an inconsistency in the aims of management and supervisors which gave rise to this position. It was this inconsistency, rather than the organisation of the inspection systems, that led to this position.

The NIIP study makes a comparison between these two firms and a third firm with female supervisors which was unpublished in the 1957 report. In this firm, there was a different attitude of the supervisors towards their role and their responsibilities. The main way in which the work differed for supervisors in the third firm was that there was far more sympathy expressed by the supervisors for the machine operators. Also, in terms of the production process, the production of a single article was over several departments, and if any problem arose over which department was responsible for a fault in the finished product supervisors from all the departments were able to reach a decision fairly and amicably.

In this third firm, the management was consciously trying to give the supervisors more status and more responsibility. Their independence was being increased and they had more opportunities for decision-making than the supervisors in the other two firms. Also, in the third firm, supervisors were assigned assistants. In sum, the third firm supervisors were given a far more responsible and prestigious task than those in the other two firms. A major consequence of this was that the third firm had no difficulties in recruiting new women to supervisory positions.

As in the other NIIP studies, it was shown that the position of the supervisor had changed over time for a variety of reasons. Variations in the quality and shortages of raw material led to difficulties. The nature of the supervised labour force called for new approaches to supervision. A higher level of skill was called for on the part of the supervisors. The discretionary part of the role had increased through a change in the nature of the technology.

The NIIP study does show that female supervisors can be different from male supervisors. It is difficult to generalise because of the variation in the nature of the role from one organisation to another, but it would appear that female supervisors are close to the work situation and part of their role is to participate in manual activities.

Another comparative study has been carried out by Rim (1965). This study compares twenty-seven female head nurses enrolled in a course in Administration and Supervision with thirty-nine male industrial supervisors. Comparison was made on their risk-taking in group decision-making. The general conclusion that was made from the study was that decisions made on a group basis are more risky than individual decisions. By using the concepts of 'consideration' and 'structure' it was also found that:

1   Male supervisors who scored high on consideration and structure, and female head nurses who scored high on structure, tended to take higher initial risks than their colleagues.
2   Men and women scoring high on both consideration and structure appeared to be the influencers in the group, leading to a shift in the risky direction. Those people who were low on both consideration and structure appeared to be the most influenced when in the group situation.

Thus, it was found that although both groups shifted their group and individual decisions in a risky direction after group discussion, consideration was a function of the initial risks of males, whilst it was not to the same extent with the females.

A different focus can be taken in discussing the question of supervisor sex. That is, instead of looking at the sex of the supervisor, the sex of the supervised can be examined to see if this has any effect upon the nature of the supervisory role. Again, there is little evidence to suggest anything either way. Blauner's study of a textile factory (1964) does give some indications. It would appear that the supervision of female labour is less problematic than the supervision of male employees. Blauner suggests that a male supervisor can adopt a paternalistic attitude towards female operators and that this attitude is accepted by them, whilst it is less likely to be so with male operators. However, this paternalistic attitude is not welcomed—it is merely accepted.

Lupton (1963) makes the point that women employees are less likely to be involved in any form of collective action; that they are more likely to be submissive because of the nature of the working class sub-culture; and that they are less likely to depend entirely upon their income. These three factors can have implications for the nature of supervision of females, whether by male or female supervisors. In many senses, the task of the supervisor is made simpler because of the submissive personality of women workers. There are unlikely to be norms relating to the restriction of output, as Lupton found in factory 'Wye'.

From this discussion of the influence of sex upon the supervisory role, it is clear that it is difficult to draw any positive conclusions because of the paucity of studies relating to the variable. Even studies which initially indicate that there are sex differences in the supervisors studied make no differentiation in the analysis of results. The Government Social Survey report, for example, indicates that 6 per cent of the supervisors were female and then makes no further distinction (GSS, 1968).

155

Age

In a study of this nature it is difficult to analyse the effects that age has upon the role performance of foremen. In other studies, age is usually considered by psychologists to determine how performance is affected by it, though the performance of shop-floor workers is usually as far as the psychologists go. Alternatively, age is mentioned in the form of a descriptive statistic—for example, in the Government Social Survey report (1968) on 598 foremen, it is mentioned that the average age of foremen was forty-six years and no more is said about this. In analytical studies concentrating upon the role of the foreman, the variable of age appears to be considered as either too simplistic or too non-theoretical for further consideration, and in many cases both aspects are considered in deciding not to investigate this variable.

Vroom's study (1959) of personality determinants found that age was not related to either the supervisor's personality variables or to attitudes to participation. Friedlander's study (1963) of the underlying sources of job satisfaction amongst supervisors and others provides further evidence relating to this variable. This was a study of all employees (approximately 10,000) in a manufacturing organisation. It was found that the younger age groups were related to one of their three factors of job satisfaction—that of intrinsic self-actualising work aspects.

Findings such as these do suggest that although a supervisor's age may not be related to a particular set of selected factors, it may account for some variance when dealing with wider or more complex variables such as the foreman's job satisfaction.

There can be little doubt that the older supervisor does in some circumstances create problems for the management of industrial organisations. It is also axiomatic to say that in a great many organisations the expectations of the supervisors by management and the capabilities of the foremen are inconsistent. In a previous section dealing with the training of foremen, the point was made that management often assumes that there is not this discrepancy between expectations and capabilities. In many of the studies concerned with foremen, there is the assumption that the loss of prestige, authority and status of the supervisor is almost entirely due to managerial policies. Whatever the truth is, a lot of argument stems from the question of selection, and the training and development of foremen.

In cases like this, the problem of the older foreman is a very real one. In an age of awareness of industrial training, managers have to deal with foremen who, in many cases, were appointed a long time ago, who have established working procedures and who are likely to resist any change, not because of bloody-mindedness on their part but merely because they have adapted to working procedures, have adhered to established value patterns, and so on, which makes it extremely difficult for management to change the existing structure. It may be in some cases that, with technological development in the plant, the older foreman has not adjusted to the development, which in a sense makes them unsuitable foremen. A study by the NIIP (1957) showed that in some of the firms investigated, managers were doing some of the work of the foremen because of this.

Various strategies have been used by industrial organisations to deal with this kind of problem. For example, foremen have been retired from the firm early, assistant foremen have been introduced to carry out those tasks that the foreman seems unable or unwilling to do. Older foremen have been 'cooled-out' such that assistants gradually take over more and more of the supervisory role.

The NIIP researchers make the point that 'it can be a serious disadvantage to have too many foremen at one time in the same age range' (p. 142). There are several reasons why such a strategy makes good sense: if supervisors are approximately in the same age range then they will all retire at approximately the same time and this leads to great organisational problems; having foremen of about the same age also means that promotion opportunities can become blocked in the organisation.

Personality factors

The personality variables associated with supervisors are obviously of importance in an understanding of the role. There are, however, two studies that deal specifically with this dimension. Most of the studies are focused on other factors and personality is viewed as a residual category. A study by Vroom (1959) does directly focus on the relationship between personality and the participation in decision-making of supervisors.

Vroom points out that while there is some acceptance by writers in this area that personality and environmental factors are important for understanding the nature of the supervisor role, few of them have systematically investigated this factor. Vroom's aim is to test whether personality determinants can affect, in any way, the participation in decision-making. He deals specifically with democratic supervisors. Two personality variables are taken—the need for independence and authoritarianism. The general hypothesis of the study is that 'participation is hypothesised to have more positive effect on the attitudes and performance of persons with strong than with weak independence needs and to have less positive effect on authoritarians than equalitarians' (Vroom, 1959, p. 323).

The study was carried out in a parcel delivery firm, the sample being made up of 108 first-, second- and third-line supervisors in the two largest plants of the firm. It was found, as elsewhere, that participation in decision-making had positive effects on job attitudes and job performance and that the magnitude of these effects was a function of personality characteristics. Thus, those supervisors with weak independence needs or who were authoritarian were not affected by the opportunity for participation. Egalitarians and those with strong independence needs, by having the opportunity to participate in decision-making, developed more positive attitudes towards the job and a greater motivation for effective performance.

As mentioned above, other studies in this area tend to be less focused than the Vroom study. Although not directly measured, it has been found that both motivation and intelligence are related to a supervisor's 'task relevance' (Cooper, 1966) and to job dissatisfaction (Sykes, 1962). These two factors have, in fact, already been dealt with in some detail. Again, a study by Di Vesta (1954) on instructor-centred and student-centred approaches to teaching a human relations course found no significant difference in supervisor's reactions as to whether the course was instructor- or student-centred.

Other studies have found certain configurations of personality factors in supervisors. For example, passive-dependent-submissive patterns have been found in supervisors in banks (McMurray, 1958) and innovators have been found in school superintendents (Carlson, 1961). The study of bank employees and supervisors related the observed patterns to the 'development of a stereotype of the right employee'. The study of school superintendents indicated that both types of superintendent found 'are conformist in the sense that their performance conforms to the expectations of their employers'. These two comments underlie and underline the relevance of personality factors in supervisors. They both have the implicit assumptions of self-selection and organisational selection. These indicate further dimensions of the relationship between personality structure and social structure, between potential and actual supervision, and the organisation in which they are located.

It has been made clear from other studies reported throughout this particular analysis that the personality of supervisors plays an important part in determining how they are to perform their role within an organisation. Perhaps of greatest relevance is the study of supervisory leadership which has already been investigated in depth. It was shown that research findings indicate that maximum performance of the work group can be achieved when the supervisor has a 'democratic' leadership style (with certain reservations that have been noted). On this whole question of personality factors, therefore, some recognition should be made of them, but it is as yet impossible to say how important a feature they are in the performance of the supervisory role. The evidence which is beginning to emerge is at times ambivalent and does demonstrate that this is clearly another area where more research work needs to be carried out.

Income and mobility

The two variables of income and mobility are not behavioural variables in the sense thay they involve the actions and interactions of supervisors. Nevertheless, they can be discussed in a meaningful way since they do have a close relationship with other more distinct behavioural variables. Really, the variable of mobility is behavioural, whereas income is not, but when the two are combined this does give a basis for the discussion of the two in this context. Also, of course, they do have far-reaching consequences for other behavioural variables.

The correlation between income and mobility can be demonstrated by reference to four studies. Form and Geschwender (1962) have shown that income is an important index of status and, as such, it is closely related to the job satisfaction of supervisors. The NIIP study of foremen (1951) indicated that there was a large variability between supervisors' incomes. McMurray (1958) has shown that industrial supervisors tend to receive considerably less payment than their counterparts in service organisations. The study of Swedish school superintendents showed that the superintendents received more payment if they were 'outsiders' than if they were 'insiders' (Carlson, 1961). The Swedish study also showed that income patterns could be related to variations in mobility, in that insiders stayed longer and were 'place-bound' in comparsion with outsiders.

From a non-empirical point of view, certain observations can be made. First, it is conceivable that the traditional differential between foremen and shop-floor workers in terms of income may have been eroded away in many instances, particularly in the last few years. The growth of productivity bargaining in Britain has been largely for manual workers in so far as their productivity is more measureable than other grades. With productivity bargaining has come a great many advantages for this grade of worker in terms of both income and benefits in working arrangements. Foremen have rarely been the subject of productivity bargaining because of both their position in the status hierarchy and the nature of their work. It is possible, therefore, that there has been an erosion of the income differential. This is certainly the case of the differential between white collar workers such as clerks and manual workers, and there have been recent attempts to re-assert the differential by white-collar workers demanding productivity agreements of their own (the case of ICI provides a good example of this).

In terms of mobility, a further observation can be made. For analytical purposes two distinct types of foremen can be distinguished again. In the first place, there is the foreman who sees his present position as being the apex of his career curve, and, second, there is the foreman who views his present position as being a 'stepping-stone' to a managerial position. In making a division such as this, there are clearly implications for an organisation. The first type of foreman is likely to be satisfied with his position and to have a 'local' orientation (Gouldner, 1959). He is likely to identify with the organisation in which he is employed and is unlikely to stress any faults there may be in his working conditions. The second type of foreman will tend to have a career-orientation, he will be 'cosmo-politan' in outlook and he will identify with management rather than with individuals on the shop-floor. He will expect to be both occupationally and geographically mobile in the course of his career. A consequence of this orientation is that he will tend to point out the faults in the employing organisation and be continually looking for something 'better'. The accommodation by the employing organisation of this type of foreman is far more difficult than the accommodation of the first type. On the other hand, since the second type of foreman desires more status, he may ensure that the productivity of his work group is high, that there is a high degree of discipline and that, in short, he continually proves his capabilities.

Conclusions

Probably the most important conclusion to emerge from this chapter is the confirmation of a prediction made at the beginning—that little is known about the individual characteristics of foremen, at least at a demographic level. Managerially, however, there are individual characteristics that foremen *ought* to have. It will be shown that in this instance there are deviations between the normative and the actual. In looking for the general characteristics of foremen, there is a similar problem to that of looking for leadership traits or the general characteristics of leaders. It was shown earlier that such attempts have not been successful and the suggestion is that the search for consistent individual characteristics of foremen is similar.

Despite this, it is consistent with one of the major themes of this study to examine individual characteristics, not on a universal basis but on a particular one—that is to take certain structural situations and in these to define the individual characteristics. Even an approach such as this has obvious difficulties. It would be wrong, for example, to expect all foremen in a given situation to exhibit exactly the same characteristics to the same degree or, for that matter, to have exactly the same characteristics. After all, in the same situation, two foremen may be equally effective in terms of performance and this very effectiveness may derive from different types of characteristics. Knowledge of individual characteristics is obviously important, since if such knowledge can be determined the *essential* characteristics in any particular situation can be recorded and foremen can be selected and/or trained with that knowledge in mind.

In addition to the specific characteristics discussed above, there is also a need to recognise what psychologists call the 'special abilities' and 'personal needs' of individuals and the way in which these affect role performance. Thus, Ghiselli (1966) has stressed the need for foremen to have special numerical, spatial, mechanical and perceptual abilities. These, of course, are in addition to verbal ability which, as Donovan (1971) points out, is closely related to effective supervisory performance. In his study a correlation of 0·31 was obtained between verbal ability and effectiveness. The need for such ability, however, probably varies with the nature of the task of the organisation and other organisational characteristics discussed in Chapter 4. For example, in Donovan's study, the supervisory sample was mainly drawn from semi-skilled production units. It might be expected that the correlation between verbal ability and performance would increase with more skilled tasks and decrease with less skilled tasks.

The other cluster of factors mentioned—'personal needs'—is also related to performance. One such need is the 'urge to achieve' which has already been analysed in the supervisory context in some detail. Where achievement needs are higher, more effective performance would be expected, and vice versa. Such a proposition is supported from evidence in the previous chapter where it was shown that those foremen with high performance goals had higher performance work groups.

Another personal need is sociability, and again it has been shown that the foreman who, psychologically, is more distant from his work group is more effective (Fiedler, 1965a). This finding, which is supported elsewhere (Zaleznick, 1966), suggests that there is an inverse relationship between the need for sociability and effective performance.

Other individual characteristics of foremen can be discussed, such as the characteristic of competency in decision-making and those of technical competence, judgmental ability, and so on, but these are best left until the next chapter where the relevance of findings in this area for managerial action is analysed. It is possible to conclude by saying that, at the individual level, certain characteristics are present that in terms of the original system model can be seen as inputs, conversions and outputs. At the sub-system level, it is important to determine the nature of the dependency of these variables, at the total system level to see how they relate to variables in other sub-systems and to the whole, and at the purely pragmatic level to analyse the relationship between such variables and foreman performance.

7 Implications and conclusions

Introduction

Among other things, this study has shown how complex the role of foremen actually is, and from this complexity some attempt needs to be made in this chapter to present the foreman role in a more simplistic form. There is a need for this, particularly with the growing increase in both the size and complexity of industrial organisations themselves. With such developments, the need for understanding a key industrial role such as the foreman is obvious, and it is suggested that such an understanding can arise by simplifying the given complex situation.

The social scientist has often been forced to adopt roles which he has no real desire to occupy. One such role is that of prophet and fortune-teller. In a study of this nature, there is an expectation that the writer should be able to predict the pattern of things to come. Some attempt can be made at such an exercise, but only on the basis of what has gone before. In order to carry out this exercise, it is felt necessary to first of all present the theoretical model of the foreman role now that the task and structural variables have been delineated and discussed.

The system approach to the foreman role

The theoretical model developed in Chapter 2 has been specifically developed throughout the study to be appropriate for the foreman role. It will be recalled that the basic model was a simple one in terms of the system having specific inputs, conversions and outputs. These three sets of variables were distinguished as being present at three general levels of analysis—the organisation, the group and the individual. These three levels have been discussed in the main body of the text in terms of the three types of variable distinguished. At its most simple, it will be recalled that the model could be expressed diagrammatically as shown in Figure 2.5, p. 26. When this over-simplified model was presented in Chapter 2, the point was made that it was not really adequate since the general model proposed is both complex and adaptive. The model presented in such a simple form implies that there is a high degree of closure, when in fact total openness is being argued for.

In the main study, attempts have been made to account for the situation of openness expressed above. For each of the three levels of analysis, the general concept of system has been applied, whilst recognising that in fact they are merely sub-systems of the total role. Equally it could be argued that the total role system is merely a sub-system of a much larger role system, and so on. In this way, the notion of openness is maintained.

In the text, each of the three levels has been regarded as a unit, as a system of inter-related parts composed of three variables—independent, intervening and dependent. The operational definition of each category or part specifies what is involved in recognising and measuring the concept in a particular situation. What the process has involved has been detailing the observations of writers by following through the inputs through conversions to outputs, and then, as it were, totalling at the end. Those detailed have generally been those that have adopted an explanatory standpoint since, as shown earlier, descriptive studies tend to melt away when exposed to a fairly rigorous framework as presented here. Obviously in a study of this size, full use has not been made of all the studies that are available, but it is felt that those studies examined together with the writer's own comments and observations do provide a basis for developing an integrated and coherence-inducing model of the foreman role.

In each of the chapters dealing with specific sub-systems at the different levels of analysis, the model of the sub-system was suggested. Now that each of them has been distinguished, the process of aggregation can take place in order to present the total system model. This exercise is best carried out diagrammatically as shown in Figure 7.1. It might be argued from the diagram that the 'slotting' of variables into a particular sub-system, or even the nature of the variable in terms of its dependency, is arbitrary. Thus, a case could be made out for the variable of 'power' not being a conversion variable at the organisational level, but that perhaps it should be an output variable in the group level sub-system. A valid case could be argued for this, but in defence of the treatment of the variables that have been distinguished it is argued that their 'position' in the model is such because of the way in which the variables have been treated in the main study. In a further study, it could easily be the

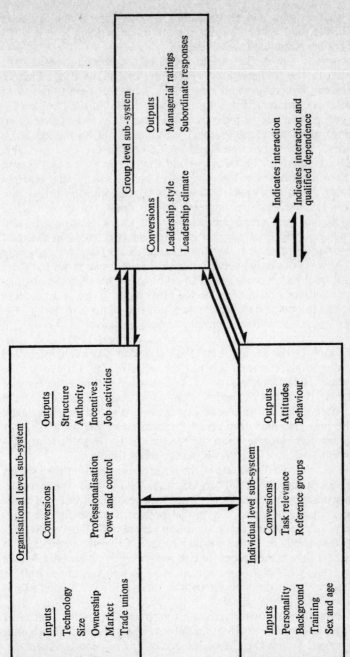

FIGURE 7.1 *System model of the foreman role*

case that there would be considerable 'shuffling' of the variables within the total system, but for the use made of them here it is felt that their positioning is adequate.

As was shown earlier, at the levels of the organisation and the individual, the trichotomised system approach was used. That is, dependent, intervening and independent variables were found to be present and in interaction with one another. But at the third level— the group—the suggestion was made that only intervening (conversion) and dependent (output) variables could be found. There obviously have to be input variables if a consistent system model is being presented, but it was suggested that the inputs at this system level are the outputs of the other two levels. That is, what emerges at the group level of analysis or what is injected into this sub-system is from the other two sub-systems. In this sense, the group level of analysis has little or no independence at all: it is structured and characterised by what goes on in the other two levels. In the total system model presented, this fact is made clear. Thus, for the group level, there is not only interaction with the other two levels but there is also 'qualified dependence'. The relationship between the organisational and individual levels, on the other hand, is one of interaction only; the notion of dependence does not enter into it.

The use of the system concept has been criticised in sociological literature during the past few years (Silverman, 1970; Gouldner, 1971), and for this reason it is felt necessary to discuss the perceived advantages of the system model over other models with respect to this study of the foreman role. This discussion will take the form of analysing the analytical and conceptual advantages that the model has. After all, it can be argued persuasively that only such a model as the one presented here could hope to cover the wide range of variables that impinge upon the foreman role—but this is a pragmatic rationale and one that is readily recognisable.

It will be recalled that one of the basic assumptions of the systems approach is that the social 'organism' being analysed—be it a role, an organisation or whatever—is seen as being composed of a set of interdependent parts. The model presented above for the foreman role demonstrates this assumption very clearly. Further assumptions that could be stated are that systems strive to survive and to grow, and that in the process of doing this they must necessarily take action and must behave in a certain way. In terms of the completed model presented, assumptions such as these can be examined to test the usefulness of the model.

Most system theorists agree that with respect to the notion of interdependency the relationship between the parts is of paramount importance. Unless there is knowledge of this relationship there can only be partial knowledge of the total system. Similarly with the assumption relating to system needs for survival, the system needs to be examined in terms of its objectives—in terms of what it is trying to achieve. And with the assumption concerning system action and behaviour, this is obviously important if the previous assumption is accepted—there must be action if a need is to be satisfied.

The system model of the foreman role presented in the study is complex, adaptive and open, in that there is recognition that there is interaction between the system and its environment. Thus, for example, with the foreman role model, it is accepted that individual foremen may bring expectations from outside the role into it. Expectations that are formed outside the work-place may significantly affect the actual operation of the role (Ingham, 1970). In this sense, the system is seen from an open perspective. One of the main advantages of such an open system perspective is that it enables certain aspects of the environment to be studied in terms of their influence upon the role itself. Thus, earlier in the study, the factor of technology, which is often regarded as a factor external to the organisation, was analysed in relation to the foreman role and it was shown that there were significant relationships between the technology of the organisation and the structure of the foreman role.

Another way of defending the use of the system concept in this study would be to ask what the alternatives would have been. There are, of course, a host of different alternatives—human relations, formal organisational, technological determinism, and so on. The main point that can be made about all of these, without examining each of them individually, is that the systems approach manages to embrace their particular individual biases of approach. Thus, in the model used in this study, the human relations perspective is embraced, particularly in discussing the group level sub-system. Technology is a dominant feature of the organisational sub-system, and so on.

But in terms of general models that attempt to incorporate all these approaches, it would appear that the recently revived social action model is the only serious rival to the systems approach. The main British advocate of this approach with reference to industrial sociology is Silverman (1968; 1970). The paradigm of the social action model examines the ends of action, the relationship between the ends of action, the means used to attain the ends, and the consequences of such action. Such an approach has much to commend itself, but its uses, it is suggested, are specific—it is not a universally applicable theory. One case where the social action model seems to be particularly inappropriate is the examination of an organisational role in the way in which this study has progressed. In the first place, the emphasis has been upon secondary data, and determination of the nature of social action with such data is impossible. Second,

167

when dealing with the study of an organisational role, there are issues of reductionism that must come into play. If a role is examined from a social action perspective, only the individual characteristics of the role would emerge. The properties at the group and organisational levels could not adequately be discussed because of reductionism problems. For these two main reasons, it was felt that the system model was the most appropriate in a study of this nature. It is not being said that other approaches are redundant, but merely that for the purposes of the present study they did appear to be inappropriate.

Now that the total system model has been presented and discussed, the implications of the study can be turned to. They are discussed under two main headings relating to the foreman role in general and to the possibilities of role effectiveness in the light of the findings of this research.

The position of the industrial foreman

Taking the present, it should by now be clear that the traditional image of the foreman—what might be called the stereotypical image—is a false one. The orthodox image is of an individual in a half-way house between the management and the workers, not belonging to either group, in an industrial organisation. The traditional view of the foreman can be seen in chants relating to what the 'working class' have to do now that an individual has 'the foreman's job at last'. Clearly such a view is far from the truth. What is closer to the truth is that foremen are undergoing rapid changes in their activities and responsibilities which provide indicators for what might occur in the future.

It will be recalled that one of the main aims of many studies of foremen is to examine the nature of their role marginality. From this traditional point of view of the foreman, he can go one of two ways. Either he becomes more securely a part of management or he identifies with and is identified as part of 'the workers'. The present indications and prospects can now be examined.

Criticisms of the traditional view of the foreman and of the marginal man thesis can be levelled from several points of view. After all, as Fletcher notes, 'Some myths have been advanced by the social sciences themselves. One such myth is the "man in the middle" thesis for industrial supervisors. It is one of sociology's most dramatic tales' (1969, p. 341).

If Fletcher is right, then one of the biggest parts of the myth is that the thesis assumes all supervisors to be 'suffering' the same stresses and strains in the performance of their roles. That is, the monolithic nature of the argument needs to be challenged. The present study has indicated that such a challenge is valid (see, for example, the section dealing with the effect of technology upon the role).

Another criticism to be made of the marginal man thesis is the way in which conflict is handled. There is the assumption that the marginality and role conflict that foremen experience derive wholly from the organisation. The nature of the system, so the thesis assumes, is responsible for the situation of the foreman being rejected by one party if he takes the view of the other. But is this so? Surely a better explanation is in terms of saying that it is not the structural characteristics of the task (albeit sometimes defined by the structure). Fletcher maintains 'A supervisor is not necessarily at odds with either worker or management, but rather *at odds with what he has to do*' (1969, p. 342).

Clearly on methodological grounds alone the marginality thesis needs re-defining. From the view of common observation there are grounds for a re-definition. More and more, the indications are that the organisational position of foreman does not represent the top of a career ladder. Increasingly, it is one of the bottom rungs of such a ladder. The influx of graduate foremen into large industrial organisations would validate such a statement. Many of the supervisory responsibilities call for specialists—for individuals who have undergone further or higher education. If supervisory positions are to be filled by people such as this, then there follows the proposition that the position of foreman can only be seen as a stepping-stone to higher things, in the managerial hierarchy. Increasingly, therefore, the modern foreman is better qualified, better educated and certainly more socially aspirant than his traditional counterpart.

A further indication of this is that some firms (notably IBM) have done away with the title 'foreman'. That is, foremen have been turned into managers, not only in terms of their functions but also in terms of their status, income, authority, and so on. For example, it has been reported that an IBM first-line manager (previously foreman) earns at least 25 per cent above the highest paid worker in his department. The position for the traditional foreman is such that many of the men over whom he has responsibility earn more than he does as a result of piece-rates, productivity bargaining, and the like.

The clear signs appear to be that the re-definition of supervisory tasks will be in managerial terms, and it must be emphasised that this does involve more than a mere change of name from foreman to, say, first-line manager. In organisational terms, the definition of new lines of communication, new structures of authority, the reward of increased status, and so on, are involved.

The other direction in which foremen can turn is towards the shop-floor. Doubtless, in the short term many foremen have done this and will continue this practice. This will continue for as long as the position of foreman is seen as being at the top of a career ladder. There are indications that this 'traditional' group of foremen exists and that they are likely to continue in existence for some time. The growth of white-collar unionism, for example, is surely more applicable to this kind of foreman than to the kind described above. It could even be that participative methods of leadership may be more appropriate for this type of foreman.

Clearly, the marginal man thesis needs re-defining and this can be done on the basis of the foregoing analysis. The first stage in this process of re-definition is to refine the so-called 'monolithic myth' of the thesis. For analytical purposes—and, as shown below, for practical purposes—it is proposed that two different and distinct types of foreman can be observed. In effect, these two categories represent the class consciousness of foremen and so for the sake of convenience it is proposed that it is possible to be able to distinguish 'working-class' foremen and 'middle-class' foremen. Each of these can be analysed in turn (see also Table 7.1).

The working-class foreman

The characteristics of the working-class foreman are those that are thought of when the 'traditional' type of foreman is thought of. The typical individual characteristics of such foremen are as follows. These foremen tend to be older than their middle-class counterparts, are unlikely to have received further or higher education, and are more likely to be products of secondary modern schools. They have probably spent most of their working lives within the one company, usually at the one plant. The family background is typically working-class—what Lockwood calls 'traditional proletarian'. There are proportionately more female supervisors in this category than in the other.

Working-class foremen tend not to be aspirantly mobile—they have realistically appraised their present position and see themselves at the top of a career ladder. In their attitudes to management, they are deferential and tend not to be critical of managerial decisions. Their orientation towards work is instrumental; they are concerned with improving their lot at that level, whilst, as noted, not being aspirant. While deferring to management, they tend to see their problems as resulting from difficulties with the men below them. Their instrumental orientation is partly expressed by the fact that this category of foreman is more likely to be unionised than the other category.

The leadership style tends to be more authoritarian. They are to be found in traditional industries, particularly unit and mass production technologies. The size of the concern (in terms of the numbers employed) can vary enormously. Until recently, there was unlikely to be a systematic training programme, although this might be changing, as the section on supervisory training has indicated.

The performance of the working-class foreman is not highly effective, arising from his attitudes, training, education, background and leadership style. In terms of reference group orientation, working-class foremen tend not to have a dominant group—they shift their point of reference as the occasion arises.

In short, the working-class foreman is the 'man in the middle'. He is likely to experience role conflict and marginality. He sees his position as being between the two dominant groups, recognising that he belongs to neither of them fully.

The middle-class foreman

This category of foreman is not the opposite of the working-class foreman; he merely represents the polar extremity. He is younger, better educated and comes from the ranks of the upper-working/lower-middle classes. Proportionately few females are represented in this category. Such foremen are socially aspirant, being both socially and geographically mobile. In terms of the attitude to management, this category of foreman is critical. He tends not to be a member of a trade union, has more of a democratic leadership style and works in the newer type of industry, particularly industry having a process technology. He will have undergone systematic training for his present position and will be sent on occasional courses. He refers continually to management and identifies with this group. Also, he is more likely to be an effective role performer.

These two categories of foremen are not 'ideal types'; they are not logical exaggerations from reality but do in fact exist. They can be regarded as polar types—as the extremes of a multi-factor index. The probability is that most foremen lie somewhere around the middle of this continuum. Although there are dangers in making qualitative or evaluative statements, it is true to say that most organisations attempt to guide their foremen towards the 'middle-class' end of the continuum and that, if this is done, there is likely to be increased effectiveness on the part of foremen.

The characteristics of the two types of foreman can be summarised as shown in Table 7.1.

Practical implications

Throughout this work there have been both direct and indirect

171

implications for the foreman role in industry. At this stage it is necessary to make explicit these implications, to see what the study might offer the practising manager, to see what the study means for the foreman himself and also to examine the implications from a training point of view. To compartmentalise the implications in these three ways is obviously wrong since any suggestions made should be as appropriate to the foreman himself as to the manager and the training specialist. Rather than do this, therefore, the approach will be more general, but will none the less be appropriate for any one of the particular orientations.

TABLE 7.1

Characteristics	Working-class	Middle-class
Age	Relatively old	Relatively young
Education	Up to secondary	Further/higher
Background	Traditional proletarian	Upper working class/ lower middle class
Sex	Most females	Few females
Mobility	Acceptance of position	Socially aspirant
Where worked	Present company	Several companies
Attitudes to management	Deferential	Critical
Problems result from	Workers	Management
Orientations to work	Instrumental	Expressive
Unionisation	Likely	Unlikely
Leadership style	Authoritarian	Democratic
Training	Unlikely	Systematic
Technology	Unit/mass	Mass/process
Performance	Relatively ineffective	Relatively effective
Reference group	Varies	Management

1 Basically, the study has concerned itself with the task and structural characteristics of the foreman role—the analysis of these two large clusters of variables leads to an important conclusion. There seems to be no doubt that at the present time there is vastly insufficient information and knowledge of the foreman role. In examining specific characteristics in the main body of the text, whether at the organisational, group or individual level, it was repeatedly necessary to point out that not enough was known about the variables to draw any specific conclusion, let alone attempt the formulation of working hypotheses for future research. But in addition to this, it became increasingly clear that it was impossible to discuss *the* foreman role because of the heterogeneity of supervisory roles.

The practical implication of this lack of knowledge is simple. If the position of foreman is to be filled by individuals who are competent, whose expectations are consistent with the job and who possess the right requirements laid down for the job, then it follows that such characteristics of the foreman position (as opposed to the person who is the incumbent of that position) need to be accurately known and stated. Yet, if nothing else, this exercise has demonstrated that such knowledge of the position is not available and cannot be stated.

There are indications that part of the problem lies with management itself. A content analysis of foreman job descriptions invariably shows that the stated requirements for the role are often inconsistent with the actual requirements. This analysis has suggested that possibly many foremen are carrying out tasks that were relevant several years ago, but with changes in task and structure the formal requirements are no longer appropriate. It has been suggested by some writers, for this very reason, that perhaps the foreman no longer has a useful role to perform in industry—in short, that he is redundant. Such a dramatic conclusion is not arrived at here, even though there is recognition of under-employment. Instead, therefore, it is suggested that schemes such as job enlargement should be examined realistically by management. Of course, it does mean that if a job enlargement exercise were to be undertaken, then the total number of foremen might have to be reduced and the number of levels in the supervisory hierarchy would have to be reduced proportionately. Such action, though perhaps swingeing in the short run, does have a long-term benefit in terms of the increased contribution the foreman has to make to the organisation.

The other point that is equally important is that the foreman himself must be made aware of his authority and responsibilities. The authority given must be sufficient to enable the attainment of the goals assigned to the role and, likewise, the responsibilities need to be such as to enable the foreman to feel that he is capable of achieving these objectives. The question of authority is obviously important here in defining the foreman role and in making suggestions and recommendations about it. As indicated earlier in the study, the nature of the authority exercised and the 'intensity' varies with the situation, which makes generalisations very difficult. Patten (1968) delineated a four-fold classification of degrees of authority in the foreman role which appear to be particularly significant here. First, there is the authority of *delegation*—that is that foremen should have the right to delegate when demands are such. Second, the authority to *act*—to have the authority to take action over specific issues without referring the problem to a superior or even reporting the action to him. Third, the authority to *act and report*. Last, the authority to *recommend*: here authority is strictly limited, particularly since recommendations are often not acted upon. Here, then, is a hierarchy of authoritative positions for foremen. There is a need for management to decide which degree of authority is most appropriate to the particular situation and by doing so a much clearer description of the foreman role is obtained.

The first major practical conclusion, therefore, is the need for a realistic appraisal to be made of actual supervisory functions and the degree of authority to be given to foremen, and for comprehensive job descriptions to be written covering foreman positions. Each of these proposals would guarantee greater effectiveness from foremen and ultimately this would mean greater effectiveness for the organisation.

2 Having defined the foreman role and position systematically as suggested, the next problem is to decide what are the personal characteristics required of persons appointed to such a position. Again, the general study points to some fairly clear recommendations. Except for obvious limitations, age and sex do not appear to be severe constraints. There are specific personality requirements, as shown in Chapter 6. Also, individuals should be endowed with special abilities as discussed earlier, particularly technical ability and decision-making ability. But combined with these is the need for a high urge to achieve and a moderate level of intelligence.

3 Even though the foreman position may be adequately described, the parameters of the role systematically defined and the individual characteristics of foremen decided upon, it would be foolish to suggest that this is all that is required to ensure foreman effectiveness. Coupled with those factors is the need for training. If the foreman is to be regarded as an integrated member of a management team, there is as much need for him to be aware of and to have the opportunity of using contemporary management techniques. Such awareness can only arise through systematic training of foremen in the sense that not only must the 'ends' of managerial objectives be stated but the 'means' to attain these ends must be taught and the opportunities to use the means must be available.

Of course, if the suggestions made under 1 and 2 are followed, management will find that its foremen have the capacity for learning by their mistakes in a kind of hit-or-miss situation. But experience suggests that methods such as these are counter-productive, expensive and frustrating. There must, then, be recognition that there is a need for training in general; this is widely recognised. What is not so widely recognised is the most appropriate particular training for foremen. There is evidence to suggest the validity of this statement. Many training programmes are designed and administered without having assessed the particular training needs, with the result that the training may finish up being a waste of time and resources—in short, that it does not lead to the increased effectiveness on the part of foremen.

If the recommendations made above concerning adequate job definition and individual characteristics definition are followed, the task of assessing training needs is made significantly easier. The first recommendation enables the determination of the requisite skills and the second enables the appraisal of individual performance. Often, more thorough jobs analysis is required for exact assessment of the training needs. It is stressed that determination of training needs is a vital prelude to any training exercise.

Once this stage has been reached a problem discussed earlier in the study appears—what form should the training take? As concluded then, there is no hard and fast line on this since training itself varies with the nature of the task, and similarly the form of training varies. In one particular situation the 'training within industry' method might be most appropriate, whereas in another situation emphasis should be placed on leadership training. One form of training that appears appropriate in most situations and in view of most training needs is what can be called 'basic skill training'.

The recognition of the need for training in basic skills derives in part from the analysis of the foreman role in this study. Consistent with the findings of Thurley and Hamblin (1963), this study recognises problem-solving to be a key element in the performance of the foreman's role. As a response to this awareness, Thurley and Hamblin suggest the need for training to include discussions of problems between foremen and their managers on the job itself, discussions about work problems off the job and, third, analysis of problems by independent 'arbitrators' in an objective fashion so that this analysis can take the form of feedback to the foreman and managers in further group discussions. Whilst agreeing that such training has much to recommend itself, it does presuppose that foremen are competent at problem-solving. Such a presupposition, it is suggested, is unwarranted in a great many cases. There is, therefore, a great need for preliminary training to take into account problem-solving (or basic skills).

As soon as a training programme has been completed (indeed, while the training is being undertaken as well), there must be evaluation in some form. Hesseling (1966) has pointed out that evaluation of training is not carried out on a large enough scale and he has suggested that at least 1 per cent of training budgets should be spent on evaluation. At present, inadequate attention is directed to training evaluation with the subsequent result that it is not known how effective particular types of training are.

Clearly, in the field of foreman training much needs to be done, but it is suggested that if the recommendations made here were to be followed—defining the training needs, finding the most appropriate form of training and assessing the results of training—then the trained foreman would be a more effective foreman.

4 In looking at the implications of the study, one important area has not been fully discussed. Thus far it has been assumed that merely by paying more careful attention to the task and structural variables, to the individual characteristics of foremen and to training, a more effective supervisory team will emerge. To a certain extent this is true, but greater effectiveness will be obtained if attention is directed to the needs of foremen themselves. Or, in current managerial terms, the foremen must be sufficiently motivated to perform. The problems of motivation are vast and to do justice to them would require a separate study in its own right. Nevertheless, some general points can be made. First of all, in terms of orientations to work,

TABLE 7.2

Factors	Description
Motivators	
Achievement	Successful completion of work, discovering a good idea or solution, seeing the results of work, being proven right
Responsibility	Opportunity to be self-responsible, given new responsibility, responsibility for the work of others
Recognition	Work noticed, work praised and possibly rewarded
Work itself	Varied, creative, opportunity to do whole job
Possibility of growth	Opportunity for growth, growth in skills or in status
Hygiene factors	
Company policy and administration	Organisation of work, personnel policies
Supervision	Competent, honest, fair, accepting suggestions, good delegation, avoidance of favouritism
Salary	Amount of salary, wage increases, wage differential
Working conditions	Social and physical surroundings, facilities, amount of work
Job security	Objective signs of security

foremen, by virtue of their position, are not purely instrumental workers, even though the instrumental orientation was taken as an index of a polar type of foreman earlier in the chapter. By accepting a position of responsibility and authority foremen show that they have relatively high expressive needs (or at least at one time they had these). Given such a situation the theories of writers such as Maslow and Herzberg should be appropriate. The two-factor motivator-hygiene theory can be summarised as shown in Table 7.2.

Looking at the motivators here brings the analysis back full circle to the suggestion that, in many cases, there is a need for more adequate description of the foreman role and that perhaps the notion of job enlargement is appropriate. Certainly the results of these two factors would act as motivators for the foreman. As with training, management needs to know all the relevant information about its foremen before any attempt can be made at motivation.

Conclusion

It is clear by now that this study has achieved some of its main aims. The many variables affecting the foreman role have been analysed, the role has been examined in terms of a strict theoretical base and the implications of changes in the foreman role have been discussed.

One final point needs to be stressed. Throughout this study it has become clear that there is insufficient information regarding foremen. Hopefully what this study has done is to integrate what information is available into a coherent framework. But a great deal of research is needed to fully comprehend the dynamics of the role. It is hoped that this analysis has made this point explicit enough and that it has pointed the way forward to further research by pin-pointing the areas where there is insufficient information. It is hoped, too, that this analysis has proved useful by high-lighting the areas of deficiency and by providing one framework of analysis which does appear to offer the possibility of integrating further research work.

In conclusion, therefore, it is felt that the tasks set at the beginning of the study have been carried out. From the point of view of the social scientist, a grounded theory of the foreman role has been provided and the areas for future research requirements have been discussed. From the point of view of foremen and managers, many useful insights into role performance are provided and although few 'recipes' for supervisory effectiveness are presented there are many indications that with this information the modern industrial foreman can take his place as a strong force in industrial organisations and that he ought, no longer, to be 'the forgotten man of industry'.

Bibliography

ALBROW, M. (1970) *Bureaucracy*, Pall Mall Press.

ANDERSON, T. R. and WARKOV, S. (1961) 'Organisational Size and Functional Complexity', *A.S.R.*, **26**, 23–8.

ANDRESKI, S. (1969) *Herbert Spencer*, Macmillan.

ANSHEN, M. (1962) 'Managerial Decisions', in J. T. Dunlop (ed.), *Automation and Technological Change*, Prentice-Hall, pp. 66–82.

ARGYLE, M., GARDNER, G. and CIOFFI, F. (1958) 'Supervisory Methods Related to Productivity, Absenteeism and Labour Turnover', *Human Relations*, **11**, 23–40.

ARGYRIS, C. (1953) *Executive Leadership*, Harper.

ARGYRIS, C. (1954) *Organization of a Bank*, Labor and Management Center, Yale University.

ARGYRIS, C. (1957) *Personality and Organisation*, Harper & Row.

ARGYRIS, C. (1962) *Interpersonal Competence and Organisational Behaviour*, Irwin-Dorsey.

ARMSTRONG, J. R. (1961) *Supervisory Training*, Institute of Personnel Management.

BADGER, A. B. (1966) *Man in Employment*, Macmillan, Chapter 28.

BAIN, G. S. (1967) *Trade Union Growth and Recognition*, Royal Commission on Trade Unions and Employers' Associations, Research Paper No. 6, HMSO.

BAKER, J. and FRANCE, A. (1954) 'Centralization and the Industrial Relations Function', *J.M.S.*, **6**, 91–123.

BALES, R. and SLATER P. (1955) 'Role Differentiation in Small Decision-making Groups', in T. Parsons (ed.), *Family, Socialisation and Interaction Process*, Free Press.

BARNARD, C. I. (1938) *The Functions of the Executive*, Harvard University Press.

BARNES COMMITTEE REPORT (1962) *Report of the Committee on the Selection and Training of Supervisors*, Ministry of Labour, HMSO.

BAUMGARTEL, H. (1956) 'Leadership, Motivation and Attitudes in Research Laboratories', *J. Soc. Issues*, **12**, 24–31.

178

BAVELAS, A. (1960) 'Leadership: Man and Function', *Admin. Sci. Qtrly*, **5**, 491–8.

BENNIS, W. G., BERKOWITZ, N., AFFINITO, M. and MALONE, M. (1958) 'Authority, Power and the Ability to Influence', *Human Relations*, **11**, 143–55.

BERGER, P. L. (1964) *The Human Shape of Work*, Collier-Macmillan.

BERLE, A. A. and MEANS, G. C. (1932) *The Modern Corporation and Private Property*, Macmillan.

BIRD, C. (1940) *Social Psychology*, Appleton-Century.

BLACKBURN, R. M. (1967) *Union Character and Social Class*, Batsford.

BLAU, P. M. (1959) *Bureaucracy in Modern Society*, Random House.

BLAU, P. M. (1963) 'The Hierarchy of Authority in Organisations', *A.J.S.*, **64**, 453–67

BLAU, P. M. (1965) 'The Comparative Study of Organisations', *Industrial and Labor Relations Review*, **18**, 323–38.

BLAU, P. M. and SCOTT, W. H. (1963) *Formal Organisations*, Routledge & Kegan Paul.

BLAUNER, R. (1964) *Alienation and Freedom*, University of Chicago Press.

BLUM, T. and NAYLOR, C. (1968) *Industrial Psychology*, Harper & Row.

BOWERS, D. G. and SEASHORE, S. E. (1966) 'Predicting Organisational Effectiveness with a Four Factor Theory of Leadership', *Admin. Sci. Qtrly*, **11**, 233–63.

BROWN, M. (1953) 'Supervision and Bureaucratic Administration', *Advanced Mgt*, **20**, 17–26.

BROWN, W. (1960) *Exploration in Management*, Heinemann.

BUCKLEY, W. (1967) *Sociology and Modern Systems Theory*, McGraw-Hill.

BUGLER, J. (1969) 'The Foreman', *Daily Mirror Magazine*, Nov. 22, pp. 4–6.

BURNHAM, J. (1962) *The Managerial Revolution*, Penguin.

BURNS, T. and STALKER, G. M. (1961) *The Management of Innovation*, Tavistock Publications.

CAMPBELL, T. (1953) 'Some Effects of Joint Consultation on the Status and Role of the Supervisor', *Occup. Psych.*, **27**, 200–6.

CANNON, I. C, (1967) 'Ideology and Occupational Community: A Study of Compositors', *Sociology*, **1**, 165–86.

CAPLOW, T. (1954) *The Sociology of Work*, McGraw-Hill.

CAPLOW, T. (1957) 'Organisational Size', *Admin. Sci. Qtrly*, **1**, 484–505.

CARLSON, S. (1961) *Executive Behaviour*, Stockholm, Strombergs.

CARTER, R. R. (1951) 'A Human Relations Program', *J. of App. Psych.*, **35**, 38–45.

CARTWRIGHT, D. (1965) 'Influence, Leadership and Control', in J. G. March (ed.), *Handbook of Organisations*, Rand McNally, pp. 1–47.

CARTWRIGHT, D. and ZANDER, A. (1968) *Group Dynamics: Research and Theory*, Tavistock Publications.

CASTLE, P. F. C. (1952) 'The Evaluation of Human Relations Training for Supervisors', *Occup. Psych.*, **26**, 191–205.

CATTELL, R. (1951) 'New Concepts for Measuring Leadership in Terms of Group Syntality', *Human Relations*, **4**, 161–84.

CHAPIN, F. S. (1951) 'The Growth of Bureaucracy: An Hypothesis', *A.S.R.*, **16**, 835–6.

CHESTER, D. and FORSYTH, K. (1961) 'Public Ownership and Individual Behaviour', *Journal of Business*, **34**, 146–60.

CLEGG, H. A. (1970) *The System of Industrial Relations in Great Britain*, Blackwell.

COCH, L. and FRENCH, J. (1948) 'Overcoming Resistance to Change', *Human Relations*, **1**, 512–32.

COOPER, R. (1966) 'Leaders' Task Relevance and Subordinate Behaviour in Industrial Work Groups', *Human Relations*, **19**, 57–84.

CROZIER, M. (1964) *The Bureaucratic Phenomenon*, Tavistock Publications.

DAHL, R. A. (1957) 'The Concept of Power', *Behav. Sci.*, **2**, 201–18.

DALTON, M. (1951) 'Informal Factors in Career Achievement', *A.J.S.*, **51**, 407–15.

DALTON, M. (1959) *Men Who Manage*, Wiley.

DANZIG, E. R. and CALENTER, E. H. (1958) *The Dynamics and Structure of Small Work Groups*, prepared for US Navy Office of Naval Research by the Institute for Research in Human Relations, Series 126, Report 7, Philadelphia.

DAVIS. L. E. and WALFER, E. S. (1966) 'Studies in Supervisory Job Design', *Human Relations*, **19**, 339–52.

DENNIS, J., HENRIQUES, C. and SLAUGHTER, C. (1956) *Coal is Our Life*, Eyre & Spottiswoode.

DEUTCH, M. and GERARD, H. B. (1958) 'A Study of Normative and Informational Power upon Individual Judgement', *J. Abnorm. Soc. Psych.*, **51**, 629–36.

DONOVAN, A. F. (1971) *Management of Supervisors*, Macmillan.

DUBIN, R. (1961) *Human Relations in Administration*, Prentice-Hall.

DUBIN, R. (1962) 'Business Behaviour Behaviourally Viewed', in G. B. Strother (ed.), *Social Science Approaches to Business Behaviour*, Tavistock Publications, pp. 11–56.

DUNKERLEY, D. (1969) 'Techniques of Analysis of Executive Behaviour', unpublished Master's Thesis, University of Wales.

DUNKERLEY, D. (1972) *The Study of Organisations*, Routledge & Kegan Paul.

EMERY, F. E. and MAREK, J. (1962) 'Some Socio-technical Aspects of Automation', *Human Relations*, **15**, 17–25.

ETZIONI, A. (1960) *A Comparative Analysis of Complex Organisations*, Free Press.

ETZIONI, A. (1961) *Complex Organisations*, Holt, Rinehart & Winston.

ETZIONI, A. (1965) 'Dual Leadership in Complex Organisations', *A.S.R.*, **30**, 688–98.

EVAN, W. M. and ZELDITCH, M. (1961) 'A Laboratory Experiment on Bureaucratic Authority', *A.S.R.*, **26**, 883–93.

FAGG, D. R., KAYSEN, C. and MCKEEN, R. N. (1958) 'What the Factory Worker Knows About his Job', *Journal of Business*, **31**, 213–34.

FIEDLER, F. E. (1965a) 'Leadership—A New Model', *Discovery*, reprinted in C. A. Gibb (ed.) *Leadership*, Penguin, 1969, pp. 230–41.

FIEDLER, F. E. (1965b) 'Engineering the Job to Fit the Manager', *Harvard Business Review*, **43**, 115–22.

FIRST REPORT OF THE COMMISSION ON INDUSTRIAL RELATIONS (1969), *Associated Octel Ltd*, Cmnd 4246, HMSO.

FLEISHMAN, E. A. (1951) *Leadership Climate and Supervisory Behaviour*, Personnel Research Board, Ohio State University.

FLEISHMAN, E. A. (1956) 'Leadership Climate, Human Relations Training and Supervisory Behaviour', *Personnel Psych.*, 6, 208–22.

FLEISHMAN, E. A., HARRIS, E. H. and BURTT, H. E. (1955) *Leadership and Supervision in Industry*, Ohio State University Educational Research Monograph, No. 33.

FLEISHMAN, E. A. and HARRIS, E. H. (1962) 'Patterns of Leadership Behaviour Related to Employee Grievance and Turnover', *Personnel Psych.*, 15, 43–56.

FLETCHER, C. (1969) 'Men in the Middle: A Reformulation of the Thesis', *Soc. Review*, 17, 341–54.

FLORENCE, P. S. (1961) *Economics and Sociology of Industry*, Watts.

FORM, W. H. and GESCHWENDER, J. (1962) 'Social Reference Basis of Job Satisfaction—The Case of the Manual Worker', *A.S.R.*, 27, 228–237.

FOX, A. (1971) *A Sociology of Work in Industry*, Collier-Macmillan.

FRASER, J. M. and BRIDGES, J. M. (1964) *The Industrial Supervisor*, Business Publications.

FRENCH, J. R. P. and RAVEN, B. H. (1959) 'The Bases of Social Power', in D. Cartwright (ed.), *Studies in Social Power*, University of Michigan Press.

FRIEDLANDER, F. (1963) 'Underlying Sources of Job Satisfaction', *J. of Applied Psych.*, 47, 246–50.

GARDNER, B. B. and WHYTE, W. F. (1945) 'The Man in the Middle: Position and Problem of the Foreman', *Applied Psych.*, 4, 1–28.

GARFORTH, F. I., LOCK, H. F. and SIDNEY, D. M. (1951) 'Selection, Training and Status of Supervisors—II Training', *Occup. Psych.*, 25, 166–80.

GEORGOPOLOUS, B. S. (1957) *The Normative Structure of Social Systems: A Study of Organisational Effectiveness*, University of Michigan.

GERTH, H. H. and MILLS, C. W. (1949) *From Max Weber: Essays in Sociology*, Routledge & Kegan Paul.

GHISELLI, E. E. (1966) 'The Validity of a Personnel Interview', *Personnel Psych.*, 19, 389–94.

GIBB, C. A. (ed.) (1969), *Leadership*, Penguin.

GLASER, B. G. and STRAUSS, A. L. (1967) *The Discovery of Grounded Theory*, Aldine Press.

GOLDTHORPE, J. H. (1959) 'Technical Organisation as a Factor in Supervisor–Worker Conflict', *B.J.S.*, 10, 213–30.

GOLDTHORPE, J. H., LOCKWOOD, D. *et al.* (1968) *The Affluent Worker: Industrial Attitudes and Behaviour*, Cambridge University Press.

GOLDTHORPE, J. H., LOCKWOOD, D. *et al.* (1969) *The Affluent Worker in the Class Structure*, Cambridge University Press.

GORDON, T. (1955) *Group-Centred Leadership*, Houghton-Mifflin.

GOULDNER, A. W. (1954) *Patterns of Industrial Bureaucracy*, Routledge & Kegan Paul.

GOULDNER, A. W. (1955) *Wildcat Strike*, Routledge & Kegan Paul.

181

GOULDNER, A. W. (1959) 'Organisational Analysis', in R. K. Merton, L. Broom and L. S. Cottrell (eds), *Sociology Today*, Harper & Row, pp. 400–28.

GOULDNER, A. W. (1971) *The Coming Crisis of Western Sociology*, Heinemann.

GOVERNMENT SOCIAL SURVEY (1968) *Workshop Industrial Relations*, HMSO.

GROSS, N., MASON, W. and MCEACHERN, A. (1958) *Exploration in Role Analysis*, Wiley.

GRUSKY, O. (1958) 'Role Conflict in Organisations: A Study of Prison Camp Officials', *Admin. Sci. Qtrly*, 3, 452–72.

GRUSKY, O. (1961) 'Corporate Size, Bureaucratisation and Managerial Succession', *A.J.S.*, 67, 269–78.

GUEST, R. M. (1962) *Organisational Change*, Tavistock.

HAIRE, M. (1959) *Modern Organisation Theories*, Wiley.

HALL, R. H. (1963) 'Bureaucracy and Small Organisations', *Sociology and Social Research*, 48, 38–46.

HALL, R. H., HAAS, J. and JOHNSON, N. J. (1967) 'Organisational Size, Complexity and Formalisation', *A.S.R.*, 32, 903–12.

HALPERN, R. (1961) 'Employee Unionisation and Foremen's Attitudes', *Admin. Sci. Qtrly*, 6, 73–88.

HALPERN, R. and WINER, B. J. (1957) 'A Factorial Study of the Leader Behaviour Questionnaire', in R. M. Stogdill and A. E. Coons (eds), *Leader Behaviour: Its Description and Management*, Bureau of Business Research, Chicago State University, pp. 39–51.

HARVEY, E. (1965) 'Technology and the Structure of Organizations', *A.S.R.*, 33, 247–59.

HAWLEY, A., BOLAND, W. and BOLAND, M. (1965) 'Population Size and Administration in Institutions of Higher Education', *A.S.R.*, 30, 252–5.

HERZBERG, F. (1965) 'The Motivation to Work Among Finnish Supervisors, *Personnel Psych.*, 18, 393–402.

HERZBERG, F., MAUSNER, B. and SNYDERMAN, B. (1959) *The Motivation to Work*, Wiley and Sons.

HESSELING, P. (1966) *Strategy of Evaluative Research*, Van Goram.

HEWITT, D. and PARFIT, J. (1953) 'A Note on Working Morale and Size of Group', *Occup. Psych.*, 27, 38–42.

HININGS, C. R., PUGH, D. and HICKSON, D. (1967) 'An Approach to the Study of Bureaucracy', *Sociology*, 1, 61–72.

HOMANS, G. C. (1951) *The Human Group*, Routledge & Kegan Paul.

HUGHES, E. C. (1959) 'The Study of Occupations', in R. K. Merton, Broom and Cottrell (eds), *Sociology Today*, Harper & Row, pp. 442–60.

INDICK, B. R. (1963) 'Some Effects of Organisational Size on Member Attitudes and Behaviour', *Human Relations*, 16, 369–84.

INDICK, B. R. (1964) 'The Relationship between Organisation Size and Supervision Ratio', *Admin. Qtrly*, 9, 301–12.

INGHAM, G. (1970) *Size of Industrial Organisation and Worker Behaviour*, Cambridge University Press.

JACQUES, E. (1951) *The Changing Culture of a Factory*, Tavistock.

JANOWITZ, M. (1959) 'Changing Patterns of Organisational Authority: The Military Establishment', *Admin. Sci. Qtrly*, 3, 473–93.

JASINSKI, F. J. (1956) 'Foremen Relations outside the Work Group', *Personnel*, 33, 105–12.

KAHN, R. L. (1956) 'The Prediction of Productivity', *J. Soc. Issues*, 12, 41–9.

KAHN, R. L. (1958) 'Human Relations on the Shop Floor' in E. M. Hugh-Jones (ed.), *Human Relations and Modern Management*, North Holland Publishing Co., pp. 43–70.

KAHN, R. L., WOLFE, D. M. *et al.* (1964) *Organisational Stress: Studies in Role Conflict and Ambiguity*, Wiley.

KATZ, D. (1949) 'Morale and Motivation in Industry', in W. Dennis (ed.), *Current Trends in Industrial Psychology*, University of Pittsburgh, pp. 145–71.

KATZ, D. and KAHN, R. L. (1951) 'Human Organization and Worker Motivation', in L. R. Tripp (ed.), *Industrial Productivity*, Industrial Relations Research Association, Wisconsin, pp. 146–71.

KATZ, D. and KAHN, R. L. (1966) *The Social Psychology of Organisations*, Wiley.

KATZ, D., MACCOBY, N. and MORSE, N. C. (1950) *Productivity, Supervision and Morale in an Office Situation*, Institute for Social Research, University of Michigan.

KELLY, J. (1966) *Is Scientific Management Possible?*, Faber & Faber.

KEPHART, W. M. (1950) 'A Quantitative Analysis of Intragroup Relationships', *A.J.S.*, 55, 544–9.

KORMAN, W. (1966) 'Authoritarian Leadership and Individual Self-Esteem', *J. of Psych. Issues*, 31, 184–91.

KRECH, D. and CRUTCHFIELD, R. (1948) *Theory and Problems in Social Psychology*, McGraw-Hill.

LENNERLÖF, L. (1968) *Supervision: Situation, Individual, Behaviour, Effect*, Swedish Council for Personnel Administration.

LEWIN, K. (1951) 'Behaviour and Development as a Function of the Total Situation', in D. Cartwright (ed.), *Field Theory in Social Science*, Harper & Row.

LIKERT, R. (1958) 'Effective Supervision: An Adaptive and Relative Process', *Personnel Psych.*, 11, 317–52.

LIKERT, R. (1961) *New Patterns of Management*, McGraw-Hill.

LIPSET, R. and BENDIX, S. (1959) *Social Mobility in Industrial Society*, Free Press.

LOCKWOOD, D. (1958) *The Black-Coated Worker*, Allen & Unwin.

LUPTON, T. (1963) *On the Shop Floor*, Pergamon.

MCGREGOR, D. (1960) *The Human Side of Enterprise*, McGraw-Hill.

MCMURRAY, R. M. (1958) 'Recruitment, Dependency and Morale in the Banking Industry', *Admin. Sci. Qtrly*, 13, 87–117.

MANN, F. C. (1962) 'Psychological and Organisational Impacts', in J. Dunlop (ed.), *Automation and Technological Change*, Prentice-Hall, pp. 43–65.

MANN, F. C. (1964) 'Towards an Understanding of the Leadership Role in Formal Organisations', in R. Dubin, G. C. Homans, and G. A. Miller (eds), *Leadership and Productivity*, Chandler.

MANN, F. C. and HOFFMAN, R. (1960) *Automation and the Worker: A Study of Social Change in Power Plants*, University of New York.

MANN, P. H. (1965) *An Approach to Urban Sociology*, Routledge & Kegan Paul.

MANNHEIM, B. F., RIM, Y. and GRINBERG, G. (1967) 'Instrumental Status of Supervisors as Related to Workers' Perceptions and Expectations', *Human Relations*, **20**, 387–97.

MARCH, J. G. (1965) *Handbook of Organisations*, Rand McNally.

MARCH, J. G. and SIMON, H. A. (1958) *Organizations*, John Wiley & Sons.

MARQUIS, D. G. (1962) 'Individual Responsibility and Group Decisions Involving Risk', *Ind. Mgt Rev.*, **3**, 8–23.

MASLOW, A. H. (1943) 'A Theory of Human Motivation', *Psychological Review*, **50**, 370–96.

MASLOW, A. H. (1954) *Motivation and Personality*, Harper.

MAURER, J. G. (1969) 'The Downward-Mobile Industrial Supervisor', *Sociology and Social Research*, **53**, 311–21.

MAYNTZ, R. (1964) 'The Study of Organisations', *Current Sociology*, **13**, 94–119.

MEADE, J. P. and GRIEG, P. W. (1966) *Supervisory Training*, HMSO.

MEIGNIEZ, J. (1963) *Industrial Training*, Gower Press.

MERTON, R. K. (1957) 'The Role Set', *B.J.S.*, **8**, 108–20.

MERTON, R. K. (1958) *Social Theory and Social Structure*, Free Press.

MERTON, R. K. and GRAY, J. M. *et al.* (1952) *Reader in Bureaucracy*, Free Press.

MILLER, D. C. and FORM, W. H. (1951) *Industrial Sociology*, Harper.

MILLERSON, G. (1964) *The Qualifying Associations*, Routledge & Kegan Paul.

MILLS, C. W. (1951) *White Collar*, Oxford University Press.

MISUMI, J. and SHIRAKUSHI, S. (1966) 'An Experimental Study of the Effects of Supervisory Behaviour on Productivity and Morale in a Hierarchical Organisation', *Human Relations*, **19**, 297–307.

MORSE, N. and REIMER, E. (1956) 'The Experimental Change of a Major Organizational Variable', *J. Abnorm. Soc. Psychol.*, **52**, 120–9.

MOUZELIS, N. (1967) *Organisation and Bureaucracy*, Routledge & Kegan Paul.

NATIONAL INSTITUTE OF INDUSTRIAL PSYCHOLOGY (1951) *The Foreman*, Staples Press.

NATIONAL INSTITUTE OF INDUSTRIAL PSYCHOLOGY (1957) *The Place of the Foreman in Management*, Staples Press.

NEWCOMBER, J. (1955) *The Big Business Executive*, Columbia University Press.

NICHOLS, T. (1969) *Ownership, Control and Ideology*, Allen & Unwin.

OECD (1963) *Evaluation of Supervisory and Management Training Methods*, OECD Project 7/07/B.

PALMER, G. J. and MCCORMICK, M. J. (1961) 'A Factor Analysis of Job Activities', *J. of Applied Psych.*, **45**, 289–94.

PARKER, S. R., BROWN, R. K., CHILD, J. and SMITH, M. A. (1967) *The Sociology of Industry*, Allen & Unwin.

PARKINSON, C. N. (1957) *Parkinson's Law*, Penguin Books.

PARSONS, T. (1956) 'Suggestions for a Sociological Approach to the Theory of Organisations', *Admin. Sci. Qtrly*, **1**, 63–85 and 224–39.

PATCHEN, M. (1962) 'Supervisory Methods and Group Performance Methods', *Admin. Sci. Qtrly*, **7**, 275–94.

PATTEN, T. H. (1968) 'The Authority and Responsibility of Supervisors in a Multi-Plant Firm', *J.M.S.*, **5**, 61–82.

PELZ, D. C. (1951) 'Leadership within a Hierarchical Organisation', *J. of Social Issues*, **7**, 49–55.

PERROW, C. (1961) 'The Analysis of Goals in Complex Organisations', *A.S.R.*, **26**, 854–67.

PERROW, C. (1970) *Organisational Analysis*, Tavistock Publications.

PFIFFNER, J. M. and FELS, M. (1964) *The Supervision of Personnel*, Prentice-Hall.

PIERSOL, D. T. (1956) 'Communication Practices of Supervisors in a Mid-Western Corporation', *Advanced Mgt*, **23**, 20–1.

PONDER, Q. D. (1958) *The Effective Manufacturing Foreman*, Industrial Relations Research Association, pp. 41–54.

PUGH, D., HICKSON, D., HININGS, C. R. *et al.* (1963) 'A Conceptual Scheme for Organisational Analysis', *Admin. Sci. Qtrly*, **8**, 289–315.

PUGH, D., HICKSON, D. and HININGS, C. R. (1968) 'Dimensions of Organization Structure', *Admin. Sci. Qtrly*, **13**, 65–105.

PUGH, D., HICKSON, D. and INKSON, J. (1970) 'Organization Structure and Context: an abbreviated replication', *Admin. Sci. Qtrly*, **15**, 318–329.

RAVEN, B. H. and FRENCH, J. R. P. (1958) 'Group Support, Legitimate Power and Social Influence', *J. of Personnel*, **26**, 400–9.

READ, R. H. (1962) 'Upward Communication in Industrial Hierarchies', *Human Relations*, **15**, 3–15.

REVANS, R. W. (1958) 'Human Relations, Management, and Size', in E. M. Hughes (ed.), *Human Relations, and Modern Management*, Amsterdam, pp. 177–220.

REVANS, R. W. (1959) *Size and Morale in the Mining Industry*, Action Research Trust.

RIM, Y. (1965) 'Leadership Attitudes and Decisions Involving Risks', *Personnel Psych.*, **18**, 423–30.

ROETHLISBERGER, F. J. (1951) 'The Foreman: Man in the Middle' in R. Dubin (ed.), *Human Relations in Administration*, Prentice-Hall, pp. 147–8.

ROETHLISBERGER, F. J. and DICKSON, W. J. (1939) *Management and the Worker*, Harvard University Press.

ROETHLISBERGER, F. J. and DICKSON, W. J. (1945) 'The Foreman: Master and Victim of Double Talk', *Harvard Business Review*, **23**, 283–98.

ROSEN, W. (1968) *The Principles and Practice of Supervision*, Pergamon.

ROSS, I. C. (1957) 'Role Specialisation in Supervision', in W. M. Evan (ed.), *Organisational Experiments* (1971), Harper & Row, pp. 221–6.

ROSSEL, R. D. (1970) 'Instrumental and Expressive Leadership in Complex Organisations', *Admin. Sci. Qtrly*, **15**, 306–17.

SADLER, P. J. (1966) *Leadership Style, Confidence in Management and Job Satisfaction*, Ashridge Management College.

SALZ, A. (1933) 'Occupations', in E. R. A. Seligman (ed.), *Encyclopedia of the Social Sciences*, vol. II, Macmillan, pp. 424–35.

SAYLES, L. R. (1958) *Behaviour of Industrial Work Groups*, Wiley.

SCHNEIDER, E. V. (1957) *Industrial Sociology*, McGraw-Hill.

SCHWARTZ, M. (1964) 'The Reciprocities Multiplier: An Empirical Investigation', *Admin. Sci. Qtrly*, **9**, 264–77.

SCOTT, W. H. and MCGIVERING, I. (1953) 'Some Impressions of Human Relations Training for Supervisors', *Occup. Psych.*, **27**, 137–51.

SEEMAN, M. (1953) 'Role Conflict and Ambivalence in Leadership', *A.S.R.*, **18**, 273–80.

SELLTIZ, C. (1959) *Research Methods in Social Relations*, Methuen.

SELZNICK, P. (1948) 'Foundations for the Theory of Organisations', *A.S.R.*, **13**, 25–35.

SELZNICK, P. (1957) *Leadership in Administration*, Row & Peterson.

SHIBUTANI, T. (1962) 'Reference Groups and Social Control', in A. M. Rose (ed.), *Human Behaviour and Social Processes*, Routledge & Kegan Paul.

SILVERMAN, D. (1968) 'Formal Organisations or Industrial Sociology?', *Sociology*, **2**, 221–38.

SILVERMAN, D. (1970) *The Theory of Organisations*, Heinemann.

SIMMONS, R. G. (1967) 'The Role Conflict of the First-Line Supervisor', *A.J.S.*, **73**, 482–95.

SIMPSON, R. L. (1959) 'Vertical and Horizontal Communication in Formal Organisations', *Admin. Sci. Qtrly*, **4**, 188–96.

SMITH, G. G. and TANNENBAUM, A. (1963) 'Organisational Control Structure', *Human Relations*, 15, 227–43.

SOROKIN, P. (1928) *Contemporary Sociological Theories*, Harper & Sons.

STINCHCOMBE, A. L. (1959) 'Bureaucratic and Craft Administration of Production', *Admin. Sci. Qtrly*, **14**, 168–87.

STOGDILL, R. (1948) 'Personal Factors Associated with Leadership', *J. of Psych.*, **25**, 35–71.

STONER, J. A. F. (1961) 'Comparison of Individual and Group Decisions Involving Risk', *School of Industrial Management*, M.I.T.

STRAUSS, G. (1954) 'The Set-Up Man: A Case Study of Organisational Change', *Hum. Org.*, **13**, 17–25.

STRAUSS, G. (1957) 'The Changing Role of the Working Supervisor', *J. of Business*, **30**, 202–11.

STRAUSS, G. (1963) 'Some Notes on Power-Equalisation', in H. J. Leavitt (ed.), *The Social Science of Organisations*, Prentice-Hall.

STURMTHAL, A. (1966) *White Collar Trade Unions*, University of Illinois Press.

SYKES, A. J. (1962) 'The Effects of a Supervisory Training Course in Changing Supervisor's Perceptions and Expectations of the Role of Management', *Human Relations*, **15**, 227–43.

TANNENBAUM, A. (1962) 'Control in Organisations: Individual Adjustment and Organisational Performance', *Admin. Sci. Qtrly*, **7**, 236–57.

TANNENBAUM, A. (1966) *Social Psychology of the Work Organisation*, Tavistock.

TANNENBAUM, A. and SEASHORE, S. (1964) 'Some Changing Conceptions and Approaches to the Study of Persons in Organizations', *XV International Congress of Applied Psychology*, Ljubljana, Yugoslavia.

TAYLOR, J. (1965) *Occupational Sociology*, Oxford University Press.

TERRIEN, F. W. and MILLS, D. L. (1955) 'The Effect of Changing Size upon the Internal Structure of Organisations', *A.S.R.*, **20**, 11–13.

THELEN, H. A. (1956) 'Emotionality and Work in Groups' in L. D. White (ed.), *The State of Social Sciences*, Chicago University Press, pp. 184–186.

THOMAS, E. J. (1959) 'Role Conceptions and Organizational Size', *A.S.R.*, **24**, 30–7.

THOMASON, G. F. (1970) *The Management of Research and Development*, Batsford.

THOMPSON, J. D. (1967) *Organisations in Action*, McGraw-Hill.

THOMPSON, J. D. and MCEWAN, W. J. (1958) 'Organisational Goals and Environment', *A.S.R.*, **23**, 23–31.

THURLEY, K. E. (1964) 'A New Deal for Foremen?—Supervision, Technology and Organisational Effectiveness', in *Human Factors and Productivity*, Association of British Chemical Manufacturers and Association of Chemical and Allied Employers, pp. 49–66.

THURLEY, K. E. and HAMBLIN, A. C. (1963) *The Supervisor and His Job*, HMSO.

TIFFIN, J. and MCCORMICK, E. J. (1966) *Industrial Psychology*, Allen & Unwin.

TOURAINE, A. (1955) *L'evolution du travail ouvrier aux usines renault*, Centre National de la Recherche Scientifique.

TOURAINE, A. (1965) *Workers' Attitudes to Technical Change*, OECD.

TRIST, E. L., HIGGIN, C. W., MURRAY, H., POLLOCK, A. B., (1963) *Organisational Choice*, Tavistock.

TSOUDEROS, J. E. (1955) 'Organisational Change in Terms of a Series of Selected Variables', *A.S.R.*, **20**, 206–10.

TUNSTALL, J. (1962) *The Fishermen*, MacGibbon & Kee.

ULRICH, D. N. (1950) *Management Behaviour and Foreman Attitude*, Harvard Business School, Division of Research.

VAN DOORN, J. A. (1963) 'Sociology and the Problem of Power', *Sociologica Nederlandica*, **1**, 3–47.

VESTA, F. J. DI (1954) 'Instructor-Centred and Student-Centred Approaches to Teaching a Human Relations Course', *J. of Applied Psych.*, **38**, 329–35.

VON BERTALANFFY, L. (1956) 'The Theory of Open Systems in Physics and Biology', *Science*, **111**, 23–9.

VROOM, V. H. (1959) 'Some Personality Determinants of the Effects of Participation, *J. of Abnorm. & Soc. Psych.*, **59**, 322–7.

VROOM, V. H. (1964) *Work and Motivation*, Wiley.

VROOM, V. H. and DECCI, E. L. (1970) *Management and Motivation*, Penguin.

WALKER, C. R. and GUEST, R. H. (1952) *The Man on the Assembly Line*, Harvard University Press.

WALKER, C. R., GUEST, R. H. and TURNER, A. N. (1956) *The Foreman on the Assembly Line*, Harvard University Press.

WARD, T. and MUMFORD, E. (1965) 'How the Computer Changes Management', *New Society*, **6**, No. 156, 6–9.

WARR, P. B. and BIRD, M. (1967) 'Assessing the Training Needs of Foremen', *J.M.S.*, **4**, 332–53.

WEBER, M. (1947) *The Theory of Social and Economic Organisation*, Free Press.

WEISS, R. (1956) *Processes of Organisation*, University of Michigan Press.

WESTERLUND, G. and STROMBERG, D. (1965) 'Measurement and Appraisal of the Performance of Foremen', *B.J.I.R.*, 3, 345–62.

WHYTE, W. F. (1944) 'Incentives for Productivity: The Bundy Tubing Case', *Applied Anthropology*, 5, 1–16.

WILENSKY, H. (1964) 'The Professionalization of Everyone', *A.J.S.*, 70, pp. 137–58.

WOODWARD, J. (1958) *Management and Technology*, HMSO.

WOODWARD, J. (1965) *Industrial Organisation*, Oxford University Press.

WRAY, D. E. (1949) 'Marginal Men of Industry: The Foreman', *A.J.S.*, 54, 298–301.

YUILL, B. (1968) *Supervision: Principles and Techniques*, Allen & Unwin.

ZALEZNICK, A. (1966) *Human Dilemmas of Leadership*, Harper & Row.

ZELDITCH, M. and HOPKINS, T. K. (1961) 'Laboratory Experiments with Organisations', in A. Etzioni (ed.), *Complex Organisations*, Holt, Rinehart & Winston.

ZINCK, C. (1958) 'The Foreman and Productivity', *Advanced Management*, 23, pp. 12–16.

ZWEIG, F. (1957) 'Two Profiles: The Shop Steward and the Foreman', *Occup. Psych.*, 31, 47–54.

Index

Routledge Social Science Series

Routledge & Kegan Paul   London and Boston

68–74 Carter Lane   London EC4V 5EL
9 Park Street   Boston   Mass 02108

Contents

*Authors wishing to submit manuscripts for any series in
this catalogue should send them to the Social Science Editor,
Routledge & Kegan Paul Ltd, 68–74 Carter Lane,
London EC4V 5EL*

●*Books so marked are available in paperback*
All books are in Metric Demy 8vo format (216 × 138mm approx.)

International Library of Sociology

General Editor John Rex

GENERAL SOCIOLOGY

Barnsley, J. H. The Social Reality of Ethics. *464 pp.*
Belshaw, Cyril. The Conditions of Social Performance. *An Exploratory Theory. 144 pp.*
Brown, Robert. Explanation in Social Science. *208 pp.*
● Rules and Laws in Sociology. *192 pp.*
Bruford, W. H. Chekhov and His Russia. *A Sociological Study. 244 pp.*
Cain, Maureen E. Society and the Policeman's Role. *326 pp.*
Gibson, Quentin. The Logic of Social Enquiry. *240 pp.*
Glucksmann, M. Structuralist Analysis in Contemporary Social Thought. *212 pp.*
Gurvitch, Georges. Sociology of Law. *Preface by Roscoe Pound. 264 pp.*
Hodge, H. A. Wilhelm Dilthey. *An Introduction. 184 pp.*
Homans, George C. Sentiments and Activities. *336 pp.*
Johnson, Harry M. Sociology: *a Systematic Introduction. Foreword by Robert K. Merton. 710 pp.*
Mannheim, Karl. Essays on Sociology and Social Psychology. *Edited by Paul Kecskemeti. With Editorial Note by Adolph Lowe. 344 pp.*
Systematic Sociology: *An Introduction to the Study of Society. Edited by J. S. Erös and Professor W. A. C. Stewart. 220 pp.*
Martindale, Don. The Nature and Types of Sociological Theory. *292 pp.*
●**Maus, Heinz.** A Short History of Sociology. *234 pp.*
Mey, Harald. Field-Theory. *A Study of its Application in the Social Sciences. 352 pp.*
Myrdal, Gunnar. Value in Social Theory: *A Collection of Essays on Methodology. Edited by Paul Streeten. 332 pp.*
Ogburn, William F., and **Nimkoff, Meyer F.** A Handbook of Sociology. *Preface by Karl Mannheim. 656 pp. 46 figures. 35 tables.*
Parsons, Talcott, and **Smelser, Neil J.** Economy and Society: *A Study in the Integration of Economic and Social Theory. 362 pp.*
●**Rex, John.** Key Problems of Sociological Theory. *220 pp.*
Discovering Sociology. *278 pp.*
Sociology and the Demystification of the Modern World. *282 pp.*
●**Rex, John** (Ed.) Approaches to Sociology. *Contributions by Peter Abell, Frank Bechhofer, Basil Bernstein, Ronald Fletcher, David Frisby, Miriam Glucksmann, Peter Lassman, Herminio Martins, John Rex, Roland Robertson, John Westergaard and Jock Young. 302 pp.*
Rigby, A. Alternative Realities. *352 pp.*
Roche, M. Phenomenology, Language and the Social Sciences. *374 pp.*
Sahay, A. Sociological Analysis. *220 pp.*
Urry, John. Reference Groups and the Theory of Revolution. *244 pp.*
Weinberg, E. Development of Sociology in the Soviet Union. *173 pp.*

FOREIGN CLASSICS OF SOCIOLOGY

●**Durkheim, Emile.** Suicide. *A Study in Sociology. Edited and with an Introduction by George Simpson. 404 pp.*
Professional Ethics and Civic Morals. *Translated by Cornelia Brookfield. 288 pp.*

●**Gerth, H. H.,** and **Mills, C. Wright.** From Max Weber: *Essays in Sociology. 502 pp.*

●**Tönnies, Ferdinand.** Community and Association. (*Gemeinschaft und Gesellschaft.) Translated and Supplemented by Charles P. Loomis. Foreword by Pitirim A. Sorokin. 334 pp.*

SOCIAL STRUCTURE

Andreski, Stanislav. Military Organization and Society. *Foreword by Professor A. R. Radcliffe-Brown. 226 pp. 1 folder.*

Coontz, Sydney H. Population Theories and the Economic Interpretation. *202 pp.*

Coser, Lewis. The Functions of Social Conflict. *204 pp.*

Dickie-Clark, H. F. Marginal Situation: *A Sociological Study of a Coloured Group. 240 pp. 11 tables.*

Glaser, Barney, and **Strauss, Anselm L.** Status Passage. *A Formal Theory. 208 pp.*

Glass, D. V. (Ed.) Social Mobility in Britain. *Contributions by J. Berent, T. Bottomore, R. C. Chambers, J. Floud, D. V. Glass, J. R. Hall, H. T. Himmelweit, R. K. Kelsall, F. M. Martin, C. A. Moser, R. Mukherjee, and W. Ziegel. 420 pp.*

Jones, Garth N. Planned Organizational Change: *An Exploratory Study Using an Empirical Approach. 268 pp.*

Kelsall, R. K. Higher Civil Servants in Britain: *From 1870 to the Present Day. 268 pp. 31 tables.*

König, René. The Community. *232 pp. Illustrated.*

●**Lawton, Denis.** Social Class, Language and Education. *192 pp.*

McLeish, John. The Theory of Social Change: *Four Views Considered. 128 pp.*

Marsh, David C. The Changing Social Structure of England and Wales, 1871-1961. *288 pp.*

Mouzelis, Nicos. Organization and Bureaucracy. *An Analysis of Modern Theories. 240 pp.*

Mulkay, M. J. Functionalism, Exchange and Theoretical Strategy. *272 pp.*

Ossowski, Stanislaw. Class Structure in the Social Consciousness. *210 pp.*

Podgórecki, Adam. Law and Society. *About 300 pp.*

SOCIOLOGY AND POLITICS

Acton, T. A. Gypsy Politics and Social Change. *316 pp.*

Hechter, Michael. Internal Colonialism. *The Celtic Fringe in British National Development, 1536–1966. About 350 pp.*

Hertz, Frederick. Nationality in History and Politics: *A Psychology and Sociology of National Sentiment and Nationalism. 432 pp.*

Kornhauser, William. The Politics of Mass Society. *272 pp. 20 tables.*

Laidler, Harry W. History of Socialism. *Social-Economic Movements: An Historical and Comparative Survey of Socialism, Communism, Cooperation, Utopianism; and other Systems of Reform and Reconstruction. 992 pp.*

Lasswell, H. D. Analysis of Political Behaviour. *324 pp.*

Mannheim, Karl. Freedom, Power and Democratic Planning. *Edited by Hans Gerth and Ernest K. Bramstedt. 424 pp.*

Mansur, Fatma. Process of Independence. *Foreword by A. H. Hanson. 208 pp.*

Martin, David A. Pacifism: *an Historical and Sociological Study. 262 pp.*

Myrdal, Gunnar. The Political Element in the Development of Economic Theory. *Translated from the German by Paul Streeten. 282 pp.*

Wootton, Graham. Workers, Unions and the State. *188 pp.*

FOREIGN AFFAIRS: THEIR SOCIAL, POLITICAL AND ECONOMIC FOUNDATIONS

Mayer, J. P. Political Thought in France from the Revolution to the Fifth Republic. *164 pp.*

CRIMINOLOGY

Ancel, Marc. Social Defence: *A Modern Approach to Criminal Problems. Foreword by Leon Radzinowicz. 240 pp.*

Cain, Maureen E. Society and the Policeman's Role. *326 pp.*

Cloward, Richard A., and **Ohlin, Lloyd E.** Delinquency and Opportunity: *A Theory of Delinquent Gangs. 248 pp.*

Downes, David M. The Delinquent Solution. *A Study in Subcultural Theory. 296 pp.*

Dunlop, A. B., and **McCabe, S.** Young Men in Detention Centres. *192 pp.*

Friedlander, Kate. The Psycho-Analytical Approach to Juvenile Delinquency: *Theory, Case Studies, Treatment. 320 pp.*

Glueck, Sheldon, and **Eleanor.** Family Environment and Delinquency. *With the statistical assistance of Rose W. Kneznek. 340 pp.*

Lopez-Rey, Manuel. Crime. *An Analytical Appraisal. 288 pp.*

Mannheim, Hermann. Comparative Criminology: *a Text Book. Two volumes. 442 pp. and 380 pp.*

Morris, Terence. The Criminal Area: *A Study in Social Ecology. Foreword by Hermann Mannheim. 232 pp. 25 tables. 4 maps.*

Rock, Paul. Making People Pay. *338 pp.*

●**Taylor, Ian, Walton, Paul,** and **Young, Jock.** The New Criminology. *For a Social Theory of Deviance. 325 pp.*

SOCIAL PSYCHOLOGY

Bagley, Christopher. The Social Psychology of the Epileptic Child. *320 pp.*

Barbu, Zevedei. Problems of Historical Psychology. *248 pp.*

Blackburn, Julian. Psychology and the Social Pattern. *184 pp.*

●**Brittan, Arthur.** Meanings and Situations. *224 pp.*

Carroll, J. Break-Out from the Crystal Palace. *200 pp.*

●**Fleming, C. M.** Adolescence: Its Social Psychology. *With an Introduction to recent findings from the fields of Anthropology, Physiology, Medicine, Psychometrics and Sociometry. 288 pp.*

● The Social Psychology of Education: *An Introduction and Guide to Its Study. 136 pp.*

Homans, George C. The Human Group. *Foreword by Bernard DeVoto. Introduction by Robert K. Merton. 526 pp.*

● Social Behaviour: *its Elementary Forms. 416 pp.*

●**Klein, Josephine.** The Study of Groups. *226 pp. 31 figures. 5 tables.*

Linton, Ralph. The Cultural Background of Personality. *132 pp.*

●**Mayo, Elton.** The Social Problems of an Industrial Civilization. *With an appendix on the Political Problem. 180 pp.*

Ottaway, A. K. C. Learning Through Group Experience. *176 pp.*

Ridder, J. C. de. The Personality of the Urban African in South Africa. *A Thematic Apperception Test Study. 196 pp. 12 plates.*

●**Rose, Arnold M.** (Ed.) Human Behaviour and Social Processes: *an Interactionist Approach. Contributions by Arnold M. Rose, Ralph H. Turner, Anselm Strauss, Everett C. Hughes, E. Franklin Frazier, Howard S. Becker, et al. 696 pp.*

Smelser, Neil J. Theory of Collective Behaviour. *448 pp.*

Stephenson, Geoffrey M. The Development of Conscience. *128 pp.*

Young, Kimball. Handbook of Social Psychology. *658 pp. 16 figures. 10 tables.*

SOCIOLOGY OF THE FAMILY

Banks, J. A. Prosperity and Parenthood: *A Study of Family Planning among The Victorian Middle Classes. 262 pp.*

Bell, Colin R. Middle Class Families: *Social and Geographical Mobility. 224 pp.*

Burton, Lindy. Vulnerable Children. *272 pp.*

Gavron, Hannah. The Captive Wife: *Conflicts of Household Mothers. 190 pp.*

George, Victor, and **Wilding, Paul.** Motherless Families. *220 pp.*

Klein, Josephine. Samples from English Cultures.

   1. Three Preliminary Studies and Aspects of Adult Life in England. *447 pp.*

   2. Child-Rearing Practices and Index. *247 pp.*

Klein, Viola. Britain's Married Women Workers. *180 pp.*

   The Feminine Character. *History of an Ideology. 244 pp.*

McWhinnie, Alexina M. Adopted Children. *How They Grow Up. 304 pp.*

● **Myrdal, Alva,** and **Klein, Viola.** Women's Two Roles: *Home and Work. 238 pp. 27 tables.*

Parsons, Talcott, and **Bales, Robert F.** Family: Socialization and Interaction Process. *In collaboration with James Olds, Morris Zelditch and Philip E. Slater. 456 pp. 50 figures and tables.*

SOCIAL SERVICES

Bastide, Roger. The Sociology of Mental Disorder. *Translated from the French by Jean McNeil. 260 pp.*

Carlebach, Julius. Caring For Children in Trouble. *266 pp.*

Forder, R. A. (Ed.) Penelope Hall's Social Services of England and Wales. *352 pp.*

George, Victor. Foster Care. *Theory and Practice. 234 pp.*
Social Security: *Beveridge and After. 258 pp.*

George, V., and **Wilding, P.** Motherless Families. *248 pp.*

● **Goetschius, George W.** Working with Community Groups. *256 pp.*

Goetschius, George W., and **Tash, Joan.** Working with Unattached Youth. *416 pp.*

Hall, M. P., and **Howes, I. V.** The Church in Social Work. *A Study of Moral Welfare Work undertaken by the Church of England. 320 pp.*

Heywood, Jean S. Children in Care: *the Development of the Service for the Deprived Child. 264 pp.*

Hoenig, J., and **Hamilton, Marian W.** The De-Segregation of the Mentally Ill. *284 pp.*

Jones, Kathleen. Mental Health and Social Policy, 1845-1959. *264 pp.*

King, Roy D., Raynes, Norma V., and **Tizard, Jack.** Patterns of Residential Care. *356 pp.*

Leigh, John. Young People and Leisure. *256 pp.*

Morris, Mary. Voluntary Work and the Welfare State. *300 pp.*

Morris, Pauline. Put Away: *A Sociological Study of Institutions for the Mentally Retarded. 364 pp.*

Nokes, P. L. The Professional Task in Welfare Practice. *152 pp.*

Timms, Noel. Psychiatric Social Work in Great Britain (1939-1962). *280 pp.*

● Social Casework: *Principles and Practice. 256 pp.*

Young, A. F. Social Services in British Industry. *272 pp.*

Young, A. F., and **Ashton, E. T.** British Social Work in the Nineteenth Century. *288 pp.*

SOCIOLOGY OF EDUCATION

Banks, Olive. Parity and Prestige in English Secondary Education: a Study in Educational Sociology. *272 pp.*

Bentwich, Joseph. Education in Israel. *224 pp. 8 pp. plates.*

● **Blyth, W. A. L.** English Primary Education. *A Sociological Description.*
1. Schools. *232 pp.*
2. Background. *168 pp.*

Collier, K. G. The Social Purposes of Education: *Personal and Social Values in Education. 268 pp.*

Dale, R. R., and **Griffith, S.** Down Stream: *Failure in the Grammar School. 108 pp.*

Dore, R. P. Education in Tokugawa Japan. *356 pp. 9 pp. plates.*

Evans, K. M. Sociometry and Education. *158 pp.*

●**Ford, Julienne.** Social Class and the Comprehensive School. *192 pp.*

Foster, P. J. Education and Social Change in Ghana. *336 pp. 3 maps.*

Fraser, W. R. Education and Society in Modern France. *150 pp.*

Grace, Gerald R. Role Conflict and the Teacher. *About 200 pp.*

Hans, Nicholas. New Trends in Education in the Eighteenth Century. *278 pp. 19 tables.*

● Comparative Education: *A Study of Educational Factors and Traditions. 360 pp.*

Hargreaves, David. Interpersonal Relations and Education. *432 pp.*

● Social Relations in a Secondary School. *240 pp.*

Holmes, Brian. Problems in Education. *A Comparative Approach. 336 pp.*

King, Ronald. Values and Involvement in a Grammar School. *164 pp.*

School Organization and Pupil Involvement. *A Study of Secondary Schools.*

●**Mannheim, Karl,** and **Stewart, W. A. C.** An Introduction to the Sociology of Education. *206 pp.*

Morris, Raymond N. The Sixth Form and College Entrance. *231 pp.*

●**Musgrove, F.** Youth and the Social Order. *176 pp.*

●**Ottaway, A. K. C.** Education and Society: An Introduction to the Sociology of Education. *With an Introduction by W. O. Lester Smith. 212 pp.*

Peers, Robert. Adult Education: *A Comparative Study. 398 pp.*

Pritchard, D. G. Education and the Handicapped: *1760 to 1960. 258 pp.*

Richardson, Helen. Adolescent Girls in Approved Schools. *308 pp.*

Stratta, Erica. The Education of Borstal Boys. *A Study of their Educational Experiences prior to, and during, Borstal Training. 256 pp.*

Taylor, P. H., Reid, W. A., and **Holley, B. J.** The English Sixth Form. *A Case Study in Curriculum Research. 200 pp.*

SOCIOLOGY OF CULTURE

Eppel, E. M., and **M.** Adolescents and Morality: *A Study of some Moral Values and Dilemmas of Working Adolescents in the Context of a changing Climate of Opinion. Foreword by W. J. H. Sprott. 268 pp. 39 tables.*

●**Fromm, Erich.** The Fear of Freedom. *286 pp.*

● The Sane Society. *400 pp.*

Mannheim, Karl. Essays on the Sociology of Culture. *Edited by Ernst Mannheim in co-operation with Paul Kecskemeti. Editorial Note by Adolph Lowe. 280 pp.*

Weber, Alfred. Farewell to European History: *or The Conquest of Nihilism. Translated from the German by R. F. C. Hull. 224 pp.*

SOCIOLOGY OF RELIGION

Argyle, Michael and **Beit-Hallahmi, Benjamin.** The Social Psychology of Religion. *About 256 pp.*

Nelson, G. K. Spiritualism and Society. *313 pp.*

Stark, Werner. The Sociology of Religion. *A Study of Christendom.*
Volume I. *Established Religion. 248 pp.*
Volume II. *Sectarian Religion. 368 pp.*
Volume III. *The Universal Church. 464 pp.*
Volume IV. *Types of Religious Man. 352 pp.*
Volume V. *Types of Religious Culture. 464 pp.*

Turner, B. S. Weber and Islam. *216 pp.*

Watt, W. Montgomery. Islam and the Integration of Society. *320 pp.*

SOCIOLOGY OF ART AND LITERATURE

Jarvie, Ian C. Towards a Sociology of the Cinema. *A Comparative Essay on the Structure and Functioning of a Major Entertainment Industry. 405 pp.*

Rust, Frances S. Dance in Society. *An Analysis of the Relationships between the Social Dance and Society in England from the Middle Ages to the Present Day. 256 pp. 8 pp. of plates.*

Schücking, L. L. The Sociology of Literary Taste. *112 pp.*

Wolff, Janet. Hermeneutic Philosophy and the Sociology of Art. *About 200 pp.*

SOCIOLOGY OF KNOWLEDGE

Diesing, P. Patterns of Discovery in the Social Sciences. *262 pp.*

●**Douglas, J. D.** (Ed.) Understanding Everyday Life. *370 pp.*

●**Hamilton, P.** Knowledge and Social Structure. *174 pp.*

Jarvie, I. C. Concepts and Society. *232 pp.*

Mannheim, Karl. Essays on the Sociology of Knowledge. *Edited by Paul Kecskemeti. Editorial Note by Adolph Lowe. 353 pp.*

Remmling, Gunter W. (Ed.) Towards the Sociology of Knowledge. *Origin and Development of a Sociological Thought Style. 463 pp.*

Stark, Werner. The Sociology of Knowledge: *An Essay in Aid of a Deeper Understanding of the History of Ideas. 384 pp.*

URBAN SOCIOLOGY

Ashworth, William. The Genesis of Modern British Town Planning: *A Study in Economic and Social History of the Nineteenth and Twentieth Centuries. 288 pp.*

Cullingworth, J. B. Housing Needs and Planning Policy: *A Restatement of the Problems of Housing Need and 'Overspill' in England and Wales. 232 pp. 44 tables. 8 maps.*

Dickinson, Robert E. City and Region: *A Geographical Interpretation* *608 pp. 125 figures.*

The West European City: *A Geographical Interpretation. 600 pp. 129 maps. 29 plates.*

● The City Region in Western Europe. *320 pp. Maps.*

Humphreys, Alexander J. New Dubliners: *Urbanization and the Irish Family. Foreword by George C. Homans. 304 pp.*

Jackson, Brian. Working Class Community: *Some General Notions raised by a Series of Studies in Northern England. 192 pp.*

Jennings, Hilda. Societies in the Making: *a Study of Development and Re-development within a County Borough. Foreword by D. A. Clark. 286 pp.*

●**Mann, P. H.** An Approach to Urban Sociology. *240 pp.*

Morris, R. N., and **Mogey, J.** The Sociology of Housing. *Studies at Berinsfield. 232 pp. 4 pp. plates.*

Rosser, C., and **Harris, C.** The Family and Social Change. *A Study of Family and Kinship in a South Wales Town. 352 pp. 8 maps.*

RURAL SOCIOLOGY

Chambers, R. J. H. Settlement Schemes in Tropical Africa: *A Selective Study. 268 pp.*

Haswell, M. R. The Economics of Development in Village India. *120 pp.*

Littlejohn, James. Westrigg: *the Sociology of a Cheviot Parish. 172 pp. 5 figures.*

Mayer, Adrian C. Peasants in the Pacific. *A Study of Fiji Indian Rural Society. 248 pp. 20 plates.*

Williams, W. M. The Sociology of an English Village: *Gosforth. 272 pp. 12 figures. 13 tables.*

SOCIOLOGY OF INDUSTRY AND DISTRIBUTION

Anderson, Nels. Work and Leisure. *280 pp.*

●**Blau, Peter M.,** and **Scott, W. Richard.** Formal Organizations: *a Comparative approach. Introduction and Additional Bibliography by J. H. Smith. 326 pp.*

Eldridge, J. E. T. Industrial Disputes. *Essays in the Sociology of Industrial Relations. 288 pp.*

Hetzler, Stanley. Applied Measures for Promoting Technological Growth. *352 pp.*

Technological Growth and Social Change. *Achieving Modernization. 269 pp.*

Hollowell, Peter G. The Lorry Driver. *272 pp.*

Jefferys, Margot, *with the assistance of Winifred Moss.* Mobility in the Labour Market: *Employment Changes in Battersea and Dagenham. Preface by Barbara Wootton. 186 pp. 51 tables.*

Millerson, Geoffrey. The Qualifying Associations: *a Study in Professionalization. 320 pp.*

Smelser, Neil J. Social Change in the Industrial Revolution: *An Application of Theory to the Lancashire Cotton Industry, 1770-1840. 468 pp. 12 figures. 14 tables.*

Williams, Gertrude. Recruitment to Skilled Trades. *240 pp.*

Young, A. F. Industrial Injuries Insurance: *an Examination of British Policy. 192 pp.*

DOCUMENTARY

Schlesinger, Rudolf (Ed.) Changing Attitudes in Soviet Russia.
2. The Nationalities Problem and Soviet Administration. *Selected Readings on the Development of Soviet Nationalities Policies. Introduced by the editor. Translated by W. W. Gottlieb. 324 pp.*

ANTHROPOLOGY

Ammar, Hamed. Growing up in an Egyptian Village: *Silwa, Province of Aswan. 336 pp.*

Brandel-Syrier, Mia. Reeftown Elite. *A Study of Social Mobility in a Modern African Community on the Reef. 376 pp.*

Crook, David, and **Isabel.** Revolution in a Chinese Village: *Ten Mile Inn. 230 pp. 8 plates. 1 map.*

Dickie-Clark, H. F. The Marginal Situation. *A Sociological Study of a Coloured Group. 236 pp.*

Dube, S. C. Indian Village. *Foreword by Morris Edward Opler. 276 pp. 4 plates.*

India's Changing Villages: *Human Factors in Community Development. 260 pp. 8 plates. 1 map.*

Firth, Raymond. Malay Fishermen. *Their Peasant Economy. 420 pp. 17 pp. plates.*

Firth, R., Hubert, J., and **Forge, A.** Families and their Relatives. *Kinship in a Middle-Class Sector of London: An Anthropological Study. 456 pp.*

Gulliver, P. H. Social Control in an African Society: a Study of the Arusha, Agricultural Masai of Northern Tanganyika. *320 pp. 8 plates. 10 figures.*

Family Herds. *288 pp.*

Ishwaran, K. Shivapur. *A South Indian Village. 216 pp.*

Tradition and Economy in Village India: *An Interactionist Approach. Foreword by Conrad Arensburg. 176 pp.*

Jarvie, Ian C. The Revolution in Anthropology. *268 pp.*

Jarvie, Ian C., and **Agassi, Joseph.** Hong Kong. *A Society in Transition. 396 pp. Illustrated with plates and maps.*

Little, Kenneth L. Mende of Sierra Leone. *308 pp. and folder.*

Negroes in Britain. *With a New Introduction and Contemporary Study by Leonard Bloom. 320 pp.*

Lowie, Robert H. Social Organization. *494 pp.*
Mayer, Adrian, C. Caste and Kinship in Central India: *A Village and its Region. 328 pp. 16 plates. 15 figures. 16 tables.*
Peasants in the Pacific. *A Study of Fiji Indian Rural Society. 248 pp.*
Smith, Raymond T. The Negro Family in British Guiana: *Family Structure and Social Status in the Villages. With a Foreword by Meyer Fortes. 314 pp. 8 plates. 1 figure. 4 maps.*

SOCIOLOGY AND PHILOSOPHY

Barnsley, John H. The Social Reality of Ethics. *A Comparative Analysis of Moral Codes. 448 pp.*
Diesing, Paul. Patterns of Discovery in the Social Sciences. *362 pp.*
●**Douglas, Jack D.** (Ed.) Understanding Everyday Life. *Toward the Reconstruction of Sociological Knowledge. Contributions by Alan F. Blum. Aaron W. Cicourel, Norman K. Denzin, Jack D. Douglas, John Heeren, Peter McHugh, Peter K. Manning, Melvin Power, Matthew Speier, Roy Turner, D. Lawrence Wieder, Thomas P. Wilson and Don H. Zimmerman. 370 pp.*
Jarvie, Ian C. Concepts and Society. *216 pp.*
Pelz, Werner. The Scope of Understanding in Sociology. *Towards a more radical reorientation in the social humanistic sciences. 283 pp.*
Roche, Maurice. Phenomenology, Language and the Social Sciences. *371 pp.*
Sahay, Arun. Sociological Analysis. *212 pp.*
Sklair, Leslie. The Sociology of Progress. *320 pp.*

International Library of Anthropology

General Editor Adam Kuper

Brown, Paula. The Chimbu. *A Study of Change in the New Guinea Highlands. 151 pp.*
Lloyd, P. C. Power and Independence. *Urban Africans' Perception of Social Inequality. 264 pp.*
Pettigrew, Joyce. Robber Noblemen. *A Study of the Political System of the Sikh Jats. 284 pp.*
Van Den Berghe, Pierre L. Power and Privilege at an African University. *278 pp.*

International Library of Social Policy

General Editor Kathleen Jones

Bayley, M. Mental Handicap and Community Care. *426 pp.*
Butler, J. R. Family Doctors and Public Policy. *208 pp.*
Holman, Robert. Trading in Children. *A Study of Private Fostering. 355 pp.*

Jones, Kathleen. History of the Mental Health Service. *428 pp.*
Thomas, J. E. The English Prison Officer since 1850: *A Study in Conflict.* *258 pp.*
Woodward, J. To Do the Sick No Harm. *A Study of the British Voluntary Hospital System to 1875. About 220 pp.*

International Library of Welfare and Philosophy

General Editors   Noel Timms and David Watson

● **Plant, Raymond.** Community and Ideology. *104 pp.*

Primary Socialization, Language and Education

General Editor   Basil Bernstein

Bernstein, Basil. Class, Codes and Control. *2 volumes.*
  1. *Theoretical Studies Towards a Sociology of Language. 254 pp.*
  2. *Applied Studies Towards a Sociology of Language. About 400 pp.*
Brandis, W., and **Bernstein, B.** Selection and Control. *176 pp.*
Brandis, Walter, and **Henderson, Dorothy.** Social Class, Language and Communication. *288 pp.*
Cook-Gumperz, Jenny. Social Control and Socialization. *A Study of Class Differences in the Language of Maternal Control. 290 pp.*
● **Gahagan, D. M.,** and **G. A.** Talk Reform. *Exploration in Language for Infant School Children. 160 pp.*
Robinson, W. P., and **Rackstraw, Susan D. A.** A Question of Answers. *2 volumes. 192 pp. and 180 pp.*
Turner, Geoffrey J., and **Mohan, Bernard A.** A Linguistic Description and Computer Programme for Children's Speech. *208 pp.*

Reports of the Institute of Community Studies

Cartwright, Ann. Human Relations and Hospital Care. *272 pp.*
●   Parents and Family Planning Services. *306 pp.*
   Patients and their Doctors. *A Study of General Practice. 304 pp.*
● **Jackson, Brian.** Streaming: *an Education System in Miniature. 168 pp.*
Jackson, Brian, and **Marsden, Dennis.** Education and the Working Class: *Some General Themes raised by a Study of 88 Working-class Children in a Northern Industrial City. 268 pp. 2 folders.*
Marris, Peter. The Experience of Higher Education. *232 pp. 27 tables.*
   Loss and Change. *192 pp.*

Marris, Peter, and **Rein, Martin.** Dilemmas of Social Reform. *Poverty and Community Action in the United States. 256 pp.*

Marris, Peter, and **Somerset, Anthony.** African Businessmen. *A Study of Entrepreneurship and Development in Kenya. 256 pp.*

Mills, Richard. Young Outsiders: *a Study in Alternative Communities. 216 pp.*

Runciman, W. G. Relative Deprivation and Social Justice. *A Study of Attitudes to Social Inequality in Twentieth-Century England. 352 pp.*

Willmott, Peter. Adolescent Boys in East London. *230 pp.*

Willmott, Peter, and **Young, Michael.** Family and Class in a London Suburb. *202 pp. 47 tables.*

Young, Michael. Innovation and Research in Education. *192 pp.*

●**Young, Michael,** and **McGeeney, Patrick.** Learning Begins at Home. *A Study of a Junior School and its Parents. 128 pp.*

Young, Michael, and **Willmott, Peter.** Family and Kinship in East London. *Foreword by Richard M. Titmuss. 252 pp. 39 tables.*

The Symmetrical Family. *410 pp.*

Reports of the Institute for Social Studies in Medical Care

Cartwright, Ann, Hockey, Lisbeth, and **Anderson, John L.** Life Before Death. *310 pp.*

Dunnell, Karen, and **Cartwright, Ann.** Medicine Takers, Prescribers and Hoarders. *190 pp.*

Medicine, Illness and Society

General Editor W. M. Williams

Robinson, David. The Process of Becoming Ill. *142 pp.*

Stacey, Margaret, *et al.* Hospitals, Children and Their Families. *The Report of a Pilot Study. 202 pp.*

Monographs in Social Theory

General Editor Arthur Brittan

●**Barnes, B.** Scientific Knowledge and Sociological Theory. *About 200 pp.*

Bauman, Zygmunt. Culture as Praxis. *204 pp.*

●**Dixon, Keith.** Sociological Theory. *Pretence and Possibility. 142 pp.*

●**Smith, Anthony D.** The Concept of Social Change. *A Critique of the Functionalist Theory of Social Change. 208 pp.*

Routledge Social Science Journals

The British Journal of Sociology. *Edited by Terence P. Morris. Vol. 1, No. 1, March 1950 and Quarterly. Roy. 8vo. Back numbers available. An international journal with articles on all aspects of sociology.*

Economy and Society. *Vol. 1, No. 1. February 1972 and Quarterly. Metric Roy. 8vo. A journal for all social scientists covering sociology, philosophy, anthropology, economics and history. Back numbers available.*

Year Book of Social Policy in Britain, The. *Edited by Kathleen Jones. 1971. Published annually.*

Printed in Great Britain by Unwin Brothers Limited
The Gresham Press Old Woking Surrey
A member of the Staples Printing Group